W9-BLR-907

Personal versus Private

Presidential Records in a Legislative Context: A Bibliographic Exploration

Peter Sezzi

The Scarecrow Press, Inc.
Lanham, Maryland • Toronto • Oxford
2005

WINGATE UNIVERSITY LIBRARY

SCARECROW PRESS, INC.

Published in the United States of America
by Scarecrow Press, Inc.
A wholly owned subsidiary of
The Rowman & Littlefield Publishing Group, Inc.
4501 Forbes Boulevard, Suite 200, Lanham, Maryland 20706
www.scarecrowpress.com

PO Box 317
Oxford
OX2 9RU, UK

Copyright © 2005 by Peter Sezzi

All rights reserved. No part of this publication may be reproduced,
stored in a retrieval system, or transmitted in any form or by any
means, electronic, mechanical, photocopying, recording, or otherwise,
without the prior permission of the publisher.

British Library Cataloguing in Publication Information Available

Library of Congress Cataloging-in-Publication Data

Sezzi, Peter H., 1977-
    Personal versus private : presidential records in a legislative context : a
bibliographic exploration / Peter H. Sezzi.
        p. cm.
    Includes index.
    ISBN 0-8108-5168-7 (pbk. : alk. paper)
    1. Presidents—United States—Archives. 2. Public records—Access
control—United States—Bibliography. 3. Archives—Law and legislation—
United States—Bibliography. I. Title: Perspma; vs. private. II. Title.

CD3029.8.S49 2005
016.35223'2387'0973—dc22   2004023939

♾™ The paper used in this publication meets the minimum requirements of
American National Standard for Information Sciences—Permanence of
Paper for Printed Library Materials, ANSI/NISO Z39.48-1992.
Manufactured in the United States of America.

To my parents,
Eduardo and Rose Ann Sezzi:
Thanks.

Contents

Preface

First, and most important, I must confess that with the writing of this book I am a librarian in an archivist's land. Despite that admitted handicap, my greatest hope for this bibliographic exploration is for it to one day be of aid to future scholars. I do not aim to be comprehensive but rather only hope to give the investigator a head start on the research of a complex topic: legislative attempts to control access to and ownership of presidential records.

The origin of this bibliographic guide can be traced back to the late summer and early fall of 2001. In the course of completing various assignments for my master's degree in library and information science at the University of California, Los Angeles, I enrolled in a class taught by Professor John V. Richardson Jr. entitled "Government Information." It was in this class that I first heard about the Presidential Records Act of 1978 (PRA). After the successful completion of the class, I remained interested in the intricacies of the PRA. My fate was sealed when I found a used copy of the *Final Report* of the National Study Commission on the Records and Documents of Federal Officials (1975-1977) for sale for $15.

During the next several months after the class was over I conducted a comprehensive literature review on all issues related to the PRA and the ownership of and access to documents created by federal officials. I submitted the final draft of my bibliography as my Master's thesis. Lack of access to primary documents and time constraints have prevented me from writing a complete history of the PRA and legislative control of presidential records. I hope this bibliographic guide will make it easier for future scholars to finish the task of creating a more complete history of the legislative control of presidential records.

Peter H. Sezzi
Pola, Croatia

Acknowledgments

Numerous—almost countless—people in my life have helped me during the creation of this work. Foremost, my entire family deserves much praise for their support, editorial comments and good-natured tolerance of my research interests during the past few years. A special thanks goes to my parents, my eldest brother and to both of my grandmothers—if I had but one-tenth their strength and fortitude, I can only imagine how improved my research would be.

So too do I need to thank the members of my thesis committee, from whence this book originates—Anne Gillian-Swetland, Jonathan Furner and John V. Richardson Jr. Without their tireless cheerleading, insightful comments and kindly suggestions, I fear to think where I would be, much less where this thesis-turned-book would be!

I am especially grateful to Professor John V. Richardson, Jr. As chair of my thesis committee, he went above and beyond the call of duty in ensuring that my work was the best possible. Under his capable guidance, I not only completed my thesis, but also turned my thesis into a manuscript ready for publication. Professor Richardson's dedication to his students is exceeded only by his dedication to scholarship. For all his guidance and help, I am immensely grateful—grateful to an extent that is difficult to express.

I would be remiss if I did not mention the debt that I owe to the always ever-patient, helpful and responsive staff of the Multimedia and Intensive Technology (MIT) in the UCLA Department of Information Studies. I shudder to think where I would be without the amazing help of the Interlibrary Loan (ILL) Department of the Young Research Library (YRL) at UCLA—no matter how obscure, obtuse or odd my request, this invaluable department always handled it with speed and professionalism.

I would also like to thank all of my friends at the Department of Information Studies at UCLA, who listened with patience and good-natured questioning to my oft-repeated stories about the development of presidential libraries and ownership of presidential records. In retrospect, my retelling of the story of the ownership of presidential records made me understand the issue more comprehensively. Many of my associates provided insightful comments, for which I am thankful. A special expression of gratitude goes to the ever-kind and helpful

Cindy Mediavilla.

My thanks also go out to the numerous academics—including, but not limited to, Anna Kasten Nelson, David A. Wallace and Alonzo L. Hamby—who so generously shared with me their time and—in some cases—their hard-to-find papers, articles or dissertations.

I am also indebted to my former employer, William Fulton, and my other coworkers at Solimar Research Group in Ventura, California. The generous in-kind support that I received from my research associates at Solimar helped to turn this thesis from an abstract idea into a tangible work. My coworkers at Ventura College— where I was an intern during the crafting of my thesis—and my former colleagues at California State University, Channel Islands all provided instrumental support and good cheer as I crafted my thesis into the present work. I owe a special debt of gratitude to my mentor in librarianship, Octavio Sifuentes. David Breslin, Paul Adalain, Loretta Wagoner and Sarah Toner also deserve special thanks for their individual contributions to this project.

Most helpful of all, and supportive of my efforts from day one, was Jill Weinreich. Jill and I were partners in a group project for Professor Richardson's "Government Information" class at UCLA. Indeed, it was Jill who first informed me about the Presidential Records Act of 1978 (PRA) after listening to a segment on National Public Radio's "Morning Edition." Without the combination of Jill and Professor Richardson, quite simply, I would not have been interested in writing about the PRA for my thesis and—subsequently—this book would not exist. An immeasurable amount of thanks would hardly express my gratefulness to these two people in the completion of this work.

I am eternally grateful for all the help by those mentioned in this short list of acknowledgments and I beg forgiveness of those who helped me with this project but whom I have absent-mindedly failed to mention. Please know that failure to mention you by name in no way lessens the importance of your help. Of course, while help has come from numerous sources in the creation of this thesis, final responsibility for the content of this work rests on my shoulders alone.

Introduction

The Presidential Records Act of 1978 (PRA) remains the United States' most noticeable effort at asserting public ownership of and access to the records of public officials (in this case, the president of the United States). Due to the PRA's unique status, a great deal of secondary material exists about the act. This bibliography allows both the seasoned researcher of the PRA and the novice to government information a way to approach the massive amount of material generated not only about the PRA, but also about the issues related to the public ownership of and access to the records and documents of federal officials.

I hope, this bibliography might in some small part help to generate renewed public and scholarly interest in the ownership of and access to the records of federal officials. This work focuses on both the specific development of the PRA and the societal, cultural and legislative attempts to control the public ownership of and public access to the records created by presidents of the United States.

Because a comprehensive overview of the literature about the PRA has not been written, this bibliography treads new ground. Future scholars interested in studying government ownership of the records created by federal officials may use this bibliography as a starting point.

In essence, the purpose of this work is to smooth the road for future scholars interested in the preservation of, ownership of and access to U.S. federal government records; specifically, on presidential records. This bibliography aims to be as comprehensive as possible in documenting all literature and relevant government materials that relate to the ownership of presidential records. Some of the materials included in this bibliography include references to federal statutes and regulations (such as sections from the United State Code [U.S.C.] and the Code of Federal Regulations [C.F.R.]) peer-reviewed journal articles, judicial opinions and monographs. In addition, this bibliography includes legislative bill tracings for relevant federal acts that relate to the ownership of presidential records. Contact information for archival centers with significant holdings of presidential materials is also included.

This bibliographic guide contains three parts. The first part presents a narrative synthesis of the PRA and other significant legislative, executive and judicial events in the history of government ownership of presidential records. The second part presents a bibliographic essay that evaluates many of the sources that I found that relate to legislative attempts to own and create access to presidential records. Not all of the sources that I found are listed in the second part, but this section lists a selection of the most helpful sources. The third part contains a comprehensive enumerative bibliography of works written about the ownership of and access to presidential records. The bibliography contains over 700 citations. While many may find the narrative portion of this book the most useful, the origin of this entire book is the bibliography presented in the third part. Finally, the appendices in this book contain much helpful information, including: a listing of executive orders that relate to presidential records; bill tracings for the legislative attempts to control ownership and access to presidential records; a table of significant case law that relates to the specific question of presidential records as well as to the larger issue of government ownership of the records created by federal employees; and, finally, a listing of archival institutions with significant holdings of presidential records.

The essay presented in the first part is an attempt to introduce a complicated topic—federal ownership of presidential records. The essay also offers subject access in a narrative form to the bibliography. Granted, the subject access value of the narrative is compromised by the fact that not every source listed in the bibliography is discussed in the essay. Some of the sources listed in the bibliography were of marginal use to the construction of the narrative and were thus excluded.

Part 1

Narrative Overview of Legislative Control of Presidential Records

1

Legislative Action Controlling
Presidential Records

Between 1974 and 1982, at least seven different scholarly articles began by lamenting the ownership status of and the lack of access to
presidential documents.[1] The reaction to Watergate and disclosure of
the Nixon-Sampson agreement created a chain reaction, the effects of
which at the least included two legislative initiatives that changed the
ownership status and the public's accessibility to presidential records.
Due to the shocking nature of the crimes leveled against the president
during the Watergate investigation, it is not surprising that "in the
Nixon administration, for the first time the question of who should own
(and thus control) presidential papers received nationwide attention."[2]

Shortly after the Watergate affair became public knowledge, the
U.S. Congress began its first effort to assert ownership over presidential records. This first attempt to affirm legislative control over and
ownership of presidential records came to be known as the Presidential
Recordings and Materials Preservation Act of 1974 (PL 93-526, hereafter PRMPA). The PRMPA was quite explicit—it allowed the federal
government to take possession of only all presidential records produced
during and by the Nixon administration. The law stopped short of providing for state ownership of the items impounded.   Whereas the
PRMPA was narrow in scope (it applied only to the possession of one
person's records), the law also was broad in some respects. For example, the PRMPA also mandated that a national commission be established. Called the National Study Commission on the Records of Federal Officials, this commission had a charge to suggest to Congress
draft legislation that would create uniform ownership standards for all
records produced by any federal employee, from the president to members of Congress and the federal judiciary.

After over two years of service, the commission ended on a divided note, providing a majority and a minority report, both of which
were released on March 31, 1977. The commission did have a sort of
détente on some issues despite the differences expressed in the two reports. Anna Kasten Nelson, a staff member of the commission, later
noted, "The 17 members of the Commission did agree on one issue:
ownership. . . . They divided on the much more difficult question of

access."[3] Unfortunately, the recommendations of the National Study were largely ignored by Congress. The fact that the commission issued two somewhat conflicting reports probably only aided Congress in ignoring its divided recommendations. Indirectly, however, the report did help generate support for the Presidential Records Act of 1978 (PL 95-591, hereafter PRA). The PRA was effected within a year of the release of the report. The statute closely advocated some of the general points of the study commission, namely, that presidential records created on or after January 20, 1981, would be owned by the federal government and shall be available for review after a specified number of years had passed. The law asserted that materials created by the chief executive are the property of the United States, to be held in trust by presidential libraries, a system of privately built but federally subsidized archival institutions.

For close to 200 years, presidential documents were treated as personal papers. In the span of little more than five years, Congress legislatively mandated that the public should have access to the records created by its chief executive. The significant change in archival practice concerning presidential records—from a system under which presidents donated their papers to the state under whose employ the papers were created to a system under which presidential records are owned by the state from the moment they are created—has no doubt led to many of the problems evident under the PRA. The fact that Congress essentially mandated control of the records created by another branch of government, while at the same time the papers created by members of Congress remain the property of individual congressmen, has also no doubt led to some negative feelings by the executive branch to the full enactment of the PRA.

Yet another difficulty present in the PRA, quite apart from the fact that it changed the custom of private ownership to state ownership of presidential records, is the fact that the PRA has little if any means of enforcement. In a government where the president is charged with executing the laws enacted by the legislative branch, is it any wonder that successive presidential administrations since the enactment of the PRA have been so slow to embrace, much less enforce, a form of legislative control over the executive branch? Indeed, the penalties outlined in the PRA can be exacted only when the archivist files a complaint. In other words, archivist in charge of a presidential materials project would be accusing his boss—the president—of neglecting the law.

The PRA legislates a more responsive government and says that the citizens have a right to know what their government is doing. This legislated attempt to mandate openness in the executive branch might be another possible reason why the PRA has been less than warmly received by successive presidential administrations.

The Presidential Records Act provides for the ownership of and access to records created by the executive branch. This legislative means of preservation and access to records exists at a level unparalleled in the other branches of the federal government. For those who complain that this legislative mandate to access of records of the executive branch creates an unbalanced playing field among the three branches of government, or that the three branches of government should be treated more equitability, it must also be remembered that ever since the presidency of Franklin D. Roosevelt, the executive branch of the federal government has grown disproportionately larger than either the legislative or judicial branch.

Rather than seeing the PRA as an inequity, it should be seen as a means to ensure a more balanced government by ensuring that citizens have a legislatively-mandated right to see the records created by the most powerful branch of government, the branch of government that some scholars such as John Hart and Edward Corwin have termed the "presidential branch." As many scholars have noted, without ready access to the primary materials created and consulted by presidents knowledge of in the discharge of their duties as federal employees, the American people are denied knowing exactly their government is doing. By mandating that records and documents created by federal officials in the discharge of their official duties are the property of the people, citizens ensure their right to know what it is that their government is doing.

However, by mandating that records and documents created by federal officials and employees are the property of the nation and its citizens, Congress created several attendant problems. Critics of the PRA and other access-to-information acts at federal, state, and local levels often complain that such legislated access ensures a so-called "Chilling Effect"—fearful of reappraisals by opposing parties or a public unaware of the situation/context in which a document or record was created who would use the information contained therein as a means to intimidate, expose or shame the records' creator., i.e., that fewer and fewer records will be created by officials. However, the chilling effect argument is fraught with external contradictions, the least of which is that since the enactment of the PRA, growth of federal records has not abated, and in fact, legislative efforts such as the Paperwork Reduction Act have been enacted to help stem the tide of records produced by the federal government. Despite the cry of critics of the PRA that the law would ensure only that high-ranking executive branch officials would not keep records, memoirs and recollections of presidential associates have grown in number over time.

In fact, so numerous are the memoirs by former high-ranking executive branch officials that a Library of Congress subject heading now exists that covers the topic: Cabinet officers—United States—Biography. Caspar Weinberger, who was a cabinet member under both Richard Nixon and Ronald Reagan, has written not one, but two accounts of his associations and dealings with the chief executives of the United States. Presidents have not been loath to publish their own tellings of their times in the White House, perhaps due as much to the Constitution's prohibition of the president receiving a pension (Art. II, Sec. 1) to a president's desire to maintain some sway and say in U.S. public life. Whereas presidential publishing is not a new phenomenon (perhaps U.S. Grant and his memoirs can be seen as the grandfather of the field), the amount of published matter produced by ex-presidents has been growing almost exponentially. Not all materials published by ex-presidents relate back to their terms as chief executive; often the writings of a president on current domestic or foreign policy can be as telling as his (perhaps fuzzy) recollection of events during his presidency.

Another cause of alarm cited by opponents of the PRA is that the act unfairly targets the executive branch as opposed to the other branches of the federal government. Granted, it was the scope of the National Study Commission on the Records of Federal Officials, to forge standards that would apply to all federally created documents and records. However, the divided report and the lack of attention that Congress paid to it severely limited the impact of the commission's findings and suggestions. Yet, despite Congress's failing to implement the breadth of access across branches advocated in both the majority and the minority reports of the commission, it must be remembered that the growth of the executive branch and the impact that it has on a citizen's everyday life has grown disproportionately in relation to the growth of the other branches of the federal government.

While the sum of these two acts, the Presidential Recordings and Materials Preservation Act and the Presidential Records Act, equated to the public ownership of the presidential records created during the Nixon administration and those records created by presidents from the Reagan administration to the present, the true mettle of the act has yet to be worked out. In effect, while it is indeed easy for Congress to legislate that presidential records shall become property of the state, it is a decidedly more difficult task to assign what constitutes a presidential record as opposed to what is a private document. Moreover, an issue of an even more timely nature to this day is that of determining access to presidential records.

As part of the PRA's provisions, ex-presidents may withhold from immediate public access certain classes of documents. The embargo from public access could last for as long as twelve years after the president leaves office. The PRA provided such a discretionary provision to the president so as to allow a sufficient period of time between when sensitive or potentially compromising documents were created and when they should become publicly available. While the PRA set limits on how long something can be sequestered, it did not fundamentally alter the fact that the president still retains the power to classify records (personal records and documents) even if the law notes that access eventually will have to be granted to the public.

The first test of the practicability of the PRA was to the scheduled release of 68,000 of President Reagan's records, which were selected for the twelve year embargo back in 1980. On November 1, 2001—

well over nine months after the withheld Reagan papers were scheduled for public release—President George W. Bush signed E.O. 13233. The executive order applies significant new restrictions on the full implementation of the Presidential Records Act of 1978. The E.O. essentially gives to a sitting president the final say over the public release status of the records of any presidential administration, not just his/her own. Tensions that were present when the PRA was enacted resurfaced.

This introductory overview will examine the development of accessibility to presidential records, especially with regard to those records that are owned by the federal government by right of the PRMPA and the PRA. This overview will discuss briefly the recent challenges that are limiting the full implementation of the PRA. Definitions of terms used frequently (e.g., records) will be discussed before proceeding to discuss the historical antecedents of the PRMPA and the PRA. Special attention will be placed on the development of the presidential library system, the Franklin D. Roosevelt Library and Museum of Hyde Park, New York, and the Presidential Libraries Act of 1955. Finally, the current status of the implementation of the PRA and how recent administrative law make a clear and straightforward interpretation of who owns presidential documents and who may access them anything but a settled issue. Taken in historical perspective, these most recent changes to the administration of the PRA are a mere blip in the 220-

plus year paradigm of relatively infrequent ready access to past presidential materials.

Indeed, despite the trauma and changes that came as a result of the Watergate affair, the same issues that haunted archivists and scholars then remain with us today: namely, who owns presidential papers (despite the PRA, much grey area still exists, particularly with regard to records created by the president that are not clearly public or private) and how to determine access to these records.

Neither the Presidential Libraries Act (1955) nor the PRA (1978) changed the discretionary nature of how the president decided what others could access.

Previous to the PRMPA and the PRA, there existed no legislative basis for personal or federal control of presidential documents. Indeed, as Pamela McKay notes, "from George Washington to Jimmy Carter, presidents viewed the papers and materials they created or caused to be created or shuffled across their desks *as their property*."[4] Indeed, the well-known Franklin D. Roosevelt biographer Arthur Schlesinger noted that "the ancient idea of presidential rather than public ownership has prevailed only in the absence of congressional legislation."[5] But before exploring how, in the words of one archivist, "the larcenous habits of Presidents from George Washington on," were changed, some key definitions for this paper must be presented.[6]

Perhaps one of the stickiest issues of dealing with presidential records is defining what exactly they are. For instance, much writing about the subject uses the terms presidential records and presidential documents in an almost synonymous fashion, indicating items created or used by the Executive Office of the President. Thus, presidential records need not emanate solely from the chief executive, but can come from one working for the president in some administrative fashion. On the other had, often the term presidential papers is used to designate works that are of a more personal nature and of a more intimate note, often relating to familial matters of the president. In a more nuanced definition, the phrase *presidential documents* embraces the entire oeuvre—an output that includes both personal and public, concealed and announced—of the president and the executive office. Similarly difficult to determining the attributes of presidential records is determining access to these records.

Notes

1. See Anna Kasten Nelson (1982), Pamela R. McKay (1982), Arnold Hirshon (1979), H.G. Jones (1975), J. Frank Cook (1975), Hirshon (1974) and "Who Owns Presidential Papers?" (1975). Complete citations for each of these articles can be found in the bibliography in Part 3. Many other works on the topic also appeared in the popular press, most notably in the *Wall Street Journal* (e.g., the Schlesinger article) or in the editorial sections of the *New York Times, Christian Science Monitor* and the *Washington Post.*

2. Jannean L. Elliott, *Presidential Papers and the Presidential Library System;* Occasional Research Paper no. 2 (Provo, UT: School of Library and Information Science, Brigham Young University, 1981), 33.

3. Anna Kasten Nelson, "The Public Documents Commission: Politics and Presidential Records," *Government Publications Review* 9: 5 (Sept.-Oct. 1982): 447.

4. Pamela R. McKay, "Presidential Papers: A Property Issue," *Library Quarterly* 52: 1 (Jan. 1982): 33.

5. Arthur Schlesinger Jr., "Who Owns a President's Papers?" *Manuscripts* 27: 3 (Summer 1975): 179.

6. H.G. Jones, "Presidential Libraries: Is There a Case for a National Presidential Library?" *American Archivist* 38: 3 (July 1975): 328.

2

Types of Presidential Documents

According to Hirshon, there are four types of presidential documents: Public Papers[1], Papers Under the Control of the Executive Office[2], Official Papers[3], and Personal Papers[4].

In addition, there are several different types of documents: White House Central Files[5], National Security Files[6], Special Files[7], Staff Files[8] and Files of Ancillary White House Offices[9].

Perhaps one of the best concise definitions for presidential papers comes from McKay, who relates her answer via a discursive method. She notes:

> What are presidential papers? "Presidential papers" is an umbrella term for a diversity of material, both written and taped. Presidential papers reflect the various roles played by the President— that of commander-in-chief, chief executive (and head diplomat), government employee and public servant, leader and member of a political party, citizen, and family member.[10]

James Rhoads, Archivist of the United States during Watergate, interestingly noted the same, stating that "the traditional view holds that it is impossible to separate the personal and political files of an elected official from the files that have a direct bearing upon his public responsibilities."[11] Likewise backing up this claim is an early user of the presidential libraries system, David D. Lloyd, who noted that "the official papers, in toto, are in a state of limbo; they are neither completely private nor public. They are 'part of the business of government, but they are not government records.' But neither are they totally private in nature."[12]

To further muddle the issue, some scholars contend that entirely different paradigms exist for understanding how presidential documents should be grouped. For example, historian Arthur Schlesinger Jr. noted that there are two main types of executive documents: White

House files and presidential files. While White House files are running files that belong to the government, presidential files belong to the individual. However, Schlesinger contends that the"answer to this, it seems, would be to enact a law defining the political and personal papers of a President as private property of a particular sort—private property clothed with a public interest and subject to public regulation."[13]

Grouping documents into either public or private can be problematic. Indeed, sometimes even ownership of records can be difficult, because "even though we have seen a distinction between the ownership and custody and control of presidential papers, the government did not see these issues as separate in Washington's time nor for many years after."[14]

Notes

1. Arnold Hirshon, "The Scope, Accessability [*sic*] and History of Presidential Papers," *Government Publications Review* 1: 4 (Fall 1974): 365.

2. Hirshon, "Presidential Papers," 365.

3. Hirshon, "Presidential Papers," 368.

4. Hirshon, "Presidential Papers," 371. The last four notes were also all cited in Pamela R. McKay, "Presidential Papers: A Property Issue," *Library Quarterly* 52: 1 (Jan. 1982): 25. I am heavily indebted to both McKay and Hirshon for this chapter.

5. National Study Commission on Records and Documents of Federal Officials, *Final Report*, March 31, 1977, 14.

6. National Study Commission, *Final Report*, 14-15.

7. National Study Commission, *Final Report*, 15.

8. National Study Commission, *Final Report*, 15.

9. National Study Commission, *Final Report*, 15. See also McKay, "Presidential Papers," 25.

10. McKay, "Presidential Papers," 24.

11. James B. Rhoads, "Who Should Own the Documents of Public Officials?" *Prologue* 7: 1 (Spring 1975): 34.

12. Hirshon, "Presidential Papers," 368, quoting David D. Lloyd, "The Harry S. Truman Library," *American Archivist* 18 (April 1955): 996.

13. Arthur Schlesinger Jr., "Who Owns a President's Papers?" *Manuscripts* 27: 3 (Summer 1975): 182.

14. "Who Owns Presidential Papers?" *Manuscripts* 27:1 (Winter 1975): 8.

Ownership of Presidential Records

The issue of ownership of and access to presidential materials is not a recent one, and unlike what many think, the issue goes back further than the Nixon problem. Indeed, the root of the historical battle over the ownership of presidential papers goes back to our first chief executive, George Washington.

From the time of Washington on, presidents have regarded the materials that they collected and used while in office as their personal property. While some claim that Franklin D. Roosevelt's creation of a presidential library fundamentally changed this situation, the fact remains that "the Boss," as his associates knew him, rigorously exerted that he was the one true owner of his presidential records, not the people of the United States. Regardless, it remains without a doubt that previous to FDR's initiative, there existed what one scholar called "the laissez-faire system" of presidential collections.[1] However, the growth of the executive branch during FDR's term of office paralleled a similar growth of paperwork and records. Realizing that maintenance of such a legacy of paper and mementos would be too much even for the Roosevelt family, FDR saw a way out of the situation by donating the materials to the United States, provided that maintenance costs would be underwritten by the federal government.

Thus, while private funding was secured for the construction of the library, the upkeep of the library was undertaken by the United States government. Presidential libraries became institutionalized and sanctioned by law with the Presidential Libraries Act of 1955. Narrow in scope, this law did nothing to change the ownership issue attendant with the creation of presidential libraries. While ownership of presidential papers was discussed when the bill that became the PLA was introduced, in the final version of the bill that became law the ownership provisos were excised. Essentially, the establishment of the presidential library system under the Roosevelt model was a financial agreement that allowed records to be kept in a place of the president's choosing, while the chief executive retained title until he wished to deed his records to the government. All the while, the library's upkeep has continued to be subsidized via public support.

Only five years after the FDR's death, percent of the records were open to research. However, for that remaining 15 percent of records, it would be over twenty-five years before the records even began to be declassified. The similarity with other documents produced by other federal agencies has not gone unnoticed, and some have even asked why presidential records should be released so quickly, whereas at other executive agencies such as the State Department, records are not available for at least twenty-five years after their creation.

Ever a plan-maker, FDR drew up plan for a museum and archive that would house all of his presidential-related materials. As Elliott notes, "Roosevelt's concept of a presidential library grew out of a need to have a place where gifts, objects and papers could go."[2] Items to be deposited ranged from paper documents and drafts of speeches to diplomatic gifts received from foreign heads of state. McKay notes much the same, stating that "Roosevelt's proposal envisioned a facility that was of necessity a library, an archives, and a museum all in one."[3]

Following in FDR's footsteps were presidential libraries of Harry S. Truman, Dwight D. Eisenhower, John F. Kennedy, Lyndon B. Johnson, Gerald R. Ford, Jimmy Carter, Ronald Reagan, George Bush and William J. Clinton, all of which are administered, the National Records and Archives Administration (NARA). Likewise, for presidential libraries Roosevelt to Carter, all were built upon what one scholar called an "underlying philosophy . . . composed of quicksand, [but] remarkably useful institutions have been built thereon."[4] Speaking years before the PRA passed, H. G. Jones continues, notes that despite their lack of legislative basis for being, presidential libraries, "unfortunately, will continue their tenuous existence until they are given a solid legal underpinning."[5] One should always keep in mind that "the presidential libraries, however, originated not in response to abstract constitutional concepts, but rather out of the intention of one man to give the American people a record of his career as president."[6]

As probably noted by the reader, the one name omitted from the list of post World War II presidents above was Richard Nixon. The house of cards (i.e., records owned by individuals but administered by a federal agency) that existed for the presidential libraries system before PRA and continues to exist for libraries from Roosevelt to Carter, began to collapse once the House Judiciary Committee subpoenaed Nixon's presidential records and recordings in 1974. As one scholar notes, "the extent of the collection was defined solely by the President as the tradition of private ownership was unchallenged."[7] With the litigation that resulted after Nixon refused to hand over the requested records and tapes in 1974, the shortcomings of the ownership of presidential records residing in the person of the president began to be revealed.

Enacted in 1955, the PLA institutionalized the system initiated by Roosevelt of private ownership but public support. However, some criticized the creation of just such a system, as noted by Ralph Brown Jr. of Yale in 1974 in the wake of Watergate, because "the Presidential Libraries Act 'can be viewed as the nation's acceptance, not of a gift, but of [the] burden' of managing such large presidential collections as now occur."[8] Indeed, many saw the PLA as bad policy. The law only provided for the financial upkeep of presidential records should a former president decide to donate the records to the country. The law contained no provision mandating that records created in the execution of the office of the president are governmental property by right. Yet, despite all of these shortcomings, "for whatever faults and problems are involved, Presidential Libraries have been immensely important because they provided [*sic*] for a uniform system of control and access to presidential papers."[9]

Announced with President Ford's pardon of Richard Nixon was the so-called "Nixon-Samson agreement." The agreement between the former president and the administrator of the General Services Administration, Arthur Sampson, created an uproar because the agreement spelled out in no uncertain terms that for the years 1974-1984, President Nixon would maintain control over his tapes and records, during which time he could decide to save or destroy the records as he saw fit. Only days later, a bill was introduced in the House (H.R. 16719) that sought to revoke this agreement, but the enactment of the Presidential Recordings and Materials Preservation Act would be one year in the making.

The PRMPA was a law of reaction. The narrowness of the PLA was brought into sharper focus when Nixon went against the main underlying assumption of the law—that a president would willingly donate his papers to a federally financed, but publicly built, presidential library. Previous to having a threat to the security of past presidential documents, no legislation was needed to mandate their control. The not-so-subtle hints of the Nixon-Sampson agreement upset the "president's agreement" that had existed for the past 200 years. As the archivist Cook notes, "clearly, the federal government trusted the preservation of the single most important body of records it generates not to the protection of the law but to the goodwill of each succeeding President."[10] Yet, Cook's argument of an implicit "president's agreement" should not appear as a black-and-white issue because many previous presidents or their heirs had destroyed presidential documents. The difference now was that the records still existed and potentially incriminated a president of both impeachable and criminal offenses.

Because no law existed that expressly said what Nixon could not do or should do with his presidential papers, he proceeded to do what all previous presidents had done—namely, whatever he wanted to do. The only difference was that in the light of Watergate, the Nixon-Sampson agreement pretty much overtly hinted at the fact that he would destroy potentially incriminating documents after a specified period of time. Although Nixon's hinting at destruction of documents in many ways only continued a tradition of previous presidents, the fact that such an agreement became public knowledge so soon after the president's ignominious resignation due to his involvement in the Watergate affair the public incensed and shocked. However, Nixon objected to the House's request to look at the Office of the President's files, and it was only through litigation that the issue was resolved.

Indeed, "the suits and counter suits which have been brought in attempts to quiet the title to those records, and the unsettled condition of the presidential libraries have revealed the weak legal and constitutional foundation supporting the traditional concepts and policies regulating presidential records."[11] Yet, when all the lawsuits had settled, the PRMPA remained in effect. Indeed, during its judicial trials, the PRMPA was not only affirmed, but a legal scholar even noted, "compared Nixon to any other federal employee working on government files with government property."[12]

In fact, judicial review was exactly what was needed to resolve the increasing dispute between the executive and the legislature. As an additional consequence of the litigation ensuing from the PRMPA and the House's requests for records, for the first time in our history, judicial review decided that presidential records belong to the public. As Cook notes, it was not "until Judge Charles R. Richey of the U.S. District Court in Washington, DC, ruled on January 31, 1975, that almost all of the records produced by the Nixon administration belong to the government, no court had ever dealt directly with the issue of ownership of presidential papers."[13]

By upholding Congress's right to abrogate the Nixon-Sampson agreement, Judge Richey upheld what the public wanted and indeed thought that it was entitled to—i.e., access to all documents, especially the potentially incriminating documents relating to the Watergate break-in and cover up. However, by no stretch of the imagination was Nixon doing what other ex-presidents had done, for they had indeed decided what to do with their papers once they left office, and thus allowed access to these documents created in the service to the nation. Nixon began to chart a different course and the Congress reacted with the Presidential Records and Materials Preservation Act.

The legislation that ultimately followed out of the PRPMA-sponsored National Study Commission on Records and Documents of Federal Officials was the Presidential Records Act of 1978. As one ebullient scholar noted, "with the passage of Presidential Records Act of 1978 (92 Stat. 2523), the law finally caught up with reality: presidential papers are now public records."[14] However, the combination of the Presidential Libraries Act with the Presidential Records Act remained flawed, because the one law implies the donation of records, with a building constructed from private funds; while the other law implies that a building exists in a vacuum and forces a president to donate records. While the PLA does not force the donation of records, the PRA does; however, the PRA does not force officials to keep records. While records that are created must indeed be kept, the fact remains that no legislation exists that forces the creation of records in the first place.

The PRA forces the president to donate materials, but the law does not stipulate where, although access issues are addressed, because most records of a presidency must be revealed within twelve years of a presidency's termination. Further, no law sets down straightforward regulations on who can enforce the provisions of the PRA, by what means the act is to be enforced or even what are the penalties of non-compliance. But perhaps the most quixotic part of the law remains the fact that it is self-enforced, because the person potentially most interested in hiding or "misfiling" papers is in charge of organizing the records in the first place.

Granted, the sitting president needs ready access to documents created by his office, so why should the president not be in charge of organizing and classifying his own records? This is not something unique to the executive branch, or even the exclusive domain of the government, for that matter. For this exact reason historians use independent verification to ensure the validity of a statement said by one source. So too is there a need for independent verification that how a president classifies documents ensures their (i.e., the documents') proper place.

In essence, while the PRA and the PLA do complement each other, both laws seem quite independent of each other, as if each was created in a vacuum. The PLA provides for maintenance costs; the PRMPA for government "control—not ownership" of Nixon's documents; the PRA provides for eventual access to presidential documents, but only from Reagan on. As to what could be accessed, that still was a matter left up to the president. The Archivist of the United States had little recourse but to force documents to be opened, because executive documents are not subject to the Freedom of Information Act (FOIA). Further, Archivists of the United States have been loath to report to Congress the possibility of infringement of the PRA by the president. Being a political appointee of the sitting president, it seems doubtful that the Archivist would go to such trouble to force open records that the president wants to remain sealed.

All in all, while the issues that effected the creation of the PRMPA and the PRA do not expressly exist today (i.e., Watergate), many of the background issues that were brought up (e.g., the chilling effect) during the course of both of the two 1970s-era bills remain with us to this day. Indeed, the issues that were brought before congressional hearings ranged from who should determine access to past presidential documents to the chilling effect that would occur if all presidential records became a part of the national trust to determining what is better, centralized or decentralized presidential libraries. Yet, these sources of friction also provide a unique opportunity for archivists, government documents librarians, records managers, policy makers and administrators to discuss how best to fulfill the promise called for in the PRA.

Granted, public officials do need some assurance that their private conversations are indeed private, but in our American experiment, the public citizenry also has a right to know what our public officials are doing and have done. Therein lies the rub: Where does one draw the line between confidentiality and public access? Nixon sensed just such an issue and it was probably for this reason that he feared disclosure of the Watergate tapes. After what amount of time does something become public domain? Five years? Ten years? Fifteen years? According to the law as noted in the PRA, most presidential documents become publicly available within twelve years. Yet Executive Order 13233 signed November 1, 2001 by President George W. Bush provides for a greater say of the sitting president to determine when and if schedules of documents should be released for public access. Despite all legislative attempts to control ownership of and access to presidential records, in 2005 access to past presidential documents seems just as capricious as in the days of the early Republic, when ownership and access were not determined by regular schedules but instead by past presidents themselves or by their heirs.

The question of ownership and accessibility of presidential documents has been asked throughout our country's history. But due to the events of Watergate, questions of ownership and access were asked more frequently in the past twenty years than ever before. Yet, many of these questions (decentralization vs. centralization; public vs. private documents; the chilling effect) remain to be answered. Some things never change, but other things only change at a glacial pace. So too is it with the Presidential Records Act, for while Executive Order 13233 changes the execution of the law to its fullest extent, the act still remains on the books. The dispute is between administrative and legislative law, an exercise in judicial review.

Somewhere in the middle of that process steps the Archivist of the United States. The position is a political appointment and the duties of that office are limited in scope and enforcement, yet it is of vital importance to ensure that documents are released when needed and classified in the proper areas, including private or public records. Some past archivists have been less than active in the area of pursuing access to or public ownership of presidential records, however.

Take, for example, Herman Kahn, a classic antidisestablishmentarist who testified before the Congress and was loath to change the present system, stating that:

> I would say we ought not radically to modify institutions which have worked well since almost the beginning of our history because of a new, unprecedented development [Watergate] which we hope will never be repeated in the future.[15]

James Rhoads, then Archivist of the United States, expressed a similar attitude, essentially advocating the less change to the system, the better:

> Functionally, archivists are supposed to be around to pick up the pieces after the events occur in which politicians and others take part. We don't ordinarily manipulate or try to control the events that we seek *only to record.*[16]

Fortunately, for those interested in access to and public ownership of presidential records, other points of view prevailed, and the

PRMPA and the PRA were both enacted. Because the Bush executive order may place presidential documents in a position of being technically accessible, if tangibly unobtainable, some have called for the extension of FOIA to presidential records. During the drafting of the PRA, critics feared that FOIA access rights eventually might be extended to executive branch records. These critics feared that FOIA-ing presidential records could lead to overclassification of documents to skirt scheduled release dates. That is, instead of a wide expanse of documents being released along a time schedule, documents would be released only when citizens requested specific records. Granting access to large segments of records via the FOIA process requires massive amounts of time and resources, as opposed to scheduled release and opening of records.

Yet another enduring tension has been the public's right to know as opposed to "a President's need for confidentiality."[17] Indeed, to trivialize this tension emanating from the Nixon-Sampson agreement would be a gross misunderstanding, because tensions between presidential expectations of confidentiality and the public's right to know has been an issue that has plagued presidents and advisors since George Washington. Yet, as Cook notes, "a desire to avoid embarrassing former officials by revealing frank discussions of political advisers can in no way be equated with the public's right to know of corruption, knavery, or unwise policy."[18] Essentially, this is a tension that can never fully be resolved, but sidestepping it completely by delaying the release of scheduled documents, not only is enmity fueled, but also is fodder is given for conspiracy theorists who create fantastic claims to explain why documents are not being released.

Notes

1. "Who Owns Presidential Papers?" *Manuscripts* 27: 1 (Winter 1975): 8.

2. Jannean L. Elliott, *Presidential Papers and the Presidential Library System* (Provo, UT: School of Library and Information Science, Brigham Young University, 1981), 5.

3. Pamela R. McKay, "Presidential Papers: A Property Issue," *Library Quarterly* 52: 1 (Jan. 1982): 29, quoting H. G. Jones, *Records of a Nation* (New York: Atheneum, 1969), 148-49.

4. H.G. Jones, "Presidential Libraries: Is There a Case for a National Presidential Library?" *American Archivist* 38: 3 (July 1975): 325.

5. Jones, "Presidential Libraries," 325.

6. J. Frank Cook, "'Private Papers' of Public Officials," *American Archi-*

vist 38: 3 (July 1975): 311.

7. Elliott, *Presidential Papers*, 4.

8. McKay, "Presidential Papers," 31, citing Ralph S. Brown Jr., "Owner-ship of Presidential Papers" (Unpublished Memorandum, New Haven, CT: Yale University Law School, 1974), 9.

9. Arnold Hirshon, "The Scope, Accessability [*sic*] and History of Presi-dential Papers," *Government Publications Review* 1:4 (Fall 1974): 374.

10. Cook, "Private Papers," 312.

11. Cook, "Private Papers," 299.

12. Cook, "Private Papers," 302.

13. Cook, "Private Papers," 302.

14. Anna Kasten Nelson, "The Public Documents Commission: Politics and Presidential Records," *Government Publications Review* 9: 5 (Sept.-Oct. 1982): 443

15. Elliott, *Presidential Papers*, 15.

16. Elliott, *Presidential Papers*, 15.

17. Cook, "Private Papers," 318.

18. Cook, "Private Papers," 319.

4

Conclusion

Q. What is the best thing that you could ever give a president in a post-Presidential Records Act world?

A. An absolutely photographic memory.

Prior to President Bush's Executive Order 13233 of November 1, 2001, the answer above would have made a bit more sense, since the major qualm of many with the PRA was that it would violate the sacred cloak of confidentiality by eventually disclosing documents to the public. The disclosure of documents would disrupt the confidentiality needed to ensure that complete candor was available between the president and his advisors in the White House. However, in light of E.O. 13233, perhaps the memos can once again be committed to paper, since the E.O. effectively makes presidential records more FOIA accessible and thus more easily controllable from the creator's end, but more difficult to access from the user's end.

Quickly claiming that the Bush executive order endangered the public's right to know, the Society of American Archivists (SAA) has rallied against the order and is currently pondering litigation against it. However, the SAA has not always been active in advocating a position on either ownership or access issues relating to presidential documents. Indeed, during the original enactment of the PRMPA and the PRA, several prominent members, including past presidents of the association, spoke out against the bills. As time has passed, the SAA has become more involved in the advocacy of openness of and access to the records of government officials. For while the issue of ownership has been decided in favor of federal possession of great majorities of executive-created materials and documents, the issues relating to access to these same records remain as lively as ever. As former Archivist of the United States and current director of the George Bush Presidential Library Don Wilson notes, "the issues and debate over Presidential records seem to mirror the political climate in our country."[1]

While laws have been put in place to control buildings and for microfilming of some presidential documents, the only sure-fire litmus test of ownership seems to be when the government out-and-out pays for documents—just as the Library of Congress did from the 1820s to the 1930s and as it recently did to end the disquiet surrounding the Nixon documents.

In the historical paradigm, the executive order promulgated by George W. Bush does not change much in the nature of accessibility of presidential papers to researchers. With regard to the trend set by FDR, timely access to records has been an issue of prominent import for researchers and one that has become a new tradition. However, by restricting when records can be disclosed, we are returning to a time when the capriciousness of individual presidents or their heirs determines who may gain access and who may not. The major change in the situation is that due to the enactment of the PRA of 1978, the ownership issue is more clearly defined; namely, that presidential records are owned by the government. Granted, issues still exist on what constitutes a record and what may be considered a document created by the president when acting in a purely unofficial manner, e.g., as a family member, common citizen, etc. Under attack now by the Bush E.O. is the accessibility of these publicly owned records. Restricting who may access them essentially guts the PRA of its second main charge: that of providing a means of access to records produced by the president when acting in his duties in the government employ.

Notes

1. Don W. Wilson, "Presidential Records: Evidence for Historians or Ammunition for Prosecutors," *Government Information Quarterly* 14: 4 (1997): 345.

Part 2

Bibliographic Essay Concerning Legislative Control of Presidential Records

5

Bibliographic Essay

The bibliographic essay that follows looks at twenty-two specific topics that relate to the use, creation and ownership of federal records and, specifically, presidential records. The topics covered in the bibliographic essay are issues that the author grappled with when trying to understand the complexities of the Presidential Records Act of 1978 (PRA). As is often the case, reading about one topic often leads to a need to find out more about the issues in a related field. An example of how this bibliographic survey became so large is the topic of administrative law.

Administrative law seems only remotely attached to the records created by federal officials, yet it is difficult to understand how federal records are processed and preserved without an appreciation for how many administrative decisions are made before presidential records of any form are preserved. This begs the question, who gives administrative agencies the power to make such decisions and can these decisions be appealed? This, in turn, leads to the topics of separation of powers and judicial review. After learning of the interplay that exists between judicial review, administrative law, and the separation of powers, one may well wonder who would ever want to explore these issues, thus the topic of how records are used and why history is studied are both broached.

Of course, discussion could be expanded so far as to become unmanageable. As with any scholarly endeavor, a delicate balance exists between providing enough contextual information without losing sight of the topic originally broached, in this case, legislative control of presidential records. While this bibliographic essay does provide access points from such widely ranging topics as "Why History" to the history of the National Study Commission on the Records and Documents of Federal Officials, each topic area covers a specific and necessary sphere of information that any scholar must understand before attempting to gain a comprehensive overview of the complex issues relating to the federal ownership of the records created by its officials.

The twenty-three topics covered in this essay are:

A. Why History?
B. How Do Historians Use Federal Government Documents and Records?
C. What Is a Record?
D. Access to Federal Records
E. Are Electronic Records Different?
F. Toward an Understanding of Administrative Law
G. Classic U.S. Administrative Concepts: Judicial Review and Separation of Powers
H. Latent Discord: Executive Privilege
I. The Development of the Presidential Branch . . .
J. . . . and of Government Secrecy
K. Privacy as a Right (?)
L. Another American Rub: Concepts of Property
M. The Fourth Amendment and Takings Law
N. Precedent: The Clark Papers Case
O. The History of the National Archives in Brief
P. Who Owns Federal Records? Q.   The Care of Presidential Papers (pre-1955)
R. The Development of the Presidential Libraries System (post-1955)
S. Histories of Individual Presidential Libraries (pre-Roosevelt)
T. Precedent: Kahn Case
U. Histories of Individual Presidential Libraries (post-Roosevelt)
V. The Past as Prologue to the Future: Richard M. Nixon's Papers
W. After Nixon: The Public Documents Commission and the Presidential Records Act of 1978'

Structurally, the framework of this essay ranges from the broadest in scope to the narrowest. In a somewhat loose fashion, a chronological framework also was applied to the essay whenever possible. Thus, events and topics covered in the essay are ordered in the manner in which they occurred. In other words, works that describe the development of the Franklin D. Roosevelt Library come before works that detail the history of the Herbert Hoover Library—even though Hoover's presidency predates Roosevelt's—because Roosevelt's presidential library opened over a decade before Hoover's did.

No bibliography can ever be 100 percent comprehensive. Many sources that appear in the bibliography in Part 3 were excluded from the essay that follows because materials selected for the essay were more current, comprehensive, concise, penetrating or well written.

While citations to legal materials are included in the bibliography, only on rare occasions does this essay list specific case names within the text of the narrative. In the case of *U.S. v. Nixon*, so much literature has appeared over the decades that several paragraphs are devoted to this legal event exclusively. For those interested in researching the legal cases listed in this essay specifically, make sure to consult the cross-indexed table of cases found in appendix C.

While the primary scope of the narrative presented in Part One of this work gives an overview of the history of the PRA and the legislative, executive and judicial control of presidential records, the primary scope of the bibliographic essay is to present a selective bibliography of all the works discovered by the author that relate to the federal control of presidential records. The succeeding paragraphs describe in detail the criteria used in discovering and selecting the works listed in the bibliography and the bibliographic essay.

A. Why History?

The specialization of the historical profession in the United States in the mid- to late-nineteenth century is often as closely associated with the alignment of the field to the social sciences as it is to the professionalization of the field and the self-imposed standards of research methods. However, roots of the professionalization of the field may in fact be traced back even further, especially if one considers that the origins of American historical editorship can be traced back to the seminal compiling efforts of Thomas Jefferson and Ebenezer Hazard, America's first historical documentary editors. Such books as Peter Novik's *That Noble Dream: The 'Objectivity Question' and the American Historical Profession* (Cambridge 1988) or Laurence Veysey's *The Emergence of the American University* (Chicago 1965) focus on the development of the historical profession, but the work that both Jefferson and Hazard undertook with their respective *Notes of Virginia* and *Historical Collections of State Papers and Other Authentic Documents* must also be credited in no small part with enabling the professsionalization of the discipline in later generations. Without the compiling and editing efforts of Jefferson, Hazard and others, the grist for the historical mill would not have been as widely available when the academic discipline professionalized and specialized in the 1800s. "There is no substitute for staying close to the primary sources," said Thomas Jefferson's biographer, Dumas Malone, to the *Washington Post* on

July 5, 1981 (quoted in Nelson 1982, 89).

For further readings on the significance of studying the past, one could not hope to do much better than to read R. G. Collingwood, *The Idea of History* (Oxford 1993). The reissued 1993 edition of Collingwood contains a helpful introduction as well as materials not available in older editions long since out of print. For more background on the pitfalls of historical thought, make sure to read David Hackett Fischer's timeless masterpiece, *Historians' Fallacies: Toward a Logic of Historical Thought* (New York 1970).

For more on Hazard and his efforts to compile the documents and records used and created by his revolutionary cohorts, see former Archivist of the United States Don W. Wilson's "Prologue in Perspective: The Legacy of Ebenezer Hazard, America's First Documentary Editor," *American Archivist* 21: 1 (Spring 1989) or Philip M. Hamer's article, "'Authentic Documents Tending to Elucidate Our History,'" *American Archivist* 25: 1 (January 1962). For further clarification on the benefits and uses of the creation and maintenance of federal records, make sure to see Anna Kasten Nelson's eloquent article entitled "Historian's Perspective: Challenge of Documenting the Federal Government in the Latter 20th Century" in *Prologue* 14: 2 (Summer 1982). Another well-written article espousing the benefits of preserving the historical record, while also understanding the archivist's dilemma that not all records can (or even should) be saved, is Helen Willa Samuels's, "Who Controls the Past," *American Archivist* 49: 2 (Spring 1986).

B. How Do Historians Use Federal Government Documents and Records?

As important as creating and saving records is how those records are used. For an introduction to the historian's use of the federal archival material, see Philip C. Brooks, "The Historian's Stake in Federal Records," *Mississippi Valley Historical Review* 43: 2 (September 1956). For another primer to the historical method—and its use of materials in presidential repositories—consult O. Lawrence Burnette Jr.'s *Beneath the Footnote: A Guide to the Use and Preservation of American Historical Sources* (Madison, WI, 1969). Make sure to see also Edward Weldon's July 1977 article in *American Archivist* entitled "Lest We Forget: Setting Priorities for the Preservation and Use of Historical Re- cords."

It is important to understand how historians use federal records in their research. Next to the first hand experience of using federal records, it is essential to recognize how other historians have made use or misuse of federal records. To gain a feel for the historical revisionism that is calling into question the historical editing of Jared Sparks and other nineteenth century U.S. historians, consult Richard N. Sheldon's "Editing a Historical Manuscript: Jared Sparks, Douglas Southall Freeman and the Battle of Brandywine," *William and Mary Quarterly* 36: 2 (April 1979). In "Jared Sparks, Robert Peel and the State Paper Office," *American Quarterly* 13: 2 (Summer 1961), author Galen Broeker explains the difficulties experienced by the fledgling history discipline in the early nineteenth century, whereas Charles K. Webster explains how a select few from the United States traversed the Atlantic to make use of British archival resources in "Some Early Applications from American Historians to Use the British Archives," *Journal of Modern History* 1: 3 (September 1929). Lester Cappon's article, "The National Archives and the Historical Profession," *Journal of Southern History* 35: 4 (November 1969), succinctly explains the development of the National Archives through the lens of the unfulfilled needs of both a government bursting at the seams with documentary evidence and a historical profession eagerly looking for new resources to use. Citations to more materials relating to the creation of the National Archives are related in fuller detail later in this essay.

Numerous monographs exist that provide narrative guides to conducting historical research, including how to use historical records and documents, as well as how documentary evidence can easily be manipulated and massaged to make one's point. Two of the more well received books on historical research are Arthur Marwick, *The Nature of History* (London 1989) and Jacques Barzun and Henry F. Graff, *The Modern Researcher* (New York 1977), as well as Fischer and Collingwood's works. A veritable plethora of works exist on the subject of the nature of history or conduct of historical research, with many more titles being produced every year, so a careful review of the modern literature will always supply this list with additional resources.

C. What Is a Record?

Before one can begin using the records of the federal government for historical purposes, one must appreciate the language and culture of those who create records (federal officials and employees).

In additionally, researchers of federal records must also understand the culture and language of those who preserve, arrange and organize the records (archivists). Complicating the issue of access to federal records is that the two respective fields (federal officials / employees and federal archivists) do not always use the same language or even necessarily espouse the same institutional values. While a significant portion of the text later on in the essay explains the organizational cultures, responsibilities and expectations of federal officials and employees, this portion introduces the reader to several introductory sources for archival materials. While nothing can take the place of actually doing archival work, several primers do exist that will present the world of fonds and provenance to the uninitiated. Perhaps the source that the student should become acquainted with first would be Maygene F. Daniels' and Timothy Walch's, eds, A *Modern Archives Reader: Basic Readings on Archival Theory and Practice* (Washington, DC 1984). Published by the National Archives, the work collates seminal works in the field of archival studies.

A monograph to consult is Trevor Livelton's *Archival Theory, Records, and the Public* (Lanham, MD, 1996), a short book that contains valuable information in accessible language. For an international perspective on the ownership of federal government records, the comprehensive scholar would be remiss if the readings of Sir Hilary Jenkinson should not make it to his or her reading list. *Selected Writings of Sir Hilary Jenkinson* (Gloucester, Eng. 1980) compiles the best and brightest of Jenkinson's writings into one convenient volume, although this text is often difficult to locate. Another source to consult for Jenkinson's opinions on the access, control and ownership of the records of government officials, is Jenkinson's *A Manual of Archive Administration* (London, Var. Ed.).

As for the legal definitions in the United States of archival terms and concepts, there is no one-stop convenient place to look other than the NARA website www.archives.gov. Regulations and definitions are often listed in numerous sources, so consulting just the U.S. Code or the Code of Federal Regulations will be time-consuming if done in print, or yield an incomplete picture if done via computer-assisted research. A handy place to start when trying to understand the legal implications of archival standards in the federal government is the American Law Reports Federal edition (ALR Fed). For example, just a few of the titles found in the ALR series are the following: Marjorie A. Shields, "What Constitutes 'Agency' for Purposes of Freedom of Information Act (5 U.S.C.A. § 552)," *American Law Reports Federal*

165 (2000, Oct. 2001 Supp.); Jo Ann F. Wasil, "What Is 'Record' Within the Meaning of Privacy Act of 1974 (5 U.S.C.A. § 552A)," *American Law Reports Federal* 121 (1994, Oct. 2001 Supp.); Donald T. Kramer, "Executive Privilege with Respect to Presidential Papers and Recordings," *American Law Reports Federal* 19 (1974, October 2001 Supp.); "What Constitutes a Public Record or Document within Statute Making Falsification, Forgery, Mutilation, Removal or Other Misuse Thereof an Offense," *American Law Reports 4th* 75 (1990, August 2001 Supp.). Although some of the articles are over twenty-five years old, updates for each article arrive on a yearly basis or until a more up-to-date version of the article supersedes the older one.

D. Access to Federal Records

After understanding how the archival and legal worlds collide and co-operate in the matrix that is the federal government, the researcher is ready to understand the tricky issue of public access to federal records. To understand who owns what—and when—with regard to federal records, one must comprehend the mechanisms in place designed to allow for ready access to government-produced materials. In other words, a full and comprehensive understanding of the workings of the Freedom of Information Act (FOIA), the Sunshine in Government Act and the Privacy Act is something the student must achieve.

For a critical analysis of the FOIA, see David A. Wallace's Ph.D. dissertation, "The Public's Use of Recordkeeping Statutes to Shape Federal Information Policy: A Study of the PROFS Case, " (University of Pittsburgh 1997). Not only does Wallace's work provide a clear and concise introduction to the quasi-clandestine means of public access to federal records, but it also provides valuable insights into what the administrative policy-making portions of the federal government have to do with regulating the public's access to documents and records created by public officials. Also especially helpful to use in understanding the FOIA and the Privacy Act is a government report by the House of Representatives, Committee on Government Reform, entitled *A Citizen's Guide on Using the Freedom of Information Act and the Privacy Act of 1974 to Request Government Records* (106th Cong., 1st sess., H. Rept. 106-50). The 1999 report not only provides a background explaining the purpose, scope and history of each act, but the report also explains how the citizen can use the two acts to request information. Also useful, but not as detailed, is the Department of Justice's webpages   on the FOIA www.usdoj.gov/04foia/referenceguidemay99.htm.

Many articles have appeared over the years on the FOIA and the Privacy Act, some of which are listed here. The articles listed here comprise but a few on the subject and were selected based on accessibility of the writing style in combination with currency of topic. In some case, these two criteria were mutually exclusive, but for the most part, the articles listed below meet both selection criteria.

One especially penetrating article written by Patricia M. Wald called "The Freedom of Information Act: A Short Case Study in the Perils and Paybacks of Legislating Democratic Values" appeared in *Emory Law Journal* 33 (Summer 1984). The article questions the merits of legislating access to information, with the author approaching the topic with a refreshingly Jeffersonian point of view. While acknowledging the tensions inherent in the FOIA, authors since the passage of the act have noted that such airs of open government could spell problems for national security as well as for prospects of ensuring limited confidentiality for government officials and employees in the discharge of their duties, which very well may involve matters dealing with national secrets or individual rights to privacy. Indeed, these are the same issues that appear when one looks at the Presidential Records Act!

Some of the articles that address the tension between open government and releasing information potentially harmful to the safety of the nation are the following: "Threshold Definitional Barriers to Disclosure: *Forsham v. Harris* and *Kissinger v. Reporters Committee for Freedom of the Press*," *Harvard Law Review* 94 (November 1980); "The Military and State Secrets Privilege: Protection for the National Security or Immunity for the Executive," *Yale Law Journal* 91 (January 1982); Susan D. Steinwall, "Appraisal and the FBI Files Case: For Whom Do Archivists Retain Records?" *American Archivist* 49: 1 (Winter 1986); Thomas Elton Brown, "The Freedom of Information Act in the Information Age: The Electronic Challenge to the People's Right to Know," *American Archivist* 58: 2 (Spring 1995); John K. Martinelli, "*United States v. Armstrong*: The United States Supreme Court's First 'Crack' at the Standard for Discovery in Selective Prosecution Challenges," *George Mason University Civil Rights Law Journal* 7 (Spring 1997); R. Kevin Bailey, "'Did I Miss Anything?' Excising the National Security Council from FOIA Coverage," *Duke Law Journal* 46: 6 (April 1997); Sasha A. Mason, "The National Security Council Is Not an Agency under the Freedom of Information Act," *George Washington Law Review* 66: 4 (April 1998).

Many other individual studies have been crafted over the years explaining the exceptions and exemptions under the FOIA, but rather than list them all here, these specialty articles and reports may be found in the bibliography attached to this report. In addition, using the *American Law Reports* (ALR) or the *American Law Reports Federal* and looking for entries about either the FOIA or the Privacy Act are fruitful ways to update one's knowledge about these ever-changing acts.

E. Are Electronic Records Different?

As the reader may surmise, many of the more recent articles written about the FOIA from the legal standpoint involve the management of electronic records and the public's right to access these records. The archival field too is concerned with discovering the applicability of the openness in government acts to electronic records. In his 1993 *American Archivist* article, "The Implications of *Armstrong v. Executive* [sic] *of the President* for the Archival Management of Electronic Records," 56: 4 (Fall 1993), David Bearman summarizes the events that led up to the infamous *Armstrong v. the Executive Office of the President* (more commonly known as the PROFS case). The case developed as a result of the Iran-Contra affair when high-ranking executive branch officials began to destroy e-mail created in the discharge of their duties. For more on Iran-Contra and how it relates to electronic recordkeeping, see Anthony Simones's article, "The Iran-Contra Affair: Ten Years Later," *UMKC Law Review* 67 (Fall 1998).

The PROFS case marks the moment when the American public at large first became acquainted with the government's use of electronic mail. Although Bearman's article is growing increasingly out of date, it conveniently introduces the concept of electronic record management and storage in an easy-to-understand manner. The litigation itself awaits its own monograph, for the five cases that are collectively called the PROFS case are in need of further research. Other than the previously mentioned dissertation of Wallace, not much scholarship has been done on this important area of governmental archival practice. For further details on the text of the messages involved in the high-profile PROFS case, make sure to consult Tom Blanton, ed., *White House E-Mail: The Top Secret Computer Messages the Reagan / Bush White House Failed to Destroy* (New York 1995). Other texts helpful in understanding the PROFS case include the following articles, all written by legal scholars: James D. Lewis, "White House Electronic Mail and Federal Recordkedeping Law: Press 'D' to Delete History," *Michigan Law Review* 93: 4 (February 1995); Christine Sgarlata Chung and David J. Byer, "The Electronic Paper Trial: Evidentiary Obstacles to Discovery and Admission of Electronic Evidence," *Boston University Journal of Science and Technology Law* 4 (Spring 1998); Catherine F. Sheehan, "Opening the Government's Electronic Mail: Public Access to National Security Council Records," *Boston College Law Review* 35; Henry H. Perritt, Jr., "Electronic Records Management and Archives," *University of Pittsburgh Law Review* 53 (Summer 1992).

Another resource not to miss is the National Academy of Public Administration's *The Effects of Electronic Recordkeeping on the Historical Record of the U.S. Government: A Report for the National Archives and Records Administration* (Washington, DC, 1989). Although contemporaneous with the first PROFS case, NAPA's report presents one of the earliest scholarly views on electronic records of the federal government. Especially helpful in the work is the manner in which NAPA dovetails electronic records management with administrative practices and standards.

F. Toward an Understanding of Administrative Law

To understand the complicated nature of federal archival practice, one must appreciate the level of influence that administrative decisions have on federal archival work. Thus, a thorough understanding of U.S. administrative law remains an essential asset for the researcher approaching the topic of government control of federal records. The specialty of administrative law is far from being a new field of study of law, yet for many decades, critics within the law field complained of the specialty's academic stagnation. Within the past twenty years, however, new scholarship has invigorated a field previously thought to be unimaginative.

A significant discourse over the nature and purpose of administrative law has ebbed and flowed over the years, but rather than listing a seemingly never-ending list of monographs and journal articles, turning to Peter H. Schuck's *Foundations of Administrative Law* (Oxford, 1994) will introduce the uninitiated to complex field. Although now nearing ten years old, Schuck's work, issued as part of Oxford's Interdisciplinary Readers in Law series, provides numerous digests of seminal articles on administrative law in the United States. Although not all of the articles are equally accessible to the reader, many provide the basics (e.g., one chapter is about the history of administrative law, another is about the Administrative Procedures Act) needed for the nascent scholar otherwise unfamiliar or uncomfortable with administrative law.

To gain a deeper understanding of the development of the American administrative state, turning to the enabling act might prove most useful, which can be found in U.S. Senate, Committee on the Judiciary, *Administrative Procedure Act Legislative History* (79th Cong., 2nd sess., Doc. No. 248). Although the act (usually abbreviated as the APA) has been modified and altered over time, the legislative history noted above provides an excellent starting point for those interested in understanding how the federal administrative state developed at the close of World War II.

Also helpful to understanding administrative law is William F. Leahy's "Recent Developments in Administrative Law: Congressional Supervision of Agency Action, the Fate of the Legislative Veto after Chadha," *George Washington Law Review* 53 (November 1984/January 1985), and Morton Rosenberg's "Congress's Prerogative over Agencies and Agency Decisionmakers: The Rise and Demise of the Reagan Administration's Theory of the Unitary Executive," *George Washington Law Review* 57 (January 1989).

G. Classic U.S. Administrative Concepts: Judicial Review and Separation of Powers

Intrinsic to the idea of a U.S. administrative state is the equally complex concept of separation of powers between the branches of the federal government. Closely associated with the idea of separation of powers is the idea of judicial review. In fact, all three concepts are closely intertwined, and in many ways, not easy to distinguish from each other. Debated vociferously since the beginnings of the American republic, the concept of judicial review is as controversial a topic today as it was in 1803, when the U.S. Supreme Court handed down its infamous precedent-setting decision in *Marbury v. Madison*. The literature surrounding judicial review has continued to grow over the years, but several introductory sources are available to the scholar approaching the topic.

Tying together nicely the fields of judicial review and administrative delegation of power is Glendon A. Schubert Jr.'s article, "Judicial Review of the Subdelegation of Presidential Power," *Journal of Poli-*

tics 12: 4 (November 1950). For a fundamental understanding of the role of the Supreme Court and justiciable issues, even though the work is slightly out of date, Otis H. Stephens's and Gregory J. Rathjen's seminal book, *The Supreme Court and the Allocation of Constitutional Power* (San Francisco 1980). Providing both selected text from significant decisions and critical analyses to accompany them, the work's first few chapters remain a great place to start one's research about judicial review. Also helpful in understanding the concept of American judicial review is Robert G. McCloskey's *The American Supreme Court* (Chicago 1994). McCloskey's work originally appeared in 1960, but the 1994 edition, revised by Sanford Levinson, a former Ph.D. student of McCloskey, contains valuable chapters on judicial review, as well as others on the development of institutional the Supreme Court over time.

An older source, but one still helpful for understanding the pre-*Marbury v. Madison* roots of judicial review, is D. O. Wagner's "Some Antecedents of the American Doctrine of Judicial Review," published in *Political Science Quarterly* 40: 4 (December 1925). Another helpful study remains Donald G. Morgan's "The Origin of Supreme Court Dissent," *William and Mary Quarterly* 10: 3 (July 1953). Already noted earlier, Carl Bretscher's "Presidential Records Act: The President and Judicial Review Under the Records Acts," is perhaps the best source available that applies the concept of judicial review to the PRA.

Another older source still valuable for its intellectual rigor on the concept of judicial review as a historical concept is the series of 1955-1958 Louis L. Jaffe articles that appeared in the widely circulated *Harvard Law Review*. For complete citations for these articles, see the "legal journals" section of Part 3. For a more recent interpretation of judicial review, make sure to see Harold H. Bruff, "Judicial Review and the President's Statutory Powers," *Virginia Law Review Association* 68: 1 (January 1982), and Steven G. Calabresi, "The President, The Supreme Court, and the Constitution: A Brief Positive Account of the Role of Government Lawyers in the Development of Constitutional Law," *Law and Contemporary Problems* 61: 1 (Winter 1998).

With regard to how the Supreme Court has approached the area of presidential power (an issue that came to bear as an important issue in the past twenty-five years in such cases as *U.S. v. Nixon, Jones v. Clinton,* as well as due to the growth of the executive branch), consult Erwin Chemerinsky, "Controlling Inherent Presidential Power: Providing a Framework for Judicial Review," *Southern California Law Review* 56: 4 (May 1983) and Paul D. Carrington, "Political Questions: The Judicial Check on the Executive," *Virginia Law Review* 42: 2 (February

1956).

For further explanation of the increasing rift between the branches of the federal government and how judicial review interacts with the increasingly siege mentality between branches, make sure to consult Jesse H. Choper, "The Supreme Court and the Political Branches: Democratic Theory and Practice," *University of Pennsylvania Law Review* 122: 4 (April 1974) and Jonathan L. Entin, "Separation of Powers, the Political Branches and the Limits of Judicial Review," *Ohio State Law Journal* 51 (Winter 1990).

Especially helpful in viewing the increased prominence of judicial review in light of the explosive growth of the executive branch is P. Allan Dionisopoulos's "New Patterns in Judicial Control of the Presidency: 1950's to 1970's," *Akron Law Review* 10: 1 (Summer 1976). Complementing Dionisopoulos is Nathaniel L. Nathanson's "From Watergate to *Marbury v. Madison*: Some Reflections on Presidential Privilege in Current Historical Perspectives," *Arizona Law Review* 16: 1 (1974), an article that argues that despite the wide-held belief that the Watergate affair presented new historical and constitutional challenges for the Republic, many of the issues—including that of executive privilege—addressed in *U.S. v. Nixon* had already been adjudicated in several seminal cases of the early Republic, including *Marbury v. Madison* and *U.S. v. Burr*.

H. Latent Discord: Executive Privilege

As the American executive branch has grown over the years, so too has the president's use of executive privilege. The concept of executive privilege remains closely aligned with the twin concepts of separation of powers and judicial review. All three of the concepts culminated perhaps most memorably in the case of *U.S. v. Nixon*, where Richard Nixon alleged that under certain circumstances, the president was immune from prosecution and only he could decide when an issue was justiciable. The court ruled against Nixon, and in so doing, paved the way for a later judicial ruling, *Nixon v. Administrator of General Services*, which led to the preservation of Nixon's White House tape recordings, thus upholding the Presidential Recordings and Materials Preservation Act.

In each case, the concept of executive privilege and immunity played a great role. Paving the way for *U.S. v. Nixon* to get to the Supreme Court was the case *Nixon v. Sirica*. For more on the *Sirica* case, see "Recent Cases—Executive Privilege: The President Does Not Have an Absolute Privilege to Withhold Evidence from a Grand Jury, *Nixon v. Sirica*, 487 F.2d 700 (D.C. Cir. 1973)," *Harvard Law Review* 87: 7 (May 1974). Also helpful is John J. Sirica, *To Set the Record Straight: The Break-in, the Tapes, the Conspirators, the Pardon* (New York, 1979), a book written by the D.C. Circuit Court judge who mandated that Nixon's tape-recorded oval office conversations be handed over for criminal prosecution.

For further explanation of the two closely aligned subjects of executive privilege and judicial review, consult Mark Rozell's *Executive Privilege: The Dilemma of Secrecy and Democratic Accountability* (Baltimore 1994). This reading should be supplemented by Rozell's more current work that appeared in the *William and Mary Bill of Rights Journal* 8 (April 2000) entitled "Restoring Balance to the Debate over Executive Privilege: A Response to Berger." This last work is the first full-length article that has taken on the heretofore expert on executive privilege, Raoul Berger.

Berger's widely cited monograph, *Executive Privilege: A Constitutional Myth* (Cambridge, MA, 1974), is best read as complementary to Rozell's more recent scholarship. For further explanation of *Nixon v. Administrator of General Services*, see Patricia L. Spencer, "Recent Cases, Constitutional Law: *Nixon v. Administrator of General Services*, 97 S.Ct. 2777 (1977)," *Akron Law Review* 11: 2 (Fall 1977). For a rather complete history of the *U.S. v. Nixon* case, make sure to locate a copy of Leon Friedman, ed. *United States v. Nixon: The President before the Supreme Court* (New York 1974), which contains an almost complete documentary history of the case as it made it to the Supreme Court. A briefer and more legalistic overview of the case may be found in "The Supreme Court, 1973 Term: Judicial Claims of Executive Privilege," *Harvard Law Review* 88: 1 (November 1974). Supplementing both Fiedman and the *Harvard Law Review* is *Political Science Quarterly* 88: 4 (December 1973), which contains the full text of the briefs filed in *U.S. v. Nixon* in a section of the journal entitled "Separation of Powers and Executive Privilege: The Watergate Briefs." Helpful for placing *U.S. v. Nixon* in a historical context is D. S. Hobbs, "*United States v. Nixon*: An Historical Perspective," *Loyola of Los Angeles Law Review* 9: 1 (December 1975).

For recent perspectives on the impact of *U.S. v. Nixon*, make sure to look at both K.A. McNeely-Johnson, "*United States v. Nixon*, Twenty Years After: The Good, the Bad and the Ugly—An Exploration of Executive Privilege," *Northern Illinois University Law Review* 14 (Fall 1993), and the *Minnesota Law Review* 83: 5 (May 1999). The latter contains eleven scholarly articles that originated as series of "panel

discussions" held at the October 1998 University of Minnesota symposium on *United States v. Nixon*. Entitled "*United States v. Nixon*: Presidential Power and Executive Privilege Twenty-Five Years Later," the
symposium's printed counterpart is an excellent secondary source to
consult to gauge the effect of *U.S. v. Nixon*. Archibald Cox, a Watergate special prosecutor who eventually was fired by President Nixon,
gives his views on executive privilege in his aptly titled "Executive
Privilege," which appeared in the *University of Pennsylvania Law Review* 122: 6 (June 1974). Dovetailing nicely with Cox's article is Leon
Jaworski's "The Most Lustrous Branch: Watergate and the Judiciary,"
Fordham Law Review 65: 6 (May 1977), and Sam Ervin Jr.'s "Controlling 'Executive Privilege,'" *Loyola Law Review* 20: 1 (Fall 1974). Jaworski was Cox's replacement as special prosecutor for Watergate,
while Ervin was a senator on the committee investigating the activities
of Nixon.

For those interested in how the limiting of executive privilege constraints the power of the president, see Randall K. Miller, "Congressional Inquests: Suffocating the Constitutional Prerogative of Executive
Privilege," *Minnesota Law Review* 81 (February 1997). For a point of
view contrary to Miller, see Luis Kutner, "Executive Privilege. . .
Growth of Power Over a Declining Congress," *Loyola Law Review* 20:
1 (Fall 1974). Also treating the subject of executive privilege is the excellent Paul A. Freund essay, "The Supreme Court, 1973 Term: Foreword—On Presidential Privilege," *Harvard Law Review* 88: 1 (November 1974). Concerned more with executive privilege as it relates to
immunity from prosecution is Theodore P. Stein, "*Nixon v. Fitzgerald*:
Presidential Immunity as a Constitutional Imperative," *Catholic University Law Review* 32 (Spring 1983), and "Supreme Court, 1996 Term
Leading Cases—Constitutional Law: Separation of Powers—
Presidential Immunity," *Harvard Law Review* 111: 1 (November
1997).

For a perspective on the interrelationship between the branches of
the federal government, as related to the growth of executive privilege
and congressional inquiries for information, make sure to see Rex
E. Lee, "Executive Privilege, Congressional Subpoena Power, and
Judicial Review: Three Branches, Three Powers, and Some Relationships," *Brigham Young University Law Review* 1978: 2 (1978).

I. The Development of the Presidential Branch . . .

While many of the resources that look at the growth of executive privilege date from the early 1970s and are contemporaneous with the Pres-

idency of Richard Nixon, works that look at the development and growth of the executive branch of government have appeared only of late. While the original works of Corwin and Schlesinger date to the mid-1950s, it was not until much more recently that scholarly attention focused on the exponential growth of the presidential side of the government, and most scholars agree that the modern presidential state of government can be traced back to the presidency of the Franklin D. Roosevelt.

Numerous works have been penned on FDR, but only one has approached Roosevelt's presidency through the prism of administrative power aggrandizement, Matthew J. Dickinson's *Bitter Harvest: FDR, Presidential Power and the Growth of the Presidential Branch* (Cambridge 1997). Another valuable place to look to gain an appreciation for the development of the "presidential branch" is John Hart, *The Presidential Branch: From Washington to Clinton* (Chatham, NJ, 1995) as well as Edward S. Corwin, *The President: Office and Powers, 1787-1984* (New York 1984), and James P. Pfiffner, *The Modern Presidency* (New York 1994). Make sure to consult also Hugh Heclo's "The Changing Presidential Office" in *Politics and the Oval Office: Toward Presidential Governance* (San Francisco 1981) for a look at the role of the executive office of the president.

Richard P. Nathan's *The Plot That Failed: Nixon and the Administrative Presidency* (New York 1975) provides a compelling case study of the administrate state that almost was under President Nixon. Nathan not only overviews Nixon's plans to create an administrative state with a characteristically Nixonian indelible thumbprint, but he also exquisitely shows how the administrative part of the executive office blossomed during the post-World War II era. Other helpful studies written about the growth of the executive, but more legal in scope, include Theodore C. Sorensen, "Making the President More Accountable to the People," *Human Rights* 5: 1 (Fall 1975), and Arthur Selwynn Miller, "Implications of Watergate: Some Proposals for Cutting the Presidency Down to Size," *Hastings Constitutional Law Quarterly* 2: 1 (Winter 1975).

For an interesting look at how the "role of presidential communication" in an increasingly sound-bite world, see Mary E. Stuckey, *The President as Interpreter-In-Chief* (Chatham, NJ, 1991). Presidential communication of a different sort is eloquently detailed in Kenneth R. Mayer, *With the Stroke of a Pen: Executive Orders and Presidential Power* (Princeton, NJ, 2001). Mayer's work is one of the most penetrating studies of the use of executive orders ever undertaken. Mayer combines both quantitative statistics and discursive analytical text that focuses on the ways that presidents have used executive orders to communicate presidential intent.

Mayer's work might best be read as a companion volume to David Sadofsky's *Knowledge as Power: Political and Legal Control of Information* (New York 1990), a monograph that contrasts political control of information against personal rights and informational needs. Finally, a work that blends the concepts of government secret, executive power and the growth of the presidential branch is Abraham D. Sofaer's "Executive Power and the Control of Information: Practice under the Framers," *Duke Law Journal* 26: 1 (March 1977). Sofaer's article seamlessly ties together the topics of governmental secrecy, executive growth and control of information, while placing his discussion in a useful historical context.

J. . . . and of Government Secrecy

Not addressed directly in this essay thus far—but touched upon tangentially—is the topic of governmental secrecy. As with so many of the other topics broached, a complete bibliography of the works associated with governmental secrecy is not the point of this essay, but an introduction to some of the major works in the field is necessary for the scholar to understand how governmental-imposed secrecy declarations affect a citizen's interactions with his or her own government.

For a historical look at how secrecy in the U.S. federal government developed during the early Republic, make sure to see Donald N. Hoffman, *Governmental Secrecy and the Founding Fathers* (Westport, CT, 1981). With regard to the president and secrecy, many may find John M. Orman's *Presidential Secrecy and Deception: Beyond the Power to Persuade* (Westport, CT 1980) a good place to start, if but the text covers material of more historical note, rather than contemporary events. More journalistic and discursive than scholarly is David Wise's *The Politics of Lying: Government Deception, Secrecy and Power* (New York 1973). A more up-to-date companion to the Orman work is the edited work of Athan G. Theoharis called *A Culture of Secrecy: The Government versus the People's Right to Know* (Lawrence, KS, 1998). Also worth consulting is Lee C. Weingart, "Who Keeps the Secrets? A Framework and Analysis of the Separation of Powers Dispute in *American Foreign Service Association v. Garfinkel*," *George Washington Law Review* 59: 1 (November 1990).

K. Privacy as a Right (?)

Contingent with the idea of governmental secrecy is the concept of the right to privacy. Much like the issue of governmental secrecy, the literature of privacy rights is much too extensive to enumerate here, although a few select sources noted in the text pertain directly to the confluence between archival theory, a right to privacy, and government documents. The seminal—and still cited—document in American legal literature concerning a right to privacy is Samuel D. Warren's and Louis D. Brandeis's classic, "The Right to Privacy," *Harvard Law Review* 4: 5 (December 1890). For further explanation of Brandeis's concepts of the "right to be left alone," make sure to see the impressive collection of Brandeis documents complied in Philippa Strum, ed., *Brandeis on Democracy* (Lawrence, KS, 1995).

For more on the way that privacy was construed at the time Warren and Brandeis penned their ground-breaking article, see "The Right to Privacy in Nineteenth Century America," *Harvard Law Review* 94 (June 1981), an article that contends that perhaps the authors were not as revolutionary as was once thought. Privacy in public documents as understood in the archival profession is perhaps best crystallized in Heather MacNeil's thesis-turned-monograph, *Without Consent: The Ethics of Disclosing Personal Information in Public Archives* (Metuchen, NJ, 1992). Another work worthy of study is Diana L. Charlton, "Secret Service Testimony Regarding Presidential Activities: The Piracy of Privacy?" *Saint Louis University Law Journal* 43: 2 (Spring 1999), which looks at the limitation of privacy rights of federal employees who work directly with the president. As for how privacy translates with regard to the president, make sure to see Joseph W. Bishop Jr.'s still fresh article, "The Executive's Right of Privacy: An Unresolved Constitutional Question," *Yale Law Journal* 66: 4 (February 1957).

L. Another American Rub: Concepts of Property

A concept almost as complex as the right to privacy, but one central to both American thought and the issues associated with the ownership of presidential records, is the idea of private property. Closely associated with the concept of private property—especially with regard to the federal government asserting ownership over the records created by federal officials and employees—is the idea of governmental takings.

Most often, takings law applies when government exerts its powers of eminent domain, but in cases such as *United States v. First Trust Company of Saint Paul* (1958, also known as the Clark Papers case), *Kenneth D. Sender v. Honorable Samuel Z. Montoya* (1963), or *United States v. Nixon* (1973)—cases that all deal centrally with the federal ownership of the records of federal officials and employees—significant parts of the cases were argued on points of takings law. Takings law addressed more in detail in the next section.

Materials relating to the Clark Papers case will be detailed later is in this essay; materials for the *U.S. v. Nixon* case have already been listed. Yet, before any of these cases came before the court, the principles outlined in *Folsom v. Marsh* delineated the landscape of intellectual property law.

Folsom v. Marsh involved ownership rights to a printed set of the works of George Washington. Adjudicated by a friend of the owner of the original documents who also happened to be a relative of the first president, the case set the tone for the future discourse on the ownership of presidential records, and indeed records created by any federal official. For further explanation of this seminal case, consult L. Ray Patterson, *"Folsom v. Marsh* and Its Legacy," *Journal of Intellectual Property Law* 5 (Spring 1998). Primary accounts as well as biographical retellings of the important case are contained in William W. Story, ed., *Life and Letters of Joseph Story* (2 vols., Boston 1851); Herbert Baxter Adams, ed., *The Life and Writings of Jared Sparks: Comprising Selections from His Journals and Correspondence.* (2 vols, Boston 1893); Mary E. Phillips, *Reminiscences of William Wetmore Story* (Chicago 1897); James McClellan, *Joseph Story and the American Constitution: A Study in Political Thought* (Norman, OK, 1990); and, to a much lesser extent, in Henry James, *William Wetmore Story and His Friends: From Letters, Diaries and Recollections*, (New York 1957).

As noted earlier, numerous works exist on the concept of private property, but only a select number pertain to private property rights and federal documents and records. Charles A. Reich's "The New Property," *Yale Law Journal* 73: 5 (April 1964) discusses the concept of governmental ownership of property couched in an economic determinism model of deconstructionist thought. Intellectual property, placed in a Lockean construct of implied and inferred rights, is in Adam D. Moore, "A Lockean Theory of Intellectual Property," *Hamline Law Review* 21 (Fall 1997). Jonathan Turley's excellent article, "Presidential Papers and Popular Government," *Cornell Law Review* 88: 2 (2003), critically reflects on how we continue to use antiquated concepts of private property to apply to presidential records. Lawrence C. Becker, in his essay "Too Much Property," *Philosophy and Public Affairs* 21: 2 (Spring 1992), summarizes the conceptual battles that have occurred in the past century over the idea of intellectual rights. A more grounded essay by Andrea Simon called "A Constitutional Analysis of Copyrighting Government-Commissioned Work," *Columbia Law Review* 84 (March 1984), looks at property rights as they apply to records and documents created for the government via contract work.

The concept of who controls the intellectual property behind government works is further explored in Steve Weinberg, *For Their Eyes Only: How Presidential Appointees Treat Public Documents as Personal Property* (Washington, DC, 1992). Weinberg's work is immediately accessible, somewhat scholarly, and an excellent beginning point for anyone interested in the disconnect between a citizen's right to know what his or her government is doing, the effects and the concept of private property ownership with regard to government-created materials.

M. The Fourth Amendment & Takings Law

As helpful as Steve Weinberg's *For Their Eyes Only* is, it fails to mention to any extent the arguments that Richard Nixon vocalized when his records were seized under Title I of the Presidential Recordings and Materials Preservation Act of 1974. Nixon claimed that such a "taking" of his theretofore personal property was unconstitutional, because of the Fourth Amendment, which provides relief against "unreasonable searches and seizures." Claims such as Nixon's against the government (which, as it turns out, was ruled in his favor after more than twenty-five years of contentious court maneuvering) are known as "takings law" cases.

As with so many other topics broached in this essay, the scope of this document is not to provide an extensive list of citations, but rather to direct the scholar to introductory sources in a potentially new field. Most often takings law and cases are related to land use or zoning, and the amount of literature produced in this combined area of takings law is immense. The literature of takings law as it applies to the records and documents produced by and the control sought by the federal government is much more manageable.

One of the seminal books on takings law that is written in plain English and is as accessible to the non-legal scholar as it is to the

lawyer is Bruce A. Ackerman's *Private Property and the Constitution*
(New Haven 1977). An excellent work directly on point with the study
of the records and documents of federal employees and officials and the
doctrine of takings law is Jennifer R. Williams's "Beyond *Nixon*: The
Application of the Takings Clause to the Papers of Constitutional Officeholders," *Washington University Law Quarterly* 71: 3 (Fall 1993).
Taking the contrary position to Williams, but equally helpful and well
written (this time by an expert in takings cases and land use law) is Michael M. Berger, "Land Use Institute: Planning, Regulation, Litigation,
Eminent Domain and Compensation, Recent Takings and Eminent
Domain Cases," *American Law Institute - American Bar Association
Continuing Legal Education* (August 18, 1993), in which pages 108-
113 focus on the precedent that Nixon had in takings law.

N. Precedent: The Clark Papers Case

Another case closely aligned to the concept of takings law and the federal government's eminent domain powers over the "private papers" of
former federal officials or employees is the so-called Clark Papers case
of 1958. Actually, *United States v. First Trust Company of Saint Paul*
took several years to wind its way through the circuit and appellate
courts in Minnesota, and the federal government's involvement actually
occurred only as an additional party to the original case,
    The case began innocuously enough as the result of an executor of
an estate decision on how to dispose of additional materials not listed in
a client's will. The contents of the material not included in the will included some original field notes created by Captain William Clark during the expedition of the Louisiana Territory by the Corps of Discovery. The federal government became involved so as to ensure that the
documents—which many had thought had long since vanished—would
be properly cared for and not capriciously scattered to disparate private
collectors. The United States asserted that its right to ownership of the
documents superseded the private property rights claimed by the defen-
dants, the First Trust Company of Saint Paul, Minnesota, the executors
of the will. Further, the United States advocated that because the documents were created by a duly appointed federal official (Lewis and
Clark had their commission handed to them directly by President Jefferson himself) in the discharge of his duties, the records remained federal property. The circuitous legal battle eventually found that the papers were drafts of official reports later submitted to the Congress (as
well as for other legal reasons) and the papers were thus indeed private

property and title could not devolve to the U.S. government.

The legal machinations that went on behind this legal battle are but one side of the story, and perhaps are told most even-handedly by the editor of the Princeton University Press edition of the Jefferson papers, Julian P. Boyd, in his article "'These Precious Monuments of . . . Our History,'" *American Archivist* 22: 2 (April 1959). The Clark Papers case also received extensive coverage in *Manuscripts*, the aptly named quarterly organ of the Manuscript Society. The coverage in *Manuscripts* varied greatly, from vitriolic accusations against the government's incursion into the sacrosanct realm of personal property to factual accounts of the case. The articles that relate to the case of *United States v. First Trust Company of Saint Paul* in *Manuscripts* are as follows: "A Government Threat to Manuscript Collections," *Manuscripts* 7: 4 (Summer 1955); Robert H. Bahmer, "The Case of the Clark Papers," *Manuscripts* 8: 2 (Winter 1956); "In the Matter of the Lewis and Clark Papers," *Manuscripts* 9: 1 (Winter 1957); Jay Edgerton, "Lewis and Clark Sequel," *Manuscripts* 9: 2 (Spring 1957); Robert F. Metzdorf, "Lewis and Clark I: A Librarian's Point of View," *Manuscripts* 9: 4 (Fall 1957).

Of course, the case made it into print in many other places, but nowhere did it receive as much attention as it did in *Manuscripts*. Indeed, the takings claim of the government on the Clark Papers is an issue almost universally unreported in the multitude of books and articles produced concerning the story of Lewis and Clark and the Corps of Discovery. At the heart of the Clark Papers case was the issue of who controls both the hard copies of and access to the records created by officials in the public employ.

As noted in the introduction, the impetus for this bibliographic essay is to provide future scholars with an introduction to the topic of the federal government's ownership of the records and documents created by its officers and employees, especially those documentary materials produced by the president. After discussing so many related areas, this essay now looks at the topic of federal ownership of the records and documents of federal employees and officers directly. Later in this bibliographic essay, the documents and records of the presidency itself will be discussed, and at great length. But before either topic is broached, it is important to note where the records—when created and saved—are processed and made accessible, i.e., the National Archives.

O. The History of the National Archives in Brief

The National Archives of the United States is the best place to go for primary materials that address many of the topics broached in this essay. From the records of the Public Documents Commission to the papers of the from presidents Hoover to Clinton, the National Archives contain the documentary evidence needed by scholars for primary research.

Established under the presidency of Herbert Hoover, and later greatly affected by Hoover Commission formed in the mid-1950s, the National Archives—in all of its acronymic incarnations—contains a rich history in need of renewed interest by historians of governmental, institutional, and personal history. Two monographs do exist on the history of the National Archives, but both date from the pre-Presidential Records Act days. Perhaps most helpful for an introductory overview on the history of the National Archives is Donald R. McCoy, *The National Archives: America's Ministry of Documents, 1934-1968* (Chapel Hill 1978). Also important to the field and somewhat more political when first penned is H. G. Jones's *The Records of a Nation: Their Management, Preservation and Use* (New York 1969). For a brief overview of National Archives since the monographs of the McCoy and Jones, see McCoy's entry on "National Archives and Records Service (NARS)" in *Government Agencies* (Westport, CT 1983) and George C. Chalou, "National Archives," in *A Historical Guide to the U.S. Government* (New York 1998).

Two other publications, issued by the National Archives itself, have also appeared on the subject of the Archives' history, *The National Archives of the United States* (New York, 1984) and *Guardian of Heritage: Essays on the History of the National Archives* (Washington, DC 1985). The first was edited by Herman Viola and the second by Timothy Walch, and although both books are geared for popular, rather than academic, audiences, each work provides valuable and colorful insights into the history of the "Ministry of Documents."

A final note: One book that may also shed light on the organizational ethos and culture of the National Archives is former Archivist of the United States Robert Warner's very personal work called *Diary of a Dream: A History of the National Archives Independence Movement, 1980-1985* (Metuchen, NJ, 1995). Although not necessarily a revelatory book (Warner warns in the preface that not enough time has passed for historical accounts to be written about the National Archives' mid-1980s attempts for "independence" as a full-fledged independent governmental agency), the work is essential for those trying to gain an insight into how the National Archives works.

P. Who Owns Federal Records?

While there are a multitude of sources available for the scholar concerned with understanding the idea of private property, the number of materials available dwindles when one begins to look for research that addresses how the concept of private property applies to the records created by federal officials and employees.

One of the first attempts to survey the ownership issue of government documents was undertaken by the Twentieth Century Fund, a research-based foundation endowed by Edward A. Feline in 1919 for the study of "major economic, political, and social institutions and issues." The Fund looked at federal records and documents from the standpoint that overclassification equated to denial of access. The report, penned by Carol M. Barker and Matthew H. Fox, can be found under the title of *Classified Files: The Yellowing Pages* (New York 1972).

Barker's and Fox's book provides a snapshot of federal practices and regulations as they existed in 1972, a time before Watergate and thus pre-Presidential Recordings and Materials Preservation Act and pre-Presidential Records Act. Also included in the appendix are several revealing letters from former Secretaries of State Dean Acheson and Dean Rusk. For a view of how the landscape had changed in just over a decade's time, consult the Committee on the Records of Government's *Report* (Malabar, FL, 1985, Rept.). The blue-ribbon committee was not called by the government but instead was an academic call for access to government records.

However, before the Committee on the Records of Government issued its *Report* or even convened, another commission had met and issued a report along the same topic of government control and access to federal government records, the National Study Commission on the Records and Documents of Federal Officials. Commonly called the Public Documents Commission, the commission convened under the auspices of Title II of the PRMPA. Meeting and researching its charge for over two years, the full impact and documentary legacy of the Public Documents Commission (also sometimes named the Brownell Commission, after the head of the commission) is discussed later in this essay.

However, before leaving the topic of the Public Documents Commission, several valid points will be discussed by comparing it with the Committee on the Records of Government. Both the committee and the commission contained a blue-ribbon panel of experts and researchers who sought to influence the government's practices of federal ownership, control, and access to government-produced records. Where the two working groups differed was in their enabling bases, for while the Public Documents Commission was governmentally created, the Committee on the Records of Government was a private enterprise that sought to effect change through its research-based findings. Also differentiating the commission from the committee is the amount of materials left in wakes, for while the *Final Report* is only the beginning of the evidence prepared by the Public Documents Commission, the *Report* of the Committee on the Records of Government comprises the entire canon of material readily available to the researcher on that working group's efforts.

On the other side of the spectrum, i.e., on disposing of records, the scholar should look at National Archives publication number 46-19, *How to Dispose of Records: A Manual for Federal Officials, Revised Edition* (Washington, DC, 1946). The document provides insight into how the federal government handled its records prior to such citizen-involvement acts as the FOIA, the Privacy Act, or even the Public Documents Act. The creation of the document shortly after the close of World War II attests to the fact that the government had undergone a document creation explosion, thus further making the guidelines within the document especially pertinent. Another government-issued report that also should be on the list of any student of government ownership of federal documents and records is the Committee on Authorities and Program Alternatives' 1989 report entitled *NARA and the Disposition of Federal Records: Laws and Authorities and Their Implementation: A Report of the Committee on Authorities and Program Alternatives* (Washington, DC 1989). Make sure to also consult the following government report: *NARA and Presidential Records: Laws and Authorities and Their Implementation: A Report of the Task Force on NARA Responsibilities for Federal Records and Related Documents* (Washington, DC 1988). The 1988 report, penned by the Task Force on NARA Responsibilities for Federal Records and Related Documentation) is discussed at greater length later in this essay.

The 1989 report, the third report of the Committee on Authorities and Program Alternatives, looked at the then-current standards and practices in place throughout the federal government for records retention and disposition and how the National Archives and Records Administration should proceed in this delicate but imperative task of determining what records to keep and for how long. In the vein of public documents and access to them, also interesting reading is the congressional hearings held in late 1974 by the Committee on House Administration, Subcommittee on Printing, entitled *The "Public*

Documents Act": Hearings on H.R. 16902 and Related Legislation, the Disposition and Preservation of Documents of Federal Officials (93rd Cong., 2nd sess.). One of the better studies on the subject of federal officials taking their records upon leaving office was penned by the U.S. General Accounting Office: *Federal Records: Removal of Agency Documents by Senior Officials Upon Leaving Office* (Washington, DC, 1989).

As far as secondary sources go, the scholarly overview by J. Frank Cook entitled "'Private Papers' of Public Officials," *American Archivist* 38: 3 (July 1975) is perhaps the best summary of ownership and access to the records of federal employees and officials. Cook's work appeared in the *American Archivist* in between the issuance of the Presidential Recordings and Materials Preservation Act and the Presidential Records Act, which might lead some to question the validity of the author's arguments. Despite its age, the article's intellectual underpinnings remain as cogent today as they did when written over some twenty-five years ago.

Cook not only provides the modern reader a snapshot of what some in the archival profession felt was the proper thing to do with the records of public officials, but the article also provides perhaps the best overview of the long and complicated history of the ownership of the records of federal government officials. The same issue of the *American Archivist* also includes other articles relating to the papers of government officials, including the following: H. G. Jones's short article, "Presidential Papers: Is There a Case for a National Presidential Library?" "The Records of Public Officials: Final Report of the Forty-Eighth American Assembly," and the one-page news note, "The Status of the Nixon Presidential Historical Materials."

The article about the American Assembly is an executive summary of the platform taken up by the American Assembly in 1975, which called for the preservation of and access to the records of federal officials. In the same year that the overview of their platform appeared in the *American Archivist*, the American Assembly published a document penned by Norman A. Graebner called *The Records of Public Officials* (New York 1975). The book by Graebner provides an overview of the ownership issue of federal records, although the subject is not treated with the same depth and breadth as in Cook's fundamental work.

Another helpful article about the public ownership of the records of public officials is the 1960 SAA presidential address of Oliver W. Holmes, entitled "'Public Records'—Who Knows What They Are?" The address may be found in the *American Archivist* 23: 1 (January

1960). Also worthy of consultation is Frederick W. Ford's "Some Legal Problems in Preserving Records for Public Use," *American Archivist* 20: 1 (January 1957), which provides an early documentation of warnings of the chilling effect as the result of ensuring public access to the records created by federal officials. Sharply contrasted to Ford's argument is the argument for preserving access to federal records taken up by Philip G. Schrag in "Working Papers as Federal Records: The Need for New Legislation to Preserve the History of National Policy," *Administrative Law Review* 46 (Spring 1994).

Indeed, Schrag not only calls for the preservation and access to the records of public officials, but he also notes that for certain portions of the government (particular the executive branch) preservation, and access to drafts of records, reports, documents, and papers should be mandated! In a historical frame, Meredith B. Colket Jr.'s "The Preservation of Consular and Diplomatic Post Records of the United States," *American Archivist* 6: 4 (October 1943), details the lengths that the State Department and its officers and employees went to preserve the documentary history of its official records and correspondence files in countries throughout the world. For those still interested in the topic of the records of federal officials, the head of the Public Documents Commission, Herbert Brownell, opines about the public ownership issue in "'Who Really Owns the Papers of Departing Federal Officials?'" *New York State Bar Journal* 50: 3 (April 1978).

Brownell's point of view in the previous article keeps him in line with the Minority Report of the *Final Report* of the Public Documents Commission. Even given the fact that Brownell's documented views from the 1970s, they do still seem intriguingly liberal given his prior stance to limited openness in government during his tenure as attorney general during the Eisenhower presidency. For more on Bronwell's attorney generalship, see the entries under his name in both the *Biographical Directory of the United States Executive Branch, 1774-1989* (New York 1990) and the *Encyclopedia of the United States Cabinet* (Santa Barbara, CA 2000). Especially, see Herbert Brownell's own memoirs, penned in conjunction with John P. Burke, called *Advising Ike: The Memoirs of Attorney General Herbert Brownell* (Lawrence, KS, 1993).

Finally, no overview of the literature of the ownership of the records of public officials could be complete without looking at James B. Rhoads, the sitting archivist during both the Presidential Recordings and Materials Preservation and Presidential Records Acts. Rhoads' opinions, an abridged and altered version of his congressional testimony given before the Public Documents Commission, may be found in the article entitled "Who Should Own the Documents of Public Officials?" *Prologue* 7: 1 (Spring 1975).

For those interested in understanding the exponential growth of federal records and documents, make sure to consult James Gregory Bradsher, "A Brief History of the Growth of the Federal Government Records, Archives, and Information, 1789-1985," *Government Publications Review* 13: 4 (July/August 1986). Bradsher's work is an excellent summary of the growth of federal records—and recordkeeping—although significant events have occurred since the article was first published: for example, the Paperwork Reduction Act of 1995. For more on the 1995 act, see Cheryl Bartel and Inna Ilinskaya, "Paperwork Reduction Act of 1995," (student paper for UCLA Information Studies 455, Fall 2001).

Helpful in understanding how different branches of the government handle their respective records is Richard Allan Baker, "Documenting the History of the United States Senate," *Government Publications Review* 10: 5 (September/October 1983). Baker's article pays tribute to the successes in preservation of and access to the records retained by the U.S. Senate Historical Office.

Q. The Care of Presidential Papers (pre-1955)

Before addressing the Presidential Recordings and Materials Preservation Act and the Presidential Records Act (PRA), one must understand the ad hoc system that had developed before the laws came into effect. For further detail on how the ad hoc system of care for presidential records in the days before the PRMPA and the PRA came into being, make sure to see Part 1 of this book.

Presidents prior to Franklin D. Roosevelt conveniently did not record their musings on the concept of ownership of presidential papers, save for two notable exceptions—Grover Cleveland and William Howard Taft. Both presidents, despite their widely varying political and ideological standings, reached a sort of consensus on the topic. To find Cleveland's famous line, consult James D. Richardson, ed., *A Compilation of the Messages and Papers of the Presidents, 1789-1902*, Vol. 8 (1881-1889) (Washington, DC 1903). Taft's similarly caustic remarks can be found in his book entitled, *Our Chief Magistrate and His Powers* (New York 1925).

For explanations of the provenance of the presidential papers previous to Richard Nixon, the scholar has no choice but to consult the last testaments of ex-presidents. Although the manner in which each president addressed his papers is treated not too surprisingly quite individualistically, Herbert R. Collins's and David B. Weaver's *Wills of the U.S. Presidents* (New York 1976) provides the full text (as well as analyses) of the wills of presidents from George Washington to Lyndon Johnson. Previous to the enactment of the PRA, the destiny of the ownership of and access to the records created by our chief executives was determined by the former presidents themselves, their families, or their executors. Capriciousness, avarice, penury, pride, and other motives caused many of the documents created by the presidents to be sold, mutilated, destroyed, preserved ad hoc, or misplaced in ways unimaginable today.

The text of the wills of the ex-presidents as contained in *Wills of the U.S. Presidents* provides future scholars a convenient place for comparing the intentions of our ex-presidents by seeing what each man said to do with his papers, a matter addressed in many of the wills.

Almost no presidential will expressly named the Library of Congress as the intended repository for presidential records. Despite this handicap, from Presidents Washington to Coolidge, with but six exceptions, the primary archival location for the papers of our past presidents from the founding of the Republic to the early twentieth century is the Library of Congress (LC). The story of how LC acquired all of these dispersed and disparate sources is one that is in need of serious study. While many articles exist on how portions of the presidential collection were assembled at the Library of Congress, no one monograph relates this story alone. Consulting Frank Veit's *Presidential Libraries and Collections* (Westport, CT 1987) Frank L. Schick's, et al., *Records of the Presidency: Presidential Papers and Libraries from Washington to Reagan* (Phoenix 1989) and Curt Smith *Windows on the Presidency: The Story of Presidential Libraries* (South Bend, IN 1997) remains de rigueur.

So too should the scholar visit Jane Aikin Rosenberg's *The Nation's Great Library: Herbert Putnam and the Library of Congress, 1899-1939* (Urbana, IL 1993). Rosenberg's work is quickly becoming a classic in the specialty field of Library of Congress history. Rosenberg's monograph explains both the growth of the Library of Congress into an institution of wider importance than just a congressional library, and albeit marginally) the simultaneous growth of the Manuscript Division of the same library. Although Rosenberg's coverage of LC activities during the early twentieth century makes it an essential place to visit for those interested in presidential papers, one should consult the book more for the flavor of LC at the time that the library collected presidential papers than for actual facts on how Putnam and the Manuscripts Division secured presidential manuscripts, records and documents.

For a timeline approach to the history of LC, make sure to use John Y. Cole, *For Congress and the Nation: A Chronological History of the Library of Congress* (Washington, DC 1979). Cole's other work, *Jefferson's Legacy: A Brief History of the Library of Congress* (available in electronic format at lcweb.loc.gov/loc/legacy), should also be consulted for scholars of the development of the Library of Congress.

Only a few written histories exist for individual collections of presidential papers in the Library of Congress. For while articles on the papers of the early presidents are more prominent than for later presidential collections, no monographic work exists that addresses the histories of individual collections at LC. Granted, for each individual collection of presidential papers, the major works written by or about each individual president should be consulted. To determine the major works of and about individual presidents, consultation of the excellent series *Bibliographies of Presidents of the United States*, published by Greenwood Press, remains the starting point for any serious research.

Constructed by subject specialist scholars, each issue in the Greenwood series contains as close to comprehensiveness as can be achieved for a subject. Usually included in each volume are introductory essays that guide scholars to sources of recent scholarship, as well highlighting archival collections. In short, the series as a whole provides a comprehensive guide to the literature of the Presidents of the United States as a group *en masse*.

There exist several introductory guides to the collections of presidential materials housed at the Library of Congress. Consulting Frank Veit's *Presidential Libraries and Collections* (Westport, CT 1987), Frank L. Schick's, et. al., *Records of the Presidency: Presidential Papers and Libraries from Washington to Reagan* (Phoenix 1989) and Curt Smith, *Windows on the Presidency: The Story of Presidential Libraries* (South Bend, IN 1997), provide varying introductions to the presidential papers housed at LC. In addition, consulting the following citations will yield benefits for the researcher: Buford Rowland, "The Papers of the Presidents," *American Archivist* 13: 3 (July 1950), Fred Shelley, "The Presidential Papers Program of the Library of Congress," and Warren R. Reid, "Public Papers of the Presidents," *American Archivist* 25: 4 (October 1962).

As noted previously, scholarship exists for individual presidential collections of the early presidents. The history of the Washington papers is one oft told; thus, consultation of sources such as Cook, Veit and Schick would prove useful as a collective introduction. John D. Knowlton's "'Properly Arranged and So Correctly Recorded,'" *American Archivist* 27: 3 (July 1964), describes with brevity but in detail how Washington proceeded to index his Revolutionary War correspondence while the war ensued. In addition, the scholar should consult W. W. Abbot, "An Uncommon Awareness of Self: The Papers of George Washington," *Prologue* 21: 1 (Spring 1989), an article that traverses much the same ground of Knowlton, but with breadth and depth.

The same issue of *Prologue* that contains the Abbot article also contains histories on the papers of John Adams and Thomas Jefferson, respectively: Richard Alan Ryerson, "Documenting the Presidency of John Adams: The Adams Papers Project," and John Catanzariti, "'The Richest Treasure House of Information': The Papers of Thomas Jefferson." For more on the history of Jefferson's papers, see Lyman H. Butterfield, "The Papers of Thomas Jefferson: Progress and Procedures in the Enterprise at Princeton," *American Archivist* 12: 2 (April 1949).

Returning to the Spring 1989 issue of *Prologue*, one will find there an article detailing the history of the papers of the nation's fourth president, James Madison: J. C. A. Stagg, "Setting the Stage for Reappraisal: The Papers of James Madison." An article even more penetrating about the history of the papers of Madison may be found in a 1958 issue of the *American Archivist*: Kate Stewart's "James Madison as an Archivist," *American Archivist* 21: 3 (July 1958).

The history of presidential papers then remains largely untold until the sixteenth president, Abraham Lincoln. In Helen Duprey Bullock, "The Robert Todd Lincoln Collection of the Papers of Abraham Lincoln," *The Library of Congress Quarterly Journal of Current Acquisitions* 5: 1 (November 1947), the riveting tale of how the papers of the Great Emancipator were narrowly saved from complete destruction. The article also tells of the extended restrictions placed on the use of the papers, a fact that makes the current use restrictions on presidential papers seem almost negligible by comparison.

As noted earlier, few presidents prior to the enactment of the Presidential Libraries Act deposited their papers in the Library of Congress, yet through the determined efforts of successive Librarians of Congress (especially Putnam), LC developed an extensive collection of presidential records. Nevertheless, the papers of presidents John Adams, John Quincy Adams, Millard Fillmore, James Buchanan, Rutherford Hayes and Warren Harding are all contained at institutions independent of the Library of Congress. Histories of the collections for each of these presidents range from journal articles to portions of books but, as with the papers housed at the Library of Congress, each collection of papers' story has not yet been told.

For the Fillmore papers, currently housed at the Buffalo Historical Society, see the short article by Charles M. Snyder, "Forgotten Fillmore Papers Examined: Sources for Reinterpretation of a Little-Known President," *American Archivist* 32: 1 (January 1969).

The saga of the Harding papers comes through poignantly in two companion articles that appeared in the February 1965 issue of *American Heritage*. Kenneth W. Duckett's article "The Harding Papers: How Some Were Burned" in *American Heritage* 16: 2 (February 1965) relates the depressing tale of the destroyed Harding papers, while Harding scholar Francis Russell's "The Harding Papers: . . . And Some Were Saved," *American Heritage* 16: 2 (February 1965), tells of Russell's discovery and "saving" of some of the more scandalous or salacious Harding materials. Also worthy of consultation for the Harding papers saga are two other Russell works: "The Shadow of Warren Harding," *Antioch Review* 36: 1 (Winter 1978), and the author's magnum opus, *The Shadow of Blooming Grove: Warren G. Harding in His Times* (New York, 1968), which relates Russell's discovery and return of several original Harding records.

R. The Development of the Presidential Libraries System (post-1955)

Although several books have been penned about presidential libraries, with one appearing only several years ago, the best place to go to understand how presidential libraries developed is journal articles. Not surprisingly, the most fruitful articles are ones found in the scholarly journals of the Society of American Archivists, *American Archivist*, and the National Archives and Records Administration, *Prologue*.

Far and away most helpful article, despite predating both the PRMPA and PRA, is J. Frank Cook's "'Private Papers' of Public Officials," *American Archivist* 38: 3 (July 1975). In Cook's seminal article, he presents in an accessible manner the complex history of ownership of presidential documents and records. Owing to its age, supplementing Cook's article with more recent scholarship is important.

Several more-recent articles complement Cook nicely, including Pamela R. McKay's "Presidential Papers: A Property Issue," *Library Quarterly* 52: 1 (January 1982), which discusses the PRA as well as introduces a convenient matrix-oriented view of the ownership issue of presidential records and documents. Complementary to McKay is Sandra E. Richetti's article, "Congressional Power Vis a Vis the President and Presidential Papers," *Duquesne Law Review* 32 (Summer 1994). Adding texture to Richetti's article, which remains centered on congressional inquests more than on the ownership issue of presidential papers, see Donald T. Kramer, "Executive Privilege with Respect to Presidential Papers and Recordings," *American Law Reports Federal* 19 (1974, October 2001 Supp.). Philip G. Schrag's article, "Working Papers as Federal Records: The Need for New Legislation to Preserve the History of National Policy," in *Administrative Law Review* 46 (Spring 1994), does not focus on presidential papers, but emphasizes that drafts, as well as final copies, of documentary evidence should be preserved, a concept perhaps most important when applied to the papers produced by the presidency.

For more introductory works concerning presidential records that approach the issue from a legal standpoint, see Carl Bretscher's "Presidential Records Act: The President and Judicial Review under the Records Acts," *George Washington Law Review* 60: 5 (June 1992). Also written from a legal standpoint, see Carl McGowan's excellent piece called "Presidents and Their Papers," *Minnesota Law Review* 68: 2 (December 1983). Raymond H. Geselbracht, an archivist with intimate knowledge of presidential libraries due to his work on the Nixon Presidential Materials Project, also provides an introduction to the topic of presidential materials in "Archivist's Perspective: The Four Eras in the History of Presidential Papers," *Prologue* 15: 1 (Spring 1983). Raymond H. Geselbracht and Daniel J. Reed in "The Presidential Library and the White House Liaison Office," *American Archivist* 46: 1 (Winter 1983), provide a somewhat technical perspective on how documents and records used and created by the executive branch turn from in-use White House records to archival materials housed in presidential libraries. Complementing Geselbracht's article is the helpful article of Brian Chandler Thompson, "The Sitting Modern President and the National Archives," *Government Information Quarterly* 12: 1 (1995), which details the current closely linked relationship between the president and NARA.

For an intense intellectual treatment of the subject of ownership of executive branch papers, read William P. Rogers, "Constitutional Law: The Papers of the Executive Branch," *American Bar Association Journal* 44: 10 (October 1958); a caustic reply to Rogers' argument appears in Bernard Schwartz, "A Reply to Mr. Rogers: The Papers of the Executive Branch," *American Bar Association Journal* 45: 5 (May 1959).

Editorials and commentaries on the subject of ownership and access to presidential papers are plenty. Some of the more cogent and well-written are the following: Blanche Wiessen Cook, "Presidential Papers in Crisis: Some Thoughts on Lies, Secrets and Silence," *Presidential Studies Quarterly* 26: 1 (Winter 1996); Russell Fridley, "Should Public Papers Be Private Property?" *Minnesota History* 44: 1 (Spring 1974); and John McDonough, et. al., "Who Owns Presidential Papers?" *Manuscripts* 27: 1 (Winter 1975).

One of the more widely circulated editorials written on the topic, penned by Arthur Schlesinger Jr., and originally appearing in the *Wall Street Journal*, "Who Owns a President's Papers?" may be found in *Manuscripts* 27: 3 (Summer 1975). Commentaries written by Archivists of the United States may be found in the following: Don W. Wilson, "Presidential Records: Evidence for Historians or Ammunition for Prosecutors," *Government Information Quarterly* 14: 4 (1997) and James B. Rhoads, "Presidential Papers: A Reply," *New York Times Book Review* (September 7, 1969). Rhoads's article was written as a response to an open letter signed by twenty scholars that appeared in the same publication called "Presidential Papers," *New York Times Book Review* (September 7, 1969).

Finally, two other helpful articles to overview are Henry F. Graff, "Preserving the Secrets of the White House," *New York Times Magazine* (December 29, 1963), and Bernard A. Weisberger, "The Paper Trust," *American Heritage* 22: 3 (April 1971).

For an interesting counterpoint view on presidential libraries, make sure to read Robert M. Warner, "The Prologue is Past," *American Archivist* 41: 1 (January 1978). The article was written as a response to the New Harmony conference, where archivists and historians together grappled over concepts about and uses of presidential records. Warner, who would later led NARA during its successful independence movement of the 1980s, eloquently explains that perhaps too much emphasis remains focused on the records and documents of the president.

Mentioned earlier in the essay, the government-commission produced *NARA and Presidential Records: Laws and Authorities and Their Implementation: A Report of the Task Force on NARA Responsibilities for Federal Records and Related Documents* (Washington, DC, 1988) provides an excellent overview on the concept of the government ownership of presidential records. In addition, this report produced by the Task Force on NARA Responsibilities for Federal Records and Related Documentation contains not only an overview of the standards and practices in place at the time of the report's production (1988) but also contains recommendations for the future. Finally, the report's appendices contain such rich material as reproductions from the *Statutes at Large*, of laws relating to presidential records, and other documents relating to the creation, care and management of executive branch documents. For a scholar new to the ownership issue of the papers of public officials, a better place to begin one's research might not be found.

Other government documents that are worthy of consultation include the Senate Committee on Governmental Affairs report for the PRA, called *The Presidential Records Act of 1978—S. 3494: Hearing on S. 3494* (95th Cong., 2nd sess., Y4.G74/9:P92) as well as the House report that accompanied H.R. 13500, simply entitled *Presidential Records Act of 1978* (95th Cong., 2nd sess., H. Rept. 95-1487). For a recent congressional view on what the intent and purpose of the PRA was, make sure to see the House Committee on Government Reform *Hearing on the Implementation and Effectiveness of the Presidential Records Act of 1978* (107th Cong., 1st sess.). The last congressional hearing came into being as a result of President George W. Bush's signing of Executive Order 13233, an act that severely calls into question the application of the Presidential Records Act. For more on the conflict between Bush's executive order and the PRA, see chapter 3.

Intertwined with the concept of who owns presidential records is the concept of who determines access to presidential records. Arnold Hirshon's research on the area of access to the materials at presidential libraries broke new ground when the articles were first published. Despite their age, Hirshon's articles, "The Scope, Accessibility and History of Presidential Papers," *Government Publications Review* 1: 4 (Fall 1974), and "Recent Developments in the Accessibility of Presidential Papers and Other Presidential Historical Materials," *Government Publications Review* 6: 4 (Fall 1979), remain required introductory reading for anyone interested in the area of access to presidential documents. Jannean L. Elliott's *Presidential Papers and Presidential Library System* (Provo, UT 1981) also remains helpful for both its overview of the presidential libraries system and for a (now historical) survey of what archivists felt were the strengths and weaknesses of the system. Also addressing the concept of access to presidential papers is the House hearing on the Committee on Government Operations, Subcommittee on the Library, *Microfilming Presidential Papers: Hearing on H.R. 7813, To Organize and Microfilm the Papers of Presidents of the United States in the Collections of the Library of*

Congress (85th Cong., 1st sess.).

Of course, to appreciate fully the access issue to presidential papers, one must understand how presidential libraries function. As noted elsewhere in this essay, Veit, Schick and Smith's triumvirate will most likely be the best place to begin one's research. One of the most recent scholarly articles written about the PRA, which overviews the legislative history of the act as well as other laws relating to presidential libraries and museums is Harold C. Reylea's "Federal Presidential Libraries" (Washington, DC 1995, 95-389-GOV). The report, which can be difficult to locate, was issued as part of the *Major Studies and Issue Briefs of the Congressional Research Service*, 1996 Supplement, and published by CIS University Publications of America, based in Bethesda, Maryland. Similar in scope and often easier to track down is another article by Reylea on the same subject, entitled "The Federal Presidential Library System"; it can be found in *Government Information Quarterly* 11: 1 (1994).

Perhaps the most academic study available on the institution that has become the presidential libraries system is Lynn Scott Cochrane's Ph.D. dissertation, "The Presidential Library System: A Quiescent Policy System" (Virginia Polytechnic Institute and State University 1998). Other helpful studies of the presidential libraries system include Linda Fischer, "The Role and Function of Presidential Libraries," (Simi Valley, CA 1991) and John Webb, "The Presidential Libraries" (Papers presented at the Institute in Archival Librarianship, University of Oregon, September 22, 1969-August 14, 1970).

Providing a more synoptic overview of the presidential libraries system are the following helpful articles: Robert F. Burk, "New Perspectives for Presidential Libraries," *Presidential Studies Quarterly* 11: 3 (Summer 1991); Victor J. Danilov, "Presidential Libraries and Museums," *Curator* 34: 3 (1991); Cynthia J. Wolff, "Necessary Monuments: The Making of the Presidential Library System," *Government Publications Review* 16: 1 (January/February 1989); Sister Louise Lovely, "The Evolution of Presidential Libraries," *Government Publications Review* 6: 1 (1979); Lester J. Cappon, "Why Presidential Libraries?" *Yale Review* 68: 1 (October 1978); Elizabeth B. Drewry, "The Role of Presidential Libraries," *Midwest Quarterly* 7: 1 (October 1965); and Garold L. Cole, "Presidential Libraries," *Journal of Librarianship: Quarterly of the Library Association* 4: 2 (April 1972).

While each of the above articles covers approximately the same material in roughly similar ways, each also provides unique insights into the organization of presidential libraries. James L. Cochrane evaluates presidential libraries from the perspective of an economic historian in "The U.S. Presidential Libraries and the History of Political Economy," *History of Political Economy* 8: 3 (Fall 1976). Also helpful to consult are the following congressional hearings and reports: House Committee on Government Operations, *Provide for the Acceptance and Maintenance of Presidential Libraries, and for Other Purposes* (84th Cong., 1st sess.); Senate Committee on Government Operations, *Providing for the Acceptance and Maintenance of Presidential Libraries* (84th Cong., 1st sess., S. Rept. 84-1189); and House Committee on Government Operations, *Presidential Libraries, to Accompany H. J. Res. 330* (84th Cong., 1st sess., H. Rept. 84-998).

For an overview of the contents of individual libraries, the web sites for each of the presidential libraries will probably be most helpful. Appendix D contains contact information and website addresses for all major repositories of presidential records. As stated elsewhere in   this essay, also helpful in determining the collection strengths of presidential libraries are the books by Veit, Schick and Smith. Make sure to also consult Nancy Kegan Smith and Mary C. Ryan, ed., *Modern First Ladies: Their Documentary Legacy* (Washington, DC, 1989) to overview the scope and locations of collections of First Lady papers and records.

For evaluative looks at presidential libraries, make sure to consult the following two Richard S. Kirkendall articles: "Presidential Libraries—One Researcher's Point of View," *American Archivist* 25: 4 (October 1962) and "A Second Look at Presidential Libraries," *American Archivist* 29: 3 (July 1966). James E. O'Neill's article "Will Success Spoil the Presidential Libraries," found in *American Archivist* 36: 3 (July 1973), provides an interesting critique of the presidential libraries, including arguments that are oft repeated elsewhere against the presidential libraries system. Regina Greenwell's "The Oral History Collections of the Presidential Libraries," *Journal of American History*, 84: 2 (September 1997), contains an excellent overview of the collections at the nation's eleven presidential library institutions.

Costs of maintaining presidential libraries became an important issue in the mid-1980s. The growth in physical plant size of presidential libraries and museums alarmed many in Congress and the press, yet, information on cost and funding for presidential libraries has largely failed to extend beyond governmental publications. One notable exception is Benjamin Hufbauer's Ph.D. dissertation, "The Father in the Temple: Memory and Masculinity in Presidential Commemoration" (University of California, Santa Barbara 1999). Hufbauer's work looks at all manifestations of presidential commemoration, including the monument-creation trend evident in the architectural style of some presidential libraries. Defending the idea behind the creation of presidential libraries, if not entirely agreeing with the escalating construction costs, is Cynthia J. Wolff's "Necessary Monuments: The Making of the Presidential Library System," *Government Publications Review* 16: 1 (January/February 1989).

As noted earlier, there exists a plethora of government-produced reports and hearings on the escalating costs of creating and maintaining presidential libraries. The easiest-to-read reports on the cost of presidential libraries are General Accounting Office (GAO) reports, *GSA Approval of Expenditures under the Former Presidents Act Has Been Reasonable* (Washington, DC, 1979) and *Former Presidents: Support Costs and Other Information* (Washington, DC, 1988). Also helpful, and incorporating only some of the provisions of the 1988 GAO report, is the Senate Committee on Governmental Affairs hearing on the *Former President's Act of 1987* (100th Cong., 2nd sess.). Make sure to also consult the following reports and hearings: House Committee on Government Operations, *Presidential Libraries: Unexplored Funding Alternatives* (97th Cong., 2nd sess., H. Rept. 97-732), House Committee on Government Operations, *Presidential Libraries Funding Proposal* (99th Cong., 1st sess., Y4.G74/7:L61/3), House Committee on Government Operations, *Presidential Libraries Funding* (98th Cong., 2nd sess., Y4.G74/7:L61/2), and Senate Committee on Governmental Affairs and Committee on Appropriations, *Cost of Former Presidents to U.S. Taxpayers* (96th Cong., 1st sess.), all of which look at the costs of presidential libraries as parts of their scope of limiting governmental spending on former presidents.

Of more recent interest, introduced in the 107th Congress were legislative attempts at policing how presidential libraries are initially funded. The hearings held for H.R. 577, the bill that would require the disclosure of the organizations that give funds to nascent presidential libraries would be an ideal place to start one's research on this bill. The hearings, in print called *Oversight Hearing on H.R. 577,* were formerly available online from the website of the former chairman of the House of Representatives Subcommittee on Government Efficiency, Financial Management and Intergovernmental Relations. Unfortunately, the hearing is now only available in print form.

S. Histories of Individual Presidential Libraries (pre-Roosevelt)

While the literature on the creation and maintenance of the presidential library system is immense, the scholarly output focused on individual libraries remains paltry as a whole and uneven among its parts. While some libraries have received widespread literary attention—especially the libraries of Roosevelt and Truman—others have had little written about them by comparison, for example, the Eisenhower, Ford and Carter libraries. In addition, several specialized institutions that focus on an individual president, such as Rutherford B. Hayes, or actions closely associated with a particular president, such as the Hoover Institution on War, Revolution and Peace, exist outside of the presidential library infrastructure maintained by NARA under the auspices of the Presidential Libraries Act of 1955. This part of the bibliographic essay begins an overview of the specialized literature centered on each presidential library institution, beginning with the non-federally supported libraries.

Since the founding of the Franklin D. Roosevelt presidential library in 1939, every president subsequent to FDR, save for Richard Nixon, has created a library under the federal system institutionalized with the Presidential Libraries Act of 1955. Yet, before the foundation of the FDR library in Hyde Park, other attempts at commemorating a president via an institutionalized setting had been attempted, most notably, the Rutherford B. Hayes Library at Spiegel Grove, Ohio. An excellent introductory work to the history of the Hayes library is Thomas A. Smith, "Before Hyde Park: The Rutherford B. Hayes Library," *American Archivist* 43: 4 (Fall 1980). An extended history of the library may be found in Myrna J. Grove's project completed for her master's in library science, entitled "Rutherford B. Hayes Presidential Center, Library and Archives: Patron Use of Collections and Services" (Kent State University, 1999). Still helpful, but not as penetrating as either Smith or Grove, is Watt Pearson Marchman, *The Hayes Memorial* (Columbus, OH, 1950).

Established at Stanford University in Palo Alto, California, by Herbert Hoover upon returning from the Paris Peace Conference after the close of World War I, the Hoover Institution on War, Revolution and Peace contains documents and records relating to the Great War that were acquired or created by Hoover. The Hoover Institution does not contain materials that specifically relate to the presidency of the library's namesake. Nonetheless, the institution remains an important part of the presidential library network. The most comprehensive treatment of the history and development of the library may be found in Gary Norman Paul's Ph.D. dissertation, "The Development of the

Hoover Institution on War, Revolution and Peace Library, 1919-1944"
(University of California, Berkeley, 1974). More readily available and
up to date than Paul's dissertation is Peter Dunigan's article found in
The Library of the Hoover Institution on War, Revolution and Peace
(Palo Alto, CA 1985) entitled "The Hoover Institution: Origin and
Growth." During the 1980s, tensions increased between Stanford and
the Hoover Institution and many reports appeared that detailed the
benefits and problems of the cooperation between the two learned institutions. All of these reports are contained in an edited volume by Martin Anderson called *Stanford and Hoover and Academic Freedom* (Palo
Alto, CA 1985). The book contains five reports, of which many include
insightful historical overviews of the development of the Hoover Institution. Also helpful for a historical perspective is Suda L. Bane, "The
Dedicatory Exercises of the Hoover Library," *American Archivist* 5: 3
(July 1942).

As a final note on non federal libraries, a presidential library almost entirely ignored by the literature on the presidential library system
as a whole is the Jefferson Davis Presidential Museum at Biloxi, Mississippi. In fact, the only article found that discusses the library of the
one and only president of the Confederate State of America is Suzan
Flanagan, "The Other Presidential Library," *Civil War Times Illustrated* 39: 4 (August 1, 2000).

Due to the founding nature of the Franklin D. Roosevelt Library, it
remains a premier institution almost without comparison amongst other
presidential libraries. Perhaps due in part to its status as the progenitor
of the federal presidential libraries system as much as to the enigmatic
person whose papers it contains, the literature on and about the FDR
Library has been significantly greater than that produced about other
presidential libraries. By no measure does the wealth of materials produced about the FDR Library constitute a large amount of published
works.

Thankfully, several of the seminal articles written about the history
of the FDR Library are easily accessible. An excellent place to begin
one's research on the history of the library remains Geoffrey Ward,
"'Future Historians Will Curse as Well as Praise Me,'" *Smithsonian* 20:
9 (December 1989), which contains exciting text with excellent full-
color photographs of some items held by the library. Perhaps the most
helpful article written on the subject remains Donald R. McCoy, "The
Beginnings of the Franklin D. Roosevelt Library," *Prologue* 7: 3 (Fall
1975), which focuses its attention on the beginning of the library.
Complementing McCoy is the account of the founding of the library

contained in the April 1940 edition of *American Archivist* simply entitled "The Franklin D. Roosevelt Library." Although written before the
library opened, the then-leader of NARS and confidant of Roosevelt,
Robert D. W. Connor, wrote the article.

For another perspective on the founding of the library, make sure
to see Waldo Gifford Leland's widely cited classic, "The Creation of
the Franklin D. Roosevelt Library: A Personal Narrative," *American
Archivist* 18: 1 (January 1955). Placing the development of the FDR
Library in the context of the presidential libraries system is Roosevelt
scholar Frank Freidel's "Roosevelt to Reagan: The Birth and Growth of
Presidential Libraries," *Prologue* 21: 2 (1989). Make sure to read also
Herman Kahn's "The Presidential Library—A New Institution," *Special Libraries* 50: 3 (March 1959), an article written a decade before
favoritism charges were levied against Kahn and the FDR Library.

T. Precedent: Kahn Case

Access to presidential materials is an issue of paramount importance to
presidential libraries. Yet, with the Franklin D. Roosevelt Library, the
issue has had special meaning—and not only because the library was
the first to house and allow access to presidential records. Rather, in the
late 1960s, several scholars complained of unfair access practices that
occurred at the FDR Library, then under the directorship of Herman
Kahn. Namely, some historians were granted privileged access to certain records, while other scholars had to wait until the records were
opened through the proper channels. As a result of the charges leveled
against the library, the American Historical Association (AHA) and the
Organization of American Historians (OAH) jointly investigated the
access policies of the FDR Library.

The report, released in 1970 by the Joint AHA-OAH Ad Hoc
Committee and called the *Final Report of the Joint AHA-OAH Ad Hoc
Committee to Investigate the Charges against the Franklin D. Roose-
velt Library and Related Matters*, also called the Leopold Report, re-
mains the first exhaustive investigation of a presidential library. Sup-
plementing the Leopold Report is Francis L. Loewenheim's   *A
Statement in Rebuttal [to the Final Report by the Joint AHA-OAH Ad
Hoc Committee to Investigate the Charges against the Franklin D.
Roosevelt Library and Related Matters]*, which outlines the grievances
of the originator of the charges against the FDR Library, Francis L.
Loewenheim.

As a side note, the bibliographic description for Loewenheim's work is complex and convoluted. Rather than describing the difficulties in ascertaining the differences between manifestations of the Loewenheim work, suffice it to say that the full work of *A Statement in Rebuttal* is ninety-three pages. Useful in clarifying the events and charges contained in both the Leopold Report and *A Statement in Rebuttal* is a House Committee on Post Office and Civil Service, Subcommittee on Census and Statistics, report issued on the topic called *Report on the Adequacy and Management of Services Furnished to Scholars and Researchers by Presidential Libraries* (92nd Cong., 2nd sess., H. Rept. 92-898).

Closely associated with the charges against the FDR Library was Yale associate university librarian, Herman Kahn, who wrote his opinions about the matter in "The Long-Range Implications for Historians and Archivists of the Charges against the Franklin D. Roosevelt Library," *American Archivist* 34: 3 (July 1971). In summary, however, the definitive history of the Leopold Report has yet to be written and the entire field of access to presidential materials is in serious need of scholarly reappraisal. Other works that specifically deal with the issue of access to presidential papers at the FDR Library, however, include the following: Herman Kahn, "World War II and Its Background: Research Materials at the Franklin D. Roosevelt Library and Policies Concerning Their Use," *American Archivist* 17: 2 (April 1954); William J. Stewart, "Opening Closed Material in the Roosevelt Library," *Prologue* 7: 4 (Winter 1975); and Lynn A. Bassanese, "The Franklin D. Roosevelt Library: Looking to the Future," *Government Information Quarterly* 12: 1 (1995).

U. Histories of Individual Presidential Libraries (post-Roosevelt)

While the Roosevelt Library was the subject of the AHA-OAH investigation, by no means did the charges of unequal access to presidential materials relate to the Franklin D. Roosevelt Library alone. In fact, before the charges were laid against the FDR Library, many scholars had grumbled at the unfair access liberties presidents took with the records of their own administrations. Kelly Alicia Woestman's Ph.D. dissertation, "Mr. Citizen: Harry S. Truman and the Institutionalization of the Ex-Presidency" (University of North Texas 1993) adroitly backs up the oft-repeated claims that Truman greatly restricted access to the presidential records of his terms as chief executive until he had penned his memoirs. Despite the delayed access to the Truman records, scholarship on the history of the Truman Library at Independence, Missouri has been great.

From memoirs, biographies and personal recollections to peer-reviewed articles, the amount of materials available on the development of the Truman Library is second only to the materials available on the FDR Library. Perhaps the most helpful article penned on the Truman Library is by presidential library scholar Raymond H. Geselbracht, "Harry S. Truman and His Library: Past Accomplishments and Plans for the Future," *Government Information Quarterly* 12: 1 (1995). Still helpful despite their age are David D. Lloyd's article "The Harry S. Truman Library, " *American Archivist* 18: 2 (April 1955), and Philip C. Brooks' "The Harry S. Truman Library—Plans and Reality," *American Archivist* 25: 1 (January 1962). Brooks's later article of 1969, called "Understanding the Presidency: The Harry S. Truman Library" and found in *Prologue* 1: 3 (Winter 1969), also remains quite useful.

Consulting Merle Miller's *Plain Speaking: An Oral Biography of Harry S. Truman* (New York 1973) provides several yarns from Truman's point of view on how his library came to be. Also helpful for their colorful accounts of the library's establishment are Richard H. Rovere, "Mr. Truman Shows Off His Library," *New York Times Magazine* of June 30, 1957, and Joe McCarthy's "A Walk Through History with Harry Truman" articles that appeared in the November and December 1963 issues of *Holiday*. As for works that discuss the uses and holdings of the Truman Presidential Library materials, consult Philip D. Lagerquist, "The Harry S. Truman Library as a Center for Research on the American Presidency," *College and Research Libraries* 25: 1 (January 1964), and Charles T. Morrissey, "Truman and the Presidency: Records and Oral Recollections," *American Archivist* 28: 1 (January 1965).

Although Hoover preceded Roosevelt chronologically as president, the establishment of the Hoover Presidential Library at West Branch, Iowa, did not occur until 1962, well after the newness of the presidential library as an institution had waned. Although few scholarly articles exist on the topic of the history of the Hoover Presidential Library, Frank T. Nye Jr.'s *Doors of Opportunity: The Life and Legacy of Herbert Hoover* (West Branch, IA, 1988) remains the only monograph written exclusively about the history and development of any presidential library. Articles written about the Hoover Library include Richard Norton Smith, "A Presidential Revival: How the Hoover Library Overcame a Mid-Life Crisis," *Prologue* 21: 2 (Summer 1989), and Timothy Walch, "Reinventing the Herbert Hoover Presidential Library," *Gov-*

ernment Information Quarterly 12: 1 (1995).

The Dwight D. Eisenhower Library in Abilene, Kansas established itself in same year as the Hoover Library. Similar to the Hoover Library, too little scholarship exists about the institutional history of Ike's library. The only two articles that could be found about the Eisenhower Library are the following: Martin M. Teasley, "No Signs of Mid-Life Crisis: The Eisenhower Library at Thirty-Something," *Government Information Quarterly* 12: 1 (1995), and John E. Wickman, "The Dwight D. Eisenhower Library," *Special Libraries* 60: 9 (November 1969). By no means should the paucity of articles belittle the Eisenhower Library, which over the years has lit the lamp of knowledge on such scholarly areas as the history of NATO. In addition, the Hoover and Eisenhower libraries mark a significant event in the scholarship written about presidential libraries. Whereas a good deal of scholarly materials exist on the history, founding, and development of the earlier presidential libraries (e.g., Roosevelt, Truman and even Hayes), the closer one gets to the founding of a presidential library, the less likely it is for published scholarly treatises to exist on the development of a library.

Indeed, the paucity of sources written about presidential libraries established later than 1962 continues right on through to the present founding of the William J. Clinton Library. Perhaps most shocking, however, is the limited amount of materials penned about the contentious history associated with the development of the John F. Kennedy Presidential Library in Boston, Massachusetts. For more on the turbulent battle over the siting of the library, see Gerry Nadel, "Johnny, When Will We Get Your Library," *Esquire* of January 1975. Dan Fenn Jr.'s "Launching the John F. Kennedy Library," *American Archivist* 42: 4 (October 1979), provides the unique perspective of the director who oversaw the opening of the Kennedy Library. For the point of view of the Kennedy Library museum curator, see Frank Rigg, "The John F. Kennedy Library," *Government Information Quarterly* 12: 1 (1995).

Due to the small number of scholarly articles available, what follows is the combined scholarly output available on the remaining presidential libraries of Presidents Lyndon B. Johnson, Gerald R. Ford, James E. Carter, Ronald W. Reagan, George H. W. Bush and William J. Clinton. Due to the special nature of the Richard M. Nixon "papers" (Nixon being the progenitor of the PRMPA and the PRA and subsequently the only president since Herbert Hoover without a federally-backed archival institution), his records will be discussed in great depth, but after the remainder of the presidential libraries.

Articles written about the Johnson library number only a few, with the most insightful being Mary K. Knill's "The Lyndon B. Johnson Library in the Information Age," *Government Information Quarterly* 12: 1 (1995). Knill's effort documents the LBJ Library's use of databases to facilitate information retrieval, especially for nontext materials. Also worth consulting is William R. Manchester's *Death of a President*, (New York 1967), especially page 403, which tells how the executive branch dealt with the transfer of title of President Kennedy's papers on the same day as his assassination.

For information about the Gerald R. Ford Library in Ann Arbor, Michigan—the only presidential institution with separate facilities for both a library and a museum—few articles are available. The only academic article encountered that discusses the Ford Library exclusively is David A. Horrocks, "Access and Accessibility at the Gerald R. Ford Library," *Government Information Quarterly* 11: 1 (Winter 1994), which focuses on the access to materials.

For information on the Jimmy Carter Library in Atlanta, Georgia, a similar lack of secondary sources exists. In "Establishing a Presidential Library: The Jimmy Carter Experience," *Prologue* 21: 2 (Summer 1989), Donald B. Schewe gives a brief historical overview of the Carter Presidential Library. Examining the Carter Library's attempts to create electronic finding aids to its archival collection may be found in another Schewe article, "The Jimmy Carter Library: An Update," *Government Information Quarterly* 11: 1 (1994). Potentially helpful too is the Senate Committee on Governmental Affairs hearings called the *Carter Presidential Library Proposal* (98th Cong., 1st sess.,).

The ninth presidential library, the Ronald W. Reagan institution at Simi Valley, California, like the Ford and Carter libraries, has only a few articles penned about its creation. The summary history of the Reagan Library exists in Dennis A. Daellenbach, "The Ronald Reagan Presidential Library," *Government Information Quarterly* 11: 1 (1994). Also helpful in understanding the Reagan Library is the opinion piece written by John Carlin, the current Archivist of the U.S., on the topic, the "Opening of the Reagan Records." The piece may be found on the NARA website at www.archives.gov/presidential_libraries/presidential_records/opening_reagan_records.html.

For information on the George H.W. Bush Presidential Library at College Station, Texas, see David E. Alsobrook, "The Birth of the Tenth Presidential Library: The Bush Presidential Materials Project, 1993-1994," *Government Information Quarterly* 12: 1 (1995).

For the William J. Clinton Library at Little Rock, Arkansas, make sure to see the *Memorandum of Understanding* [MOU] *between the National Archives and Records Administration and the Executive Office of the President Concerning the Continuation and Completion, After January 20, 2001, of the Tape Restoration, 'Multi Host,' and Reformatting Projects for the Clinton-Gore Administration Electronic Mail Records Associated with Automatic Records Management System.* The MOU between Clinton/Gore and the National Archives and Records Administration is available at www.archives.gov/ presidetial_libraries/presidential_records/clinton_gore_email_ records_memo.html.

Also worthy of consultation for the researcher is Brian Chandler Thompson's "The Sitting Modern President and the National Archives," *Government Information Quarterly* 12: 1 (1995). Thompson details the current closely linked relationship between the president and NARA. Since the article appeared during the Clinton presidency, special attention is given to Clinton-NARA relations. While newspaper articles exist about President George W. Bush's gift of his gubernatorial papers to his father's presidential library—thus breaking with the Texas tradition of depositing governor's papers at Texas State Archives and possibly also violating Texas law—no articles have appeared about the current President Bush's plans for a presidential library.

While numerous newspaper accounts exist for the establishment of all presidential libraries, they seem especially numerous regarding the creation of the Reagan Library. However, as noted in the introduction to this essay, while newspaper cites are included in the bibliography, they are not included in this essay because their inclusion would make the subject access element of the essay unnecessarily large and unwieldy.

That said, however, short of going to each individual presidential library, there is no better way to discover the uniqueness and intricacies of each library than to scope through the newspaper articles written about each institution. Granted, the amount and quality of articles written about each institution vary as much as the institutions that they cover, but on the whole, a good number of newspaper articles exist for each library, and citations to a portion of those articles may be found in the bibliography (Part 3).

V. The Past as Prologue to the Future: Richard M. Nixon's Papers

Purposely not mentioned in the above section on presidential libraries
is the Richard M. Nixon Library and Birthplace. The only post-World
War II president without a federally sponsored library, Nixon nonetheless does have a presidential library of sorts. The Richard M. Nixon Library and Birthplace is the only presidential library that lacks presidential records. Nixon's institution came about through private initiative.
Lacking primary materials used and created by Nixon during his presidential years, the library functions in a significantly different sphere
from other presidential libraries. Yet, despite the fact that the library
lacks records from the Nixon presidency, it is for this very same reason
that presidential libraries from Ronald Reagan on will both own (in the
name of the people) and provides access to all presidential records.

The details of how President Nixon's records came into public
ownership are detailed in Part 1 of this work. The sources that document how these records and documents came to be public property
number in the hundreds, of which only the most helpful are listed here.
Useful as an introduction, as well as a place to look for more sources,
are the following two bibliographies: Dale E. Casper, *Richard M.
Nixon: A Bibliographic Exploration* (New York 1988), and Myron J.
Smith Jr., *Watergate: An Annotated Bibliography of Sources in English, 1972-1982* (Metuchen, NJ 1983). Although Smith's work is now
almost twenty years old, it provides an essential starting point for those
beginning more extensive research on the Watergate affair, which is the
historical event that eventually led to such reform legislation as the
Presidential Recordings and Materials Preservation Act of 1974.

The Presidential Recordings and Materials Preservation Act of
1974, as explained in Part 1, was legislation quickly drafted and enacted that invalidated an agreement that ex-President Nixon signed with
the Administrator of the General Services Administration (GSA). The
GSA at that time was the parent agency to the National Archives and
Records Service, which had no say in the agreement between the former chief executive and Administrator Arthur Sampson, a Nixon-
appointed Pennsylvania Republican chosen to lead the GSA. The text
of the infamous so-called Nixon-Sampson agreement exists in several
places, including "Presidential Materials of Richard Nixon," *Weekly
Compilation of Presidential Documents* 10, pt. 37 (September 8, 1974).
Immediately following the agreement in the *Weekly Compilation of
Presidential Documents* 10, pt. 37 (September 8, 1974), is the explanation that Sampson gave for his drafting the document, which entitled
the ex-president to control access to and retain ownership of all the records (both print and, more significantly, tape recordings) created while

Nixon was president.

The highly controversial agreement eventually led to legislative efforts to overturn the Nixon-Sampson document. The agreement also indirectly led to the Presidential Records Act of 1978, the legislation that guarantees public ownership of and access to presidential records. For a comprehensive view of the legislative efforts that eventually became the PRMPA, make sure to use the legislative history for this act. It is found in appendix B.

In the legal community, numerous articles have been penned about the ownership issue of Richard Nixon's records. Articles on the topic have also appeared in the literature of political science, history and information studies. Although some of the articles are now over twenty-five years old, they remain excellent in-depth treatments of the topic of federal ownership of Nixon's presidential materials. Equally useful are "Government Control of Richard Nixon's Presidential Material," *Yale Law Journal* 87: 8 (July 1978), which provides an early view but also one of the most comprehensive perspectives, and Joan Hoff, "The Endless Saga of the Nixon Tapes," in *A Culture of Secrecy: The Government versus the People's Right to Know* (Lawrence, KS, 1998), which updates the saga.

Designed more for an audience of information professionals, yet also one of the best written pieces about the Nixon tapes, is Bruce P. Montgomery's "Nixon's Legal Legacy: White House Papers and the Constitution," *American Archivist* 56: 4 (Fall 1993). However, significant changes have occurred in the Nixon tapes saga even since Hoff's piece was published in 1998. Supplement both of the articles mentioned above with newspaper accounts of the June 2000 judicial ruling that found that the government needed to pay the heirs of Nixon for his papers.

While numerous monographs and edited works exist on the Watergate affair, few address the development of the PRMPA as a direct effect of the infamous bungled third-rate burglary. Of the few books that do mention the topic of increased legislative control of presidential records as a result of the Watergate affair, some incorporate the topic better than others. Perhaps the only monograph that adequately addresses the topic of Nixon's presidential papers is one of the more recent works, Stanley I. Kutler, *The Wars of Watergate: The Last Crisis of Richard Nixon* (New York 1990). Kutler touches on and explores the crucial topic of ownership of presidential papers throughout his text without ever dwelling on the topic extensively. Of course, one of the better treatments of the Watergate affair in general, Theodore H.

White's *Breach of Faith: The Fall of Richard Nixon* (New York 1975), also brushes on the public ownership issue, although not as much as one would hope. For a chronological assessment of the Watergate affair presented in narrative form, one could do no better than Elizabeth Drew, *Washington Journal: The Events of 1973-1974* (New York 1975). Granted, Drew's work lacks almost any mention of the PRMPA, but her journalistic account provides an excellent overview of the Watergate affair.

As noted earlier, numerous articles on the Nixon saga exist. The following paragraph lists some of the written sources on the Nixon tapes controversy. The following shorter articles are helpful overviews: William D. Ford and Daniel H. Pollitt, "Who Owns the Tapes?" *North Carolina Central Law Journal* 6: 2 (Spring 1975); Joe Morehead, "Tennis Elbow of the Soul: The Public Papers of Richard Nixon, 1973-1974," in *Essays on Public Documents and Government Policies* (New York 1986); and Ruth P. Morgan, "Nixon, Watergate and the Study of the Presidency," *Presidential Studies Quarterly* 26: 1 (Winter 1996). For a comparative law point of view between several high-profile cases in Malaysia and their counterparts with Nixon (including one Nixon case directly on point with the ownership of federal records—*Nixon v. Sirica*), make sure to look at Myint Zan, "The Three Nixon Cases and Their Parallels in Malaysia," *St. Thomas Law Review* 13 (Spring 2001).

U.S. v. Nixon, Nixon v. Sirica, Nixon v. Administrator of General Services—it is easy for the cases to blur into one confusing legal nightmare for all but the most dedicated. While this essay points to numerous articles that explain the intricate and nuanced differences between these important cases, they still lack personality to all but the legal scholar. Several of the major personages involved in these three cases have written accounts of their involvement.

Perhaps the most readable—and, in some ways, most exciting—account comes from the pen of the judge who ordered that President Nixon remand the infamous Oval Office tape recordings over to the judiciary. Judge John J. Sirica's *To Set the Record Straight: The Break-in, the Tapes, the Conspirators, the Pardon* (New York 1979) presents an interesting and important account of the Watergate judicial history. Complementing Sirica is Leon Jaworski's *The Right and the Power: The Prosecution of Watergate* (New York 1976). Jaworski was the Watergate special prosecutor who took the case *U.S. v. Nixon* to the Supreme Court. Upon adjudication, the court upheld that the president was not immune from prosecution and the Oval Office tapes must be handed over to fulfill the congressional requests for them. Extremely helpful in explaining why Jaworski replaced Archibald Cox as special prosecutor and other legal maneuvering is James Doyle's *Not above the Law: The Battles of Watergate Prosecutors Cox and Jaworski* (New York 1977). Doyle's work details the intricate events involved in the Saturday Night Massacre, when Cox was "fired" by Nixon, which led to Jaworski being named special prosecutor. Placing Sirica, Cox and Jaworski in an entirely different context is Richard Nixon's own account of his Watergate legal troubles, which can be found in Nixon's enormous *RN: The Memoirs of Richard Nixon* (New York 1978).

Thirty years and several long and drawn-out lawsuits after the Watergate break-in, the ownership of President Nixon's papers has finally been definitively settled. In the meantime, efforts at creating a Nixon library met with success and documented best in the following articles: Susan Naulty, "Creating an Archives at the Richard Nixon Library and Birthplace," *Government Information Quarterly* 11: 1 (1994) and Charles F. Lyons Jr., "The Nixon Presidential Materials Staff," *Government Information Quarterly* 12: 1 (1995). To place the development of the Nixon Library in context of the legal battles over Nixon archival material, be sure to consult Maarja Krusten, "Watergate's Last Victim," *Presidential Studies Quarterly* 26: 1 (Winter 1996). Also helpful to consult is the section entitled "Researching the Nixon Presidency: Documents and Evidence," in Leon Friedman and William F. Levantrosser, eds., *Watergate and Afterward* (Westport, CT, 1992). The entire book is the result of a conference held on Nixon's legacy at Hofstra University in 1987. The work contains many other chapters of potential benefit (i.e., there are chapters on topics mentioned elsewhere throughout this essay, such as the growth of the executive branch, rise of executive power/privilege, etc.).

While all of the above sources provide adequate introductions to the battles that raged from the early 1970s to the year 2000 over the fate of Nixon's presidential records, there can be no substitute for actually consulting the material itself. However, because consulting the original material is an option available to the few, even with the release of tapes to the public, several resources do exist for the scholar. The portions of the tapes submitted to the House Committee on the Judiciary are available in *White House Transcripts* (New York 1974). Complementary to this work is the Senate Committee on Government Operations report entitled *Preservation, Protection, and Public Access with Respect to Certain Tape Recordings and Other Materials, to Accompany S. 4106* (93rd Cong., 2nd sess., S. Rept. 93-1181) and the

House Committee on House Administration report, *Presidential Recordings and Materials Preservation Act, to Accompany S. 4016* (93rd Cong., 2nd sess., H. Rept. 93-1507).

Later Congresses also dealt with the problems associated with Richard Nixon's presidential material. About one year after the PRMPA passed Congress, attempts arose that sought to limit certain specific parts of the act. For more information on these attempts at legislative delimiting, make sure to read the following two congressional reports: House Committee on House Administration, *Disapproving Regulations Proposed by the General Services Administration Implementing the Presidential Recordings and Materials Act, to Accompany H. Res 710* (94th Cong., 1st sess., H. Rept. 94-560), and Senate Committee on Government Operations, *Disapproving the Regulations Proposed by the General Services Administration Implementing the Presidential Recordings and Materials Preservation Act, To Accompany S. Res. 244* (94th Cong., 1st sess., S. Rept. 94-368).

A considerably longer, yet very helpful treatment of Congress's hand-wringing over how to implement the PRMPA may be found in the documented hearings that Congress held in the mid 1970s. The published hearings held in each chamber of Congress provide insights into the issues that Congress' proposed altering in the PRMPA. See House Committee on House Administration, Subcommittee on Printing, *GSA Regulations to Implement Title I of the Presidential Recordings and Materials Preservation Act: Hearings on S. 4016 to Protect and Preserve Tape Recordings of Conversations Involving Former President Richard M. Nixon and Made during His Tenure as President, and for Other Purposes* (94th Cong., 1st sess., Y4.H81/3:P92), and Senate Committee on Government Operations, *GSA Regulations Implementing Presidential Recordings and Materials Preservation Act* (94th Cong., 1st sess., Y4.G74/6:P92).

The congressional attempts to alter the PRMPA and the control of Richard Nixon presidential records did not end with the closing of the first session of the 94th Congress. In the second session of that same Congress, attempts were once again initiated to alter specific portions of the PRMPA. For further details, see House Committee on House Administration, *Disapproving Certain Regulations Proposed by the General Services Administration Implementing Section 104 of the Presidential Recordings and Materials Preservation Act, to Accompany H. R. 1505* (94th Cong., 2nd sess., H. Rept. 94-1485), and Senate Committee on Government Operations, *Disapproving Regulations Proposed by the Administrator of General Services Under Section 104 of the Presidential Recordings and Materials Act on S. Res. 428* (94th Cong., 2nd sess., S. Rept. 94-748).

Attempts to alter the functions and structure of the PRMPA died down after the release of the *Final Report* of the National Study Commission on the Records and Documents of Federal Officials, a document that indirectly led to the Presidential Records Act (PRA) of 1978. The PRA is discussed in greater detail later, but before leaving the scope of congressional actions that focus on Nixon's records, several more reports and hearings should be mentioned. In 1986, at the same time that Congress explored alternative ways to reduce or defray the operating costs of presidential libraries, it also reassessed the access to Nixon presidential materials.

Especially helpful and detailed is a published hearing from the House Committee on Government Operations, Government Information, Justice, and Agriculture Subcommittee entitled *Review of Nixon Presidential Materials Access Regulations* (99th Cong., 2nd sess., Y4.G74/7:N65). Make sure to see also the corresponding committee report, which almost acts as an executive summary to the findings recorded in the hearing. The citation for the report is as follows: House Committee on Government Operations, *Access to the Nixon Presidential Materials Should Be Governed by NARA Regulations, Not OMB or DOJ Actions* (99th Cong., 2nd sess., S. Rept. 99-961)

W. After Nixon: The Public Documents Commission and the Presidential Records Act of 1978

Title II of the Presidential Recordings and Materials Preservation Act called for the creation of a blue-ribbon committee that would present to Congress a report of its findings on the historical, legal and cultural implications of the federal government's ownership of the records created by federal officials. The National Study Commission on the Records and Documents of Federal Officials—also called the Public Documents Commission or the Brownell Commission, after its chairman, Herbert Brownell—has largely been neglected as a cause for historical or archival research. The records of the Public Documents Commission are stored at the College Park, Maryland, NARA storage facility—the same location as the Nixon records.

Although the original materials produced, consulted, and used by the commission are of paramount importance for the study of the Public Documents Commission, the working group also produced a significant published record of its activity. A good number of materials created by the commission are available to the scholar who cannot travel to the National Archives and request the primary materials of the commission. However, before consulting any of the documents produced by the Public Documents Commission, reading Anna Kasten Nelson's "The Public Documents Commission: Politics and Presidential Records," *Government Publications Review* 9: 5 (September-October 1982), provides the reader with a fascinating look at the internal dynamics of the government-sponsored committee. Kasten, who was a staff member of the Public Documents Commission, has her views of how the commission operated placed in high relief when one reads Herbert Bronwell assessment of the commission in "'Who Really Owns the Papers of Departing Federal Officials?'" *New York State Bar Journal* 50: 3 (April 1978). Fifteen years' time somewhat mellowed Brownell's opinions on the Public Documents Commission, as pages 312-318 of his memoirs written with journalist John P. Burke show in *Advising Ike: The Memoirs of Attorney General Herbert Brownell* (Lawrence, KS, 1993).

An excellent primer for the copious amounts of materials produced by the Public Documents Commission crystallized in an edited version of all the reports generated by the commission. The edited volume by Anna Kasten Nelson is entitled *The Records of Federal Officials: A Selection of Materials from the National Study Commission on Records and Documents of Federal Officials* (New York 1978). The work contains selections from the numerous reports of the commission, ranging from looking at the ownership issue of records produced by each branch of the federal government, to the position of the National Archives under the General Services Administration, to issues of access to federally produced records. Nelson provides access to all of the commission's reports via an extensive listing at the end of her edited work, something especially helpful given the fact that all of the Public Documents Commission reports are available, albeit primarily on microfilm. The only depository document issued by the commission was its *Final Report*. Perhaps even more perplexing, though, was the Public Document Commission's decision to issue all of the supporting material to its *Final Report* on microfilm.

The decision to make the supporting material to the *Final Report* on microfilm was a space-saving measure that has made tracking down individual supporting reports an especially difficult job even for the most dedicated of researchers. (For more on why the commission issued the supporting reports on microform, see Nelson's article "The Public Documents Commission: Politics and Presidential Records.")

While most of the commission's reports are available on microfilm or as the original documents of the commission housed at the National Archives, a few of the twenty-six reports produced by the National Study Commission are available in print. Three of the more readily available National Study Commission on Records and Documents of Federal Officials reports include the following: *Study of the Records of Supreme Court Justices: A Survey of the Collections of Personal Papers of Supreme Court Justices*, prepared by Alexandra K. Wigdor (Washington, DC, 1977), *Memorandum of Findings on Existing Law, Fact and Opinion* (Washington, DC, 1977), and *Public Hearings Background Memorandum* (Washington, DC, 1977).

The *Study of the Records of Supreme Court Justices* divides its subject matter in two. The first half of the report presents an essay on past and current practices of preservation of records of Supreme Court justices. The much larger second half describes the locations, provenance, and scope of the collections of papers of justices from the founding of the Republic up to the then-current court. While both parts of the report contain valuable information, a more up-to-date version of the second half of the report is available on the Federal Judiciary Center's web site, air.fjc.gov.

In addition to soliciting the opinions of various department heads within the federal government, the Public Documents Commission also held several public hearings. The commission held four public hearings at different locations across the country and comments from the public were recorded, although the most hearings seem to have attracted only academics. Nelson's *The Records of Federal Officials* contains a full listing of where and when each hearing was held, as well as who submitted materials at each hearing.

Prior to holding a public hearing, the commission created a booklet that explained the scope and purpose of both the hearings and the commission. Called the *Public Hearings Background Memorandum* (Washington, DC, 1977), this lithe booklet that counts fewer than 100 pages provides a brief overview of the complex problems that the commission was charged with answering. Perhaps most useful due to its size, the small book presents in a clear and concise manner the policy considerations of the commission, the laws then in force concerning federal records, and historical practices of preservation and access to government records.

Contrasting with the conciseness of the *Public Hearings Background Memorandum* are the *Memorandum of Findings on Existing Law, Fact and Opinion* and the *Memoranda of Law*, the two other readily available print reports of the National Study Commission. Both reports are well over 300 pages long and filled with dense legal text. For those interested in the legal issues of private property, executive privilege, public access and right-to-know laws, separation of powers and other constitutional issues should consult the commission's *Memoranda of Law*. The commission's *Memorandum of Findings on Existing Law, Fact and Opinion*, places the law memo in a broader social context of an information-rich society that prides itself on access.

Regardless of whether one is interested in the supporting material created and consulted by the commission, of vital importance for anyone interested in the topic of public access and ownership of federally created materials, one must read the National Study Commission on Records and Documents of Federal Officials' *Final Report* (Washington, DC, 1977, Y3.R24/2:1/977). Titled deceptively, the *Final Report* actually includes two reports—the majority reported signed by all but two commission members and the minority report, drafted and signed by Brownell (the chair of the commission) and one other commission member.

The *Final Report* synthesizes much of the information contained in the more specific reports listed the above paragraphs, but such a synopsizing of the commission reports should not deter the scholar from consulting the original reports. Despite—or perhaps because of—its inclusion of two reports, the *Final Report* made little impact when it was reported to both chambers of Congress in late March/early April of 1977.

Although effectively ignored when it made it before Congress, residual effects from the reports did lead to the Presidential Records Act of 1978. The House hearings held on the PRA spanned several days in late February and early March 1978. The hearings produced a behemoth of a government document, rich with various sources, personal statements and appendices. This House Committee on Government Operations, Subcommittee on Government Information and Individual Rights hearing is called the *Presidential Records Act of 1978: Hearings on H.R. 10998 and Related Bills, to Amend the Freedom of Information Act to Insure Public Access to the Official Papers of the President, and for Other Reasons* (95th Cong., 2nd sess., Y4.G74/7:P92/5). Also helpful and not as intimidating and verbose as the House hearings are the Senate Committee on Governmental Affairs hearings called *The Presidential Records Act of 1978—S. 3494: Hearing on S. 3494, To Amend Title 44 to Insure the Preservation of and Public Access to the Official Records of the President, and for Other Purposes* (95th Cong., 2nd sess., Y4.G74/9:P92). See also the House Committee on Government Operations report, *Presidential Records Act of 1978* (95th Cong., 2nd sess., H. Rept. 95-1487).

Conclusion

Fundamental to any understanding of the complexities of the issues involved with and surrounding the topic of public ownership and access to the Records of government officials is an appreciation of both information-seeking behavior of researchers, and how knowledge is dispersed through organizations and networks. The literature of information seeking behavior is immensely rich, yet, at the present, no exclusive stand-alone volume exists on the topic. As for the subject of how information in social and institutionalized settings is shared, possessed and controlled, almost countless sources exist. Especially helpful in the formation of this bibliographic essay and the narrative found in Part One of this book were two books by Max H. Boisot, *Information and Organizations: The Manager as Anthropologist* (London 1987) and *Information as Space: A Framework for Learning in Organizations, Institutions and Culture* (London 1995). Each work by Boisot presents nuanced versions of a similar thesis on how information sharing and control works in institutionalized settings.

Part 3

Bibliography

6

Introduction to the Bibliography

The works present in the bibliography originate from almost every step in the publication cycle. The standard bibliographic practice of including only items personally inspected by the author ensured the veracity of all the items listed, yet this also generated another problem—what to do with the archival collections of presidential libraries. To compensate for materials deemed significant, but not consulted first hand by the author, Appendix D contains a list of presidential libraries as well as other select archival institutions.

Formats that were searched extensively for materials included the areas of monographic literature, periodical literature and government documents. Searched to a lesser extent were the publishing spheres of newspaper articles and broadcast media. For the most part, the Internet was used as a means to facilitate searching for information via proprietary electronic databases. The World Wide Web was used as a resource its own right but it yielded only a few valuable results.

Both print and electronic indexes were used in addition to online sources to ensure comprehensiveness. The list that follows records in no specific order the database used in the author's literature review. The information in parentheses indicates index provider, acronym for the index, or—in some cases—both.

The following databases were consulted over the span of six months, from November 2001 to April 2002: Library and Information Science Abstracts File (Dialog); Library Literature and Information Science (H.W. Wilson); Current Index to Legal Periodicals (WestLaw); Index to Legal Periodicals and Books, ILP (WestLaw); Essay and General Literature (H.W. Wilson); Congressional Universe (CIS); *CIS Index to Executive Orders*; Lord's *Presidential Executive Orders* (vol. 2); Newspapers File (Dialog); America: History and Life (ABC-Clio); InfoTrac (Gale); Lexis-Nexis Academic Universe (Lexis-Nexis);Thomas (Library of Congress); Dissertation Abstracts International (ProQuest UMI); ProQuest; ERIC (CSA); GPO Access; JSTOR; Project Muse; Web of Science—Arts, Humanities and Social Sciences and Citation Indexes (ISI); Expanded Academic ASAP (EBSCO); Public Affairs Information Service, PAIS (OCLC); Periodicals Contents Index (PCI); PapersFirst (OCLC); ProceedingsFirst (OCLC); World Cat (OCLC); Research Libraries Group (RLIN); Current Contents (OVID); ORION (UCLA's OPAC); and MELVYL (University of California Union Catalog). Also consulted were the print counterparts for PAIS, ILP, the *Los Angeles Times*, the *New York Times*, and the *Christian Science Monitor.* The dates for each of these print indexes varied widely. Of course, also used were the following government-based indexes: *Congressional Record* (stand-alone individual session indexes), *Digest of Public General Bills and Resolutions*, the *House Journal* and the *Senate Journal.*

Listing every search string and query used would require reams of paper and would be of only marginal usefulness. However, to give the reader an idea of how the above databases and print indexes were used, each resource consulted was approached via both narrow search strings (e.g., using the phrase "Hoover Institution on War, Revolution and Peace" as a descriptor) and broad strings (e.g., searching using the keywords "presidential" and "records"). Using both the complete and short titles of each of the presidential libraries from Hayes to Clinton yielded beneficial results. Other helpful terms used across databases included "presidential libraries," "presidential records," "government records," "president—united states—papers" and "presidential papers." Using open-ended search terms that yielded numerous results helped when first approaching a database, for after a few hits came back, search strings could then be altered accordingly.

In general, bibliographic formatting has followed the *Chicago Manual of Style (CMS)*, 14th ed., although the principles outlined in *A Uniform System of Citation* (the Bluebook), 17th edition, have been followed for legal cases.

This bibliography is arranged by format. Within each format, entries are organized alphabetically via word-by-word organization, ignoring the initial articles "the," "a" and "an." Thus, works authored by the Committee on Government Operations appear before works by the Committee on Governmental Affairs. Unsigned works (e.g., newspaper or magazine articles) have been separated from signed works for most formats. Thus, unsigned newspaper articles precede signed newspaper articles, although in both sections, alphabetical, word-by-word filing is strictly obeyed.

In some cases, citations are given to parts of a single bibliographic unit. For instance, the published conference proceedings for the New Harmony Conference is cites as follows:

Hamby, Alonzo L. and Edward Weldon, eds. *Access to the Papers of Recent Public Figures: The New Harmony Conference*. Bloomington, IN: Organization of American Historians, 1977.

Yet, because this book contains numerous citations that the reader may well be interested in, listing the citation above without also listing the chapters included in the book would deprive the user of numerous helpful works. For example, included within the conference proceedings listed above is the following chapter:

Berkeley, Edmund, Jr. "The Archivist and Access Restrictions." In *Access to the Papers of Recent Public Figures: The New Harmony Conference*, edited by Alonzo L. Hamby and Edward Weldon, 57-59. Bloomington, IN: Organization of American Historians, 1977.

In the example of the New Harmony Conference, citations are included to most of the fourteen papers included within the work. In addition to the New Harmony Conference, several other works include citations to both parts as well as entire bibliographic units.

Federal government works are filed according to the rubrics laid out in the following two paragraphs.

Works where the responsibility resides with the U.S. Congress are filed alphabetically from body of government down to the title of the document level. In other words, responsibility begins from the highest authority (e.g., U.S. Congress), down to the lowest (e.g., subcommittees or special committees). The citations reflect this organization. According to these rules, House documents precede Senate documents and documents issued by Subcommittee Y of Committee X follow works issued by Committee X alone. In the few cases where a document was issued jointly by two committees or subcommittees, the work is filed under the first committee/subcommittee listed.

The same principles used for congressional documents have been applied to congressional statements, thus collecting together all *Congressional Record* items. Statutory laws are filed under the heading Public Law, rather than Statute at Large, because Public Laws appear prior to the Statutes at Large.

Presidential documents are collocated together by the convention of substituting the issuing president's personal name with the title "President. Proclamation." Citations for presidential documents refer to the *Weekly Compilation of Presidential Documents* (*WCPD*), rather than the *Public Papers of the Presidents* series because the *WCPD* often includes materials not found in the *Public Papers*.

Parallel citations for legal cases have been provided whenever available, following the rules set forth in the Bluebook. Due to the ephemeral nature of tracking down legal briefs, citations are included only when the briefs are widely and freely available, usually via an electronic format. Short titles for cases and legal briefs replace the respective full titles. The abbreviated term U.S. is used uniformly for United States for all cases. However, a cross-referenced and indexed table of cases included in these bibliographies may be found in appendix C.

7

Bibliography

Congressional Record

U.S. Congress. House. Congressman Allen Ertel of Pennsylvania Commended. 95th Cong., 1st sess., *Congressional Record* (March 28, 1977), 123, pt. 8, 9284-85. [Bound edition].

U.S. Congress. House. Establishment and Maintenance of the Franklin D. Roosevelt Library. 76th Cong., 1st sess., *Congressional Record* (June 5, 1939), 84, pt. 6, 6607. [Bound edition].

U.S. Congress. House. Franklin D. Roosevelt Library. 76th Cong., 1st sess., *Congressional Record* (June 5, 1939), 84, pt. 6, 6622-29. [Bound edition].

U.S. Congress. House. Franklin D. Roosevelt Library. 76th Cong., 1st sess., *Congressional Record* (July 13, 1939), 84, pt. 8, 9037-66. [Bound edition].

U.S. Congress. House. Franklin D. Roosevelt Library. 76th Cong., 1st sess., *Congressional Record* (July 17, 1939), 84, pt. 9, 9282. [Bound edition].

U.S. Congress. House. The Nixon Papers Decision: An Inducement for Congressional Action. 95th Cong., 1st sess., *Congressional Record* (July 13, 1977), 123, pt. 18, 22722-23. [Bound edition].

U.S. Congress. House. Presidential Libraries. 84th Cong., 1st sess., *Congressional Record* (August 1, 1955), 120, pt. 10, 12649-50. [Bound edition].

U.S. Congress. House. Presidential Recordings and Materials Preservation Act. 93rd Cong., 2nd sess., *Congressional Record* (December 3, 1974), 120, pt. 28, 37898-906. [Bound edition].

U.S. Congress. House. Presidential Records Act of 1978. 95th Cong., 2nd sess., *Congressional Record* (October 5, 1978), 124, pt. 25, 33860-62. [Bound edition].

U.S. Congress. House. Presidential Records Act of 1978. 95th Cong., 2nd sess., *Congressional Record* (October 10, 1978), 124, pt. 26, 34892-97. [Bound edition].

U.S. Congress. House. Presidential Records Act of 1978. 95th Cong.,

2nd sess., *Congressional Record* (October 14, 1978), 124, 38283-84. [Bound edition].

U.S. Congress. House. Protecting and Preserving Tape Recordings Involving Former President Richard M. Nixon. 93rd Cong., 2nd sess., *Congressional Record* (December 9, 1974), 120, pt. 29, 38645-47. [Bound edition].

U.S. Congress. House. Providing Acceptance and Maintenance of Presidential Libraries. 84th Cong., 1st sess., *Congressional Record* (July 5, 1955), 120, pt. 8, 9934-38. [Bound edition].

U.S. Congress. House. United States Code Amending Chapter 33 of Title 44. 94th Cong., 2nd sess., *Congressional Record* (March 31, 1976), 122, pt. 7, 8884-85. [Bound edition].

U.S. Congress. Senate. Acceptance and Maintenance of Presidential Libraries. 84th Cong., 1st sess., *Congressional Record* (June 20, 1955), 101, pt. 7, 8655. [Bound edition].

U.S. Congress. Senate. Acceptance and Maintenance of Presidential Libraries. 84th Cong., 1st sess., *Congressional Record.* (July 30, 1955), 120, pt. 10, 12230. [Bound edition].

U.S. Congress. Senate. Franklin D. Roosevelt Library. 76th Cong., 1st sess., *Congressional Record* (April 20, 1939), 84, pt. 4, 4543-44. [Bound edition].

U.S. Congress. Senate. Franklin D. Roosevelt Library. 76th Cong., 1st sess., *Congressional Record* (July 14, 1939), 84, pt. 9, 9141-42. [Bound edition].

U.S. Congress. Senate. Preservation of and Public Access to Official Records of the President. 95th Cong., 2nd sess., *Congressional Record* (October 13, 1978), 124, pt. 27, 356843-46. [Bound edition].

U.S. Congress. Senate. Presidential Recordings and Materials Preservation Act. 93rd Cong., 2nd sess., *Congressional Record* (October 3, 1974), 120, pt. 25, 33849-76. [Bound edition].

U.S. Congress. Senate. Presidential Recordings and Materials Preservation Act. 93rd Cong., 2nd sess., *Congressional Record* (October 4, 1974), 120, pt. 25, 33958-76. [Bound edition].

U.S. Congress. Senate. Presidential Recordings and Materials Preservation Act. 93rd Cong., 2nd sess., *Congressional Record* (December 9, 1974), 120, pt. 29, 38529-37. [Bound edition].

U.S. Congress. Senate. Public Documents Act Amendments. 94th Cong., 2nd sess., *Congressional Record* (March 30, 1976), 122, pt. 7, 8621. [Bound edition].

U.S. Congress. Senate. S. 4016—Unanimous-Consent Agreement. 93rd Cong., 2nd sess., *Congressional Record* (October 3, 1978), 120, pt.

25, 33878. [Bound edition].

U.S. Congress. Senate. Statements on Introduced Bills and Joint Resolutions: S. 4016. 93rd Cong., 2nd sess., *Congressional Record*
(September 18, 1974), 120, pt. 24, 31549-51. [Bound edition].

Congressional Hearings

U.S. Congress. House. Committee on Government Operations. Government Information and Individual Rights Subcommittee. *Presidential Records Act of 1978: Hearings on H.R. 10998 and Related
Bills, to Amend the Freedom of Information Act to Insure Public
Access to the Official Papers of the President, and for Other Reasons*. 95th Cong., 2nd sess., February 23, 28; March 2, 7, 1978.
Y4.G74/7:P92/5.

U.S. Congress. House. Committee on Government Operations. Government Information, Justice, and Agriculture Subcommittee. *Review of Nixon Presidential Materials Access Regulations*. 99th
Cong., 2nd sess., April 29, 1986. Y4.G74/7:N65.

U.S. Congress. House. Committee on Government Operations. Gov-
ernment Information, Justice, and Agriculture Subcommittee.
*Presidential Libraries Funding Proposal: Hearing on H.R. 1349,
To Reduce the Costs of Operating Presidential Libraries, and for
Other Purposes*. 99th Cong., 1st sess., March 26, 1985.
Y4.G74/7:L61/3.

U.S. Congress. House. Committee on Government Operations. Government Information, Justice, and Agriculture Subcommittee.
*Presidential Libraries Funding: Hearings on H.R. 3138 and Re-
lated Bills, to Improve the Preservation and Management of Presidential Records and for Other Purposes*. 98th Cong., 2nd sess.,
February 23, 1984. Y4.G74/7:L61/2.

U.S. Congress. House. Committee on Government Operations. Special
Subcommittee. *To Provide for the Acceptance and Maintenance of
Presidential Libraries, and for Other Purposes: Hearings on H.J.
Res. 330, H.J. Res. 331 and H.J. Res 332, Bills to Provide for the
Acceptance and Maintenance of Presidential Libraries, and for
Other Purposes*. 84th Cong., 1st sess., June 13, 1955.
Y4.G74/7:L61

U.S. Congress. House. Committee on Government Operations. Sub-
committee on the Library. *Microfilming Presidential Papers:
Hearing on H.R. 7813, To Organize and Microfilm the Papers of
Presidents of the United States in the Collections of the Library of*

Congress. 85th Cong., 1st sess., June 21, 1957. Y4.H81/3:M58.

U.S. Congress. House. Committee on Government Reform. Subcommittee on Government Efficiency, Financial Management and Intergovernmental Relations. *Hearing on the Implementation and Effectiveness of the Presidential Records Act of 1978*. 107th Cong., 1st sess., November 6, 2001.

U.S. Congress. House. Committee on Government Reform. Subcommittee on Government Efficiency, Financial Management and Intergovernmental Relations. *Oversight Hearing on H.R. 577, A Bill to Require Any Organization That Is Established for the Purpose of Raising Funds for the Creation of a Presidential Archival Depository to Disclose the Sources and Amounts of Any Funds Raised*. 107th Cong., 1st sess., April 5, 2001.

U.S. Congress. House. Committee on House Administration. Subcommittee on Printing. *GSA Regulations to Implement Title I of the Presidential Recordings and Materials Preservation Act: Hearings on S. 4016 to Protect and Preserve Tape Recordings of Conversations Involving Former President Richard M. Nixon and Made During His Tenure as President, and for Other Purposes*. 94th Cong., 1st sess., May 22 and June 3, 1975. Y4.H81/3:P92.

U.S. Congress. House. Committee on House Administration. Subcommittee on Printing. *The "Public Documents Act": Hearings on H.R. 16902 and Related Legislation, the Disposition and Preservation of Documents of Federal Officials*. 93rd Cong., 2nd sess., September 30 and October 4, 1974. Y4.H81/3:P96/2.

U.S. Congress. Senate. Committee on Government Operations. *GSA Regulations Implementing Presidential Recordings and Materials Preservation Act*. 94th Cong., 1st sess., May 13, 1975. Y4.G74/6:P92.

U.S. Congress. Senate. Committee on Governmental Affairs. *Carter Presidential Library Proposal*. 98th Cong., 1st sess., November 9, 1983. Y4.G74/9:S.hrg.98-1124.

U.S. Congress. Senate. Committee on Governmental Affairs. *The Presidential Records Act of 1978—S. 3494: Hearing on S. 3494, To Amend Title 44 to Insure the Preservation of and Public Access to the Official Records of the President, and for Other Purposes*. 95th Cong., 2nd sess., September 15, 1978. Y4.G74/9:P92.

U.S. Congress. Senate. Committee on Governmental Affairs and Committee on Appropriations. Subcommittee on Civil Service and General Services and Subcommittee on Treasury, Postal Service, and General Government. *Cost of Former Presidents to U.S. Tax-*

payers: Special Hearing. 96th Cong., 1st sess., November 6-8, 1979. Y4.Ap6/2:P92.

U.S. Congress. Senate. Committee on Governmental Affairs. *Benefits to Former Presidents: Hearing on S. 1325, to Reform Laws Relating to Former Presidents.* 97th Cong., 2nd sess., September 22, 1982.

U.S. Congress. Senate. Committee on Governmental Affairs. Subcommittee on Civil Service and General Services. *Oversight on the Former Presidents* [Sic] *Act and the Presidential Transition Act.* 96th Cong., 1st sess., May 16, 1979. Y4.G74/9:S.hrg.100-726.

U.S. Congress. Senate. Committee on Governmental Affairs. Subcommittee on Federal Spending, Budget and Accounting. *Former President's Act of 1987: Hearing on S. 1647, to Reform the Laws Relating to Former Presidents.* 100th Cong., 2nd sess., March 3, 1988. Y4.G74/9:S.hrg.103-847.

U.S. Congress. Senate. Committee on Governmental Affairs. Subcommittee on Regulation and Government Information. *Public Papers of Supreme Court Justices: Assuring Preservation and Access.* 103rd Cong., 1st sess., June 11, 1993. Y4.G74/9:S.hrg.103-847.

Congressional Reports and Prints

U.S. Congress. House. Committee on Government Operations. *Presidential Libraries, to Accompany H. J. Res. 330.* 84th Cong., 1st sess., June 29, 1955. H. Rept. 84-998, Serial Set No. 11823-3.

U.S. Congress. House. Committee on Government Operations. *Presidential Libraries: Unexplored Funding Alternatives.* 97th Cong., 2nd sess., August 12, 1982. H. Rept. 97-732, Calendar No. 452, Y1.1/8:97-732.

U.S. Congress. House. Committee on Government Operations. Government Information and Individual Rights Subcommittee. *Presidential Records Act of 1978: Hearings on H.R. 10998 and Related Bills, to Amend the Freedom of Information Act to Insure Public Access to the Official Papers of the President, and for Other Reasons.* 95th Cong., 2nd sess., February 23, 28; March 2, 7, 1978. Y4.G74/7:P92/5.

U.S. Congress. House. Committee on Government Operations. Government Information, Justice, and Agriculture Subcommittee. *Review of Nixon Presidential Materials Access Regulations.* 99th Cong., 2nd sess., April 29, 1986. Y4.G74/7:N65.

U.S. Congress. House. Committee on Government Operations. Government Information, Justice, and Agriculture Subcommittee. *Presidential Libraries Funding Proposal: Hearing on H.R. 1349, To Reduce the Costs of Operating Presidential Libraries, and for Other Purposes.* 99th Cong., 1st sess., March 26, 1985. Y4.G74/7:L61/3.

U.S. Congress. House. Committee on Government Operations. Government Information, Justice, and Agriculture Subcommittee. *Presidential Libraries Funding: Hearings on H.R. 3138 and Related Bills, to Improve the Preservation and Management of Presidential Records and for Other Purposes.* 98th Cong., 2nd sess., February 23, 1984. Y4.G74/7:L61/2.

U.S. Congress. House. Committee on Government Operations. Special Subcommittee. *To Provide for the Acceptance and Maintenance of Presidential Libraries, and for Other Purposes: Hearings on H.J. Res. 330, H.J. Res. 331 and H.J. Res 332, Bills to Provide for the Acceptance and Maintenance of Presidential Libraries, and for Other Purposes.* 84th Cong., 1st sess., June 13, 1955.

U.S. Congress. House. Committee on Government Operations. Subcommittee on the Library. *Microfilming Presidential Papers: Hearing on H.R. 7813, To Organize and Microfilm the Papers of Presidents of the United States in the Collections of the Library of Congress.* 85th Cong., 1st sess., June 21, 1957. Y4.H81/3:M58.

U.S. Congress. House. Committee on Government Reform. Subcommittee on Government Efficiency, Financial Management and Intergovernmental Relations. *Hearing on the Implementation and Effectiveness of the Presidential Records Act of 1978.* 107th Cong., 1st sess., November 6, 2001.

U.S. Congress. House. Committee on Government Reform. *A Citizen's Guide on Using the Freedom of Information Act and the Privacy Act of 1974 to Request Government Records.* 106th Cong., 1st sess., H. Rept. 106-50. Y1.T/8:106-50.

U.S. Congress. House. Committee on Government Reform. Subcommittee on Government Efficiency, Financial Management and Intergovernmental Relations. *Oversight Hearing on H.R. 577, A Bill to Require Any Organization That Is Established for the Purpose of Raising Funds for the Creation of a Presidential Archival Depository to Disclose the Sources and Amounts of Any Funds Raised.* 107th Cong., 1st sess., April 5, 2001.

U.S. Congress. House. Committee on House Administration. Subcommittee on Printing. *GSA Regulations to Implement Title I of the Presidential Recordings and Materials Preservation Act: Hearings* on S. 4016 to Protect and Preserve Tape Recordings of Conversations Involving Former President Richard M. Nixon and Made During His Tenure as President, and for Other Purposes. 94th Cong., 1st sess., May 22 and June 3, 1975. Y4.H81/3:P92.

U.S. Congress. House. Committee on House Administration. Subcommittee on Printing. The "Public Documents Act": Hearings on H.R. 16902 and Related Legislation, the Disposition and Preservation of Documents of Federal Officials. 93rd Cong., 2nd sess., September 30 and October 4, 1974. Y4.H81/3:P96/2.

U.S. Congress. House. Committee on Post Office and Civil Service. Subcommittee on Census and Statistics. Report on the Adequacy and Management of Services Furnished to Scholars and Researchers by Presidential Libraries. 92nd Cong., 2nd sess., March 2, 1972. H. Rept. 92-898, Serial Set No. 12976-1A, Calendar No. 451.

U.S. Congress. Senate. Committee on Government Operations. GSA Regulations Implementing Presidential Recordings and Materials Preservation Act. 94th Cong., 1st sess., May 13, 1975. Y4.G74/6:P92.

U.S. Congress. Senate. Committee on Government Operations. Providing for the Acceptance and Maintenance of Presidential Libraries, to Accompany H. J. Res. 330. 84th Cong., 1st sess., July 28, 1955. S. Rept. 84-1189, Serial Set No. 11817-3, Calendar No. 1205.

U.S. Congress. Senate. Committee on Governmental Affairs. Amending Title 44, United States Code, to Require any Organization that is established for the Purpose of Raising Funds for Creating, Maintaining, Expanding, or Conducting Activities at a Presidential Archival Depository or Any Facilities Relating to a Presidential Archival Depository to Disclose the Sources and Amounts of Funds Raised, and for Other Purposes. 107th Cong., 2nd sess., June 11, 2002.

U.S. Congress. Senate. Committee on Governmental Affairs. Carter Presidential Library Proposal. 98th Cong., 1st sess., November 9, 1983.

U.S. Congress. Senate. Committee on Governmental Affairs. The Presidential Records Act of 1978—S. 3494: Hearing on S. 3494, To Amend Title 44 to Insure the Preservation of and Public Access to the Official Records of the President, and for Other Purposes. 95th Cong., 2nd sess., September 15, 1978. Y4.G74/9:P92.

U.S. Congress. Senate. Committee on Governmental Affairs and Committee on Appropriations. Subcommittee on Civil Service and

General Services and Subcommittee on Treasury, Postal Service, and General Government. *Cost of Former Presidents to U.S. Taxpayers: Special Hearing*. 96th Cong., 1st sess., November 6-8, 1979.

U.S. Congress. Senate. Committee on Governmental Affairs. *Benefits to Former Presidents: Hearing on S. 1325, to Reform Laws Relating to Former Presidents*. 97th Cong., 2nd sess., September 22, 1982. Y4.G74/9:B43/3.

U.S. Congress. Senate. Committee on Governmental Affairs. Subcommittee on Civil Service and General Services. *Oversight on the Former Presidents* [Sic] *Act and the Presidential Transition Act*. 96th Cong., 1st sess., May 16, 1979. Y4.G74/9:P92/2.

U.S. Congress. Senate. Committee on Governmental Affairs. Subcommittee on Federal Spending, Budget and Accounting. *Former President's Act of 1987: Hearing on S. 1647, to Reform the Laws Relating to Former Presidents*. 100th Cong., 2nd sess., March 3, 1988. Y4.G74/9:S.hrg.103-847.

U.S. Congress. Senate. Committee on Governmental Affairs. Subcommittee on Regulation and Government Information. *Public Papers of Supreme Court Justices: Assuring Preservation and Access*. 103rd Cong., 1st sess., June 11, 1993. Y4.G74/9:S.hrg.103-847.

U.S. Congress. Senate. Select Committee on Intelligence. *Were Relevant Documents Withheld from the Congressional Committees Investigating the Iran-Contra Affair*. 101st Cong., 1st sess., June 1989. S. Committee Print 101-44. Y4.In8/19:S.prt.101-44.

Statutes

Public Law 84-373. 69 Stat. 695. 84th Cong., 1st sess., August 12, 1955. *Presidential Libraries: Acceptance and Maintenance*.

Public Law 93-526. 88 Stat. 1695. 93rd Cong., 2nd sess., December 19, 1974. *Preservation of Presidential Recordings and Materials*.

Public Law 94-261. 90 Stat. 326. 94th Cong., 2nd sess., April 11, 1976. *National Study Commission on Records and Documents—Federal Officials*.

Public Law 95-591. 92 Stat. 2553. 95th Cong., 2nd sess., October 13, 1978. *Presidential Records Act of 1978*.

Public Law 98-497. 98 Stat. 2280. 98th Cong., 2nd sess., October 3, 1984. *National Archives and Records Administration Act of 1984*.

Public Law 99-323. 100 Stat. 495. 99th Cong., 2nd sess., May 27, 1986. *An Act to Reduce the Costs of Operating Presidential Li-*

braries.

Presidential Documents (Print)

President. Proclamation. "Availability of Information from Presidential Tapes." *Weekly Compilation of Presidential Documents* 9, pt. 42 (Oct. 19, 1973): 1265-1266.

President. Proclamation. "Court Order Requiring Production of Recordings and Documents." *Weekly Compilation of Presidential Documents* 9, pt. 37 (Sept. 10, 1973): 1100-1122.

President. Proclamation. "Donation of the President's Papers to the Government." *Weekly Compilation of Presidential Documents* 12, pt. 51 (Dec. 14, 1976): 1709-1714.

President. Proclamation. "Donation of the President's Papers to the Government." *Weekly Compilation of Presidential Documents* 12, pt. 51 (Dec. 14, 1976): 1714-1719.

President. Proclamation. "Executive Order 8248: Establishing the Divisions of the Executive Office of the President and Defining Their Functions and Duties." *Federal Register* 4 (Sept. 8, 1939): 3864.

President. Proclamation. "Executive Order 12667: Presidential Records." *Federal Register* 54 (Jan. 18, 1989): 3403.

President. Proclamation. "Executive Order 13231: Critical Infrastructure Protection in the Information Age." *Federal Register* 66 (Oct. 18, 2001): 53063-53071.

President. Proclamation. "Executive Order 13233: Further Implementation of the Presidential Records Act." *Federal Register* 66 (Nov. 5, 2001): 56025-56029.

President. Proclamation. "Pardon and Agreement on Presidential Materials of Richard Nixon." *Weekly Compilation of Presidential Documents* 10, pt. 37 (Sept. 10, 1974): 1123-1129.

President. Proclamation. "Pardon for Former President Nixon." *Weekly Compilation of Presidential Documents* 10, pt. 42 (Oct. 17, 1974): 1301-1316.

President. Proclamation. "Presidential Recordings and Materials Preservation Act." *Weekly Compilation of Presidential Documents* 10, pt. 51 (Dec. 19, 1974): 1595.

President. Proclamation. "Presidential Tapes." *Weekly Compilation of Presidential Documents* 9, pt. 43 (Oct. 23, 1973): 1275-1283.

President. Proclamation. "Presidential Tapes and Documents." *Weekly Compilation of Presidential Documents* 9, pt. 46 (Nov. 12, 1973): 1329-1331.

President. Proclamation. "Presidential Tapes and Documents." *Weekly Compilation of Presidential Documents* 9, pt. 48 (Nov. 26, 1973): 1370-1377.

President. Proclamation. "Presidential Tapes and Materials." *Weekly Compilation of Presidential Documents* 10, pt. 1 (Jan. 4, 1974): 11-12.

President. Proclamation. "Presidential Materials of Richard Nixon." *Weekly Compilation of Presidential Documents* 10, pt. 37 (Sept. 8, 1974): 1104-1105.

President. Proclamation. "Presidential Materials of Richard Nixon." *Weekly Compilation of Presidential Documents* 10, pt. 37 (Sept. 8, 1974): 1105-1119.

President. Proclamation. "Presidential Records Act of 1978." *Public Papers of the President, Jimmy Carter: 1978*, pt. 2 (Nov. 6, 1978): 1965-1966.

Presidential Documents (Microform)

President. Proclamation. "Executive Order 206." *Presidential Executive Orders* [Library of Congress Photoduplication Service, Microfilm] Reel 1 (March 9, 1903).

President. Proclamation. "Executive Order 449." *Presidential Executive Orders* [Library of Congress Photoduplication Service, Microfilm] Reel 1 (May 23, 1906).

President. Proclamation. "Executive Order 1499." *Presidential Executive Orders* [Library of Congress Photoduplication Service, Microfilm] Reel 3 (March 16, 1912).

President. Proclamation. "Executive Order 3554: Transfer of the Declaration of Independence and the Constitution from the Department of State to the Library of Congress." *Presidential Executive Orders* [Library of Congress Photoduplication Service, Microfilm] Reel 5 (Sept. 29, 1921).

President. Proclamation. "Executive Order 3594: Transfer of Certain Historical Papers from the Department of State to the Library of Congress." *Presidential Executive Orders* [Library of Congress Photoduplication Service, Microfilm] Reel 6 (Dec. 19, 1921).

Non-Congressional Government Documents and Reports

Committee on Authorities and Program Alternatives. *NARA and the Disposition of Federal Records: Laws and Authorities and Their Implementation: A Report of the Committee on Authorities and Program Alternatives.* Washington, DC: National Archives and Records Administration, 1989.

Library of Congress, Manuscript Division, Reference Department. *The Presidential Papers Program of the Library of Congress.* Washington, DC: Government Printing Office, [1960 ?].

National Archives. *How to Dispose of Records: A Manual for Federal Officials.* Rev. ed. Washington, DC: National Archives, 1946. Publication No. 46-19.

National Archives and Records Administration. "Presidential Libraries Manual." Reprint. Washington, DC: National Archives and Records Administration, 1992.

National Archives and Records Administration. *Ready Access to Essential Evidence: The Strategic Plan of the National Archives and Records Administration, 1997-2007.* Washington, DC: National Archives and Records Administration, 2000.

National Study Commission on Records and Documents of Federal Officials. *Study of the Records of Supreme Court Justices: A Survey of the Collections of Personal Papers of Supreme Court Justices.* Prepared by Alexandra K. Wigdor. Washington, DC: Government Printing Office, 1977.

————. *Memorandum of Findings on Existing Law, Fact and Opinion.* Washington, DC: Government Printing Office, 1977.

————. *Final Report.* Washington, DC: Government Printing Office, 1977. Y3.R24/2:1/977.

————. *Memoranda of Law.* Washington, DC: Government Printing Office, [1977 ?].

————. *Public Hearings Background Memorandum.* Washington, DC: Government Printing Office, [1977 ?].

Task Force on NARA Responsibilities for Federal Records and Related Documentation. *NARA and Presidential Records: Laws and Authorities and Their Implementation: A Report of the Task Force on NARA Responsibilities for Federal Records and Related Documents.* Washington, DC: National Archives and Records Administration, 1988.

U.S. General Accounting Office. *GSA Approval of Expenditures Under the Former Presidents Act Has Been Reasonable.* Washington, DC: U.S. General Accounting Office, 1979.

————. *Former Presidents: Support Costs and Other Information.*

Washington, DC: U.S. General Accounting Office, 1988.

————. *Federal Records: Removal of Agency Documents by Senior Officials Upon Leaving Office.* Washington, DC: U.S. General Accounting Office, 1989.

Cases

AHA v. Peterson. 876 F.Supp. 1300, 63 U.S.L.W. 2557 (1995).

Allen v. Carmen. 578 F.Supp. 951, 1983 U.S.Dist. LEXIS 10286 (1983).

Armstrong v. Bush. 721 F.Supp. 343, 58 U.S.L.W. 2184 (1989).

Armstrong v. Bush. 924 F.2d 282, 288 U.S.App.D.C. 38 (1991).

Armstrong v. EOP. 810 F.Supp. 335, 61 U.S.L.W. 2427 (1993).

Armstrong v. EOP. 1 F.3d 1274, 303 U.S.App.D.C. 107, 62 U.S.L.W. 2109 (1993).

Armstrong v. EOP. 877 F.Supp. 750, 1995 U.S.Dist. LEXIS 2334 (1995).

Armstrong v. EOP. 90 F.3d 553, 319 U.S.App.D.C. 330, 65 U.S.L.W. 2140 (1996).

Brandon v. Eckard. 569 F.2d 683, 187 U.S.App.D.C. 28, 1977 U.S.App. LEXIS 5518 (1977).

Dellums v. Powell. 642 F.2d 1351, 206 U.S.App.D.C. 383, 30 Fed.R.Serv. 333 (1981).

EPA v. Mink. 410 U.S. 73, 93 S.Ct. 827, 35 L.Ed.2d 119 (1973).

Eyre v. Higbee. 1861 WL (N.Y.Sup.Gen.Term) 5315, 22 How.Pr. 198, 35 Barb. 502 (1861).

Folsom v. Marsh. 9 F.Cas. 342, 6 Hunt Mer.Mag. 342, 2 Story 100, No. 4901 (1841).

Hist. Soc. of New Mex. v. Montoya. 74 N.M. 285, 393 P.2d 21, 1964 N.M. LEXIS 2204 (1964).

In re Roosevelt's Will. 73 N.Y.S.2d 821, 190 Misc. 341, 1947 N.Y.Misc. LEXIS 3141 (1947).

In re Sealed Case. 116 F.3d 550, 325 U.S.App.D.C. 206, 46 Fed.R.Evid.Serv. 1188 (1997).

INS v. Chadha. 462 U.S. 919, 103 S.Ct. 2764, 77 L.Ed.2d 317 (1983).

Kissinger v. Reporters Committee for Freedom of the Press. 445 U.S. 136, 100 S.Ct. 960, 63 L.Ed.2d 267 (1980).

Kutler v. Carlin. 139 F.3d 237, 1998 U.S.App. LEXIS 6313 (1998).

Marbury v. Madison. 5 U.S. 137, 1 Cranch 137, 2 L.Ed. 60 (1803).

New York v. Dewitt. 1868 WL (N.Y.Sup.Gen.Term) 5939, 51 Barb. 19 (1868).

Nixon v. Administrator. 433 U.S. 425, 97 S.Ct. 2777, 53 L.Ed.2d 867 (1977).

Nixon v. Freeman. 670 F.2d 346, 216 U.S.App.D.C. 188, 8 Media L.Rep. 1001 (1982).

Nixon v. Richey. 513 F.2d 430, 168 U.S.App.D.C. 172 (1975).

Nixon v. Sampson. 389 F.Supp. 107 (1975).

Nixon v. Sirica. 487 F.2d 700, 159 U.S.App.D.C. 58, 19 A.L.R. Fed. 343 (1973).

Nixon v. U.S. 782 F.Supp. 634 (1991).

Nixon v. U.S. 978 F.2d 1269, 298 U.S.App.D.C. 249, 61 USLW 2325 (1992).

Nixon v. U.S. 935 F.Supp. 1, 1995 U.S.Dist. LEXIS 17626 (1995).

Public Citizen v. Carlin. 2 F.Supp.2d 18 (1998).

Public Citizen v. DOJ. 111 F.3d 168, 324 U.S.App.D.C. 126 (1997).

Public Citizen v. Sampson. 1974 U.S.Dist. LEXIS 12721, 180 U.S.P.Q. (BNA) 497 (1974).

Public Citizen v. Sampson. 379 F.Supp. 662, 1974 U.S.Dist. LEXIS 7468, 20 Cont.Cas.Fed. (CCH) P83, 198 (1974).

Senate Select Committee v. Nixon. 366 F.Supp. 51 (1973).

Sender v. Montoya. 73 N.M. 287, 387 P.2d 860, 1963 N.M. LEXIS 2081 (1963).

U.S. v. Burr. 25 F.Cas. 1 (No. 14694a-h), 1807 U.S.App. LEXIS 497 (1807).

U.S. v. First Trust Company of Saint Paul. 251 F.2d 686, 116 U.S.P.Q. 172 (1958).

U.S. v. Mitchell. 425 F.Supp. 917, 1976 U.S.Dist. LEXIS 11702 (1976).

U.S. v. Reynolds. 345 U.S. 1, 73 S.Ct. 528, 97 L.Ed. 727 (1953).

Wolfe v. Dept. of Health and Human Serv. 539 F.Supp. 276, 1982 U.S.Dist. LEXIS 12607, 8 Media L.Rep. 1649 (1982).

Youngstown v. Sawyer. 343 U.S. 579, 72 S.Ct. 863, 96 L.Ed. 1153 (1952).

Legal Briefs and Attorney General Opinions

Amici Curiae Brief in Support of Plaintiffs in American Historical Association et al. v. National Archives and Records Administration. [Electronic resource]. United States District Court, District of Columbia, February 28, 2002.

Before the Opinion Committee of the Office of Attorney General of the State of Texas, Brief of Public Citizen Concerning Request No. 0468-JC. [Electronic resource]. Texas Attorney General's Office,

January 3, 2002 [cited April 25 2002]. Available from www.publiccitizen.org/print_article.cfm?ID=6638.

Brief for Plaintiffs in American Historical Association et. al. v. National Archives and Records Administration and John Carlin. [Electronic resource]. United States District Court, District of Columbia, November 28, 2001 [cited April 25 2002]. Available from www.archives.gov/presidential_libraries/presidential_records/complaint.txt.

Caraley, Demetrios and Frances Penn. "Separation of Powers and Executive Privilege: The Watergate Briefs." *Political Science Quarterly* 88: 4 (December 1973): 582-654.

Memorandum of Points and Authorities in Support of Plaintiffs' Motion for Preliminary Injunction. Brief for the Plaintiffs in American Historical Association v. Trudy Peterson. [Electronic resource]. United States District Court, District of Columbia, January 18, 1995. Available from www.cpsr.org/cpsr/foia/PROFS_CASE/Legal__Memo_Pts._against.

Title to Pres. Papers. 43 Op. Att'y Gen. 11, 1974 U.S.AG LEXIS 1 (1974).

Edited Works

Adams, Herbert Baxter, ed. *The Life and Writings of Jared Sparks: Comprising Selections from His Journals and Correspondence.* 2 vols. Boston: Houghton, Mifflin and Co., Riverside Press, 1893.

Blanton, Tom, ed. *White House E-Mail: The Top Secret Computer Messages the Reagan/Bush White House Failed to Destroy.* New York: New Press, 1995.

Cappon, Lester J., ed. *The Adams-Jefferson Letters: The Complete Correspondence between Thomas Jefferson and John Adams.* Reprint (2 vol. in 1). New York: Simon and Schuster, 1971.

Daniels, Maygene F. and Timothy Walch, eds. *A Modern Archives Reader: Basic Readings on Archival Theory and Practice.* Washington, DC: National Archives and Records Service, 1984.

Edwards, George C., III and Stephen J. Wayne, eds. *Studying the Presidency.* Knoxville, TN: University of Tennessee Press, 1983.

Firestone, Bernard J. and Alexej Ugrinsky, eds. *Gerald R. Ford and the Politics of Post-Watergate America.* 2 vols. Contributions in Political Science No. 300. Westport, CT: Greenwood Press, 1993.

Friedman, Leon, ed. *United States v. Nixon: The President before the Supreme Court.* New York: Chelsea House and R. R. Bowker Co.,

1974.

Friedman, Leon and William F. Levantrosser, eds. *Watergate and Afterward*. Contributions in Political Science, No. 274. Westport, CT: Greenwood Press, 1992.

Hernon, Peter and Charles R. McClure, eds. *Federal Information Policies in the 1980's: Conflicts and Issues*. Information Management, Policy and Services Series. Norwood, NJ: Ablex Publishing Corp., 1987.

Hernon, Peter, Charles R. McClure and Harold C. Relyea, eds. *Federal Information Policies in the 1990s: Views and Perspectives*. Information Management, Policy and Services Series. Norwood, NJ: Ablex Publishing Corp., 1996.

McClure, Charles R. and Peter Hernon, eds. *United States Scientific and Technical Information (STI) Policies: Views and Perspectives*. Information Management, Policy and Services Series. Norwood, NJ: Ablex Publishing Corp., 1989.

McClure, Charles R., Peter Hernon and Harold C. Relyea, eds. *United States Government Information Policies: Views and Perspectives*. Information Management, Policy and Services Series. Norwood, NJ: Ablex Publishing Corp., 1989.

Nelson, Anna Kasten, ed. *The Records of Federal Officials: A Selection of Materials from the National Study Commission on Records and Documents of Federal Officials*. Foreword by Arthur Schlesinger Jr. New York: Garland Publishing, 1978.

Richardson, James D., ed. *A Compilation of the Messages and Papers of the Presidents, 1789-1902*. Vol. 8 (1881-1889). Washington, DC: Bureau of National Literature and Art, 1903.

Smith, Nancy Kegan and Mary C. Ryan, eds. *Modern First Ladies: Their Documentary Legacy*. Washington, DC: National Archives and Records Administration, 1989.

Smith, Richard Norton and Timothy Walch, eds. *Farewell to the Chief: Former Presidents in American Public Life*. Foreword by Don W. Wilson. Worland, WY: High Plains Publishing Co., 1990.

Story, William W., ed. *Life and Letters of Joseph Story*. 2 vols. Boston: Charles C. Little and James Brown, 1851.

Strum, Philippa, ed. *Brandeis on Democracy*. Lawrence, KS: University Press of Kansas, 1995.

Theoharis, Athan G., ed. *A Culture of Secrecy: The Government versus the People's Right to Know*. Lawrence, KS: University Press of Kansas, 1998.

Walch, Timothy, ed. *Guardian of Heritage: Essays on the History of the National Archives.* Washington, DC: National Archives and Records Administration, 1985.

Monographs

Ackerman, Bruce A. *Private Property and the Constitution.* New Haven, CT: Yale University Press, 1977.

American Library Association, Washington Office. *Less Access to Less Information by and about the U.S. Government: A 1988-1991 Chronology.* Washington, DC: American Library Association, 1992.

Anderson, Martin, ed. *Stanford and Hoover and Academic Freedom: A Collection of Published Reports on the Relationship between Stanford University and the Hoover Institution.* [Palo Alto, CA: Hoover Institution on War, Revolution and Peace and Stanford University], 1985.

Barker, Carol M. and Matthew H. Fox. *Classified Files: The Yellowing Pages.* New York: Twentieth Century Fund, 1972.

Barzun, Jacques and Henry F. Graff. *The Modern Researcher.* New York: Harcourt Brace Jovanovich, 1977.

Berger, Raoul. *Executive Privilege: A Constitutional Myth.* Cambridge, MA: Harvard University Press, 1974.

Boisot, Max H. *Information and Organizations: The Manager as Anthropologist.* London: Fontana Paperbacks, 1987.

————. *Information as Space: A Framework for Learning in Organizations, Institutions and Culture.* London: Routledge, 1995.

Brownell, Herbert and John P. Burke. *Advising Ike: The Memoirs of Attorney General Herbert Brownell.* Lawrence, KS: University Press of Kansas, 1993.

Burger, Robert H. *Information Policy: A Framework for Evaluation and Policy Research.* Information Management, Policy and Services Series. Norwood, NJ: Ablex Publishing Corp., 1993.

Burnette, O. Lawrence, Jr. *Beneath the Footnote: A Guide to the Use and Preservation of American Historical Sources.* Madison, WI: State Historical Society of Wisconsin, 1969.

Cole, John Y. *For Congress and the Nation: A Chronological History of the Library of Congress.* Washington, DC: Library of Congress, 1979.

Collingwood, R.G. *The Idea of History.* Edited by Jan ver der Dussen.

Rev. ed. Oxford: Oxford University Press, 1993.

Collins, Herbert R. and David B. Weaver. *Wills of the U.S. Presidents.* New York: Communication Channels, 1976.

Corwin, Edward S. *The President: Office and Powers, 1787-1984.* 5th ed. New York: New York University Press, 1984.

Dickinson, Matthew J. *Bitter Harvest: FDR, Presidential Power and the Growth of the Presidential Branch.* Cambridge: Cambridge University Press, 1997.

Doyle, James. *Not Above the Law: The Battles of Watergate Prosecutors Cox and Jaworski.* New York: William Morrow and Co., 1977.

Drew, Elizabeth. *Washington Journal: The Events of 1973-1974.* New York: Random House, 1975.

Elliott, Jannean L. *Presidential Papers and the Presidential Library System.* Occasional Research Paper, No. 2. Provo, UT: Brigham Young University, 1981.

Fischer, David Hackett. *Historians' Fallacies: Toward a Logic of Historical Thought.* New York and Evanston, IL: Harper and Row, 1970.

Graebner, Norman A. *The Records of Public Officials.* New York: American Assembly, Columbia University, 1975.

Hamilton, Alexander, James Madison and John Jay. *The Federalist Papers.* Introduction by Clinton Rossiter. New York: New American Library, 1961.

Hart, John. *The Presidential Branch: From Washington to Clinton.* 2 nd ed. Chatham, NJ: Chatham House Publishers, 1995.

Hecht, Marie B. *Beyond the Presidency: The Residues of Power.* New York: Macmillan Publishing Co., 1976.

Hess, Stephen. *Organizing the Presidency.* Rev. ed. Washington, DC: Brookings Institution, 1988.

Hoffman, Donald N. *Governmental Secrecy and the Founding Fathers.* Contributions in Legal Studies, No. 17. Westport, CT: Greenwood Press, 1981.

James, Henry. *William Wetmore Story and His Friends: From Letters, Diaries and Recollections.* Reprint (2 vol. in 1). New York: Grove Press, 1957.

Jaworski, Leon. *The Right and the Power: The Prosecution of Watergate.* New York: Reader's Digest Press; Houston: Gulf Publishing Co., 1976.

Jenkinson, Hilary. *A Manual of Archive Administration Including the Problems of War Archives and Archive Making.* Edited by James

T. Shotwell. *Economic and Social History of the World War* (British Series). Oxford: Clarendon Press, 1922.

———. *Selected Writings of Sir Hilary Jenkinson*. Glocester, England: Alan Sutton Publishing, 1980.

Jones, H. G. *The Records of a Nation: Their Management, Preservation, and Use*. New York: Atheneum, 1969.

Kling, Robert E., Jr. *The Government Printing Office*. Praeger Library of U.S. Government Departments and Agencies, No. 26. New York: Praeger, 1970.

Kutler, Stanley I. *The Wars of Watergate: The Last Crisis of Richard Nixon*. New York: Alfred A. Knopf, 1990.

Livelton, Trevor. *Archival Theory, Records, and the Public*. Lanham, MD: Society of American Archivists and Scarecrow Press, 1996.

MacNeil, Heather. *Without Consent: The Ethics of Disclosing Personal Information in Public Archives*. Metuchen, NJ: Society of American Archivists and Scarecrow Press, 1992.

Manchester, William R. *Death of a President*. New York: Harper and Row, 1967.

Marchman, Watt Pearson. *The Hayes Memorial*. Columbus, OH: Ohio State Archaeological and Historical Society, 1950.

Marwick, Arthur. *The Nature of History*. 3rd ed. New York: Macmillan Publishing Co., 1989.

Mayer, Kenneth R. *With the Stroke of a Pen: Executive Orders and Presidential Power*. Princeton, NJ: Princeton University Press, 2001.

McClellan, James. *Joseph Story and the American Constitution: A Study in Political Thought*. Reprint. Norman, OK: University of Oklahoma Press, 1990.

McCloskey, Robert G. *The American Supreme Court*. 2nd ed. Chicago: University of Chicago Press, 1994.

McCoy, Donald R. *The National Archives: America's Ministry of Documents, 1934-1968*. Chapel Hill: University of North Carolina Press, 1978.

Miller, Merle. *Plain Speaking: An Oral Biography of Harry S. Truman*. New York: Berkeley Publishing Co., 1973.

Morehead, Joe. *Essays on Public Documents and Government Policies*. New York: Haworth Press, 1986. Reprint, also published in *Technical Services Quarterly* 3: 3/4 (Spring/Summer 1986).

Nash, Bradley D., et al. *Organizing and Staffing the Presidency*. Proceedings. Vol. 3, No. 1. New York: Center for the Study of the

Presidency, 1980.

Nathan, Richard P. *The Plot That Failed: Nixon and the Administrative Presidency.* New York: John Wiley and Sons, 1975.

National Academy of Public Administration. *The Effects of Electronic Recordkeeping on the Historical Record of the U.S. Government: A Report for the National Archives and Records Administration.* Washington, DC: National Academy of Public Administration, 1989.

Nixon, Richard M. *RN: The Memoirs of Richard Nixon.* New York: Grosset and Dunlap, 1978.

Novick, Peter. *That Noble Dream: The 'Objectivity Question' and the American Historical Profession.* Cambridge: Cambridge University Press, 1988.

Nye, Frank T., Jr. *Doors of Opportunity: The Life and Legacy of Herbert Hoover.* West Branch, IA: Herbert Hoover Presidential Library Association, 1988.

Orman, John M. *Presidential Secrecy and Deception: Beyond the Power to Persuade.* Contributions in Political Science, No. 43. Westport, CT: Greenwood Press, 1980.

Patterson, Bradley H., Jr. *The Ring of Power: The White House Staff and Its Expanding Role in Government.* New York: Basic Books, 1988.

Pfiffner, James P. *The Modern Presidency.* New York: St. Martin's Press, 1994.

Phillips, Mary E. *Reminiscences of William Wetmore Story.* Chicago: Rand, McNally and Co., 1897.

Roosevelt, James and Sidney Shalett. *Affectionately, F.D.R.: A Son's Story of a Courageous Man.* London: George G. Harrap and Co., 1966.

Rosenberg, Jane Aikin. *The Nation's Great Library: Herbert Putnam and the Library of Congress, 1899-1939.* Urbana and Chicago: University of Illinois Press, 1993.

Rozell, Mark J. *Executive Privilege: The Dilemma of Secrecy and Democratic Accountability.* Baltimore: Johns Hopkins University Press, 1994.

Russell, Francis. *The Shadow of Blooming Grove: Warren G. Harding in His Times.* New York: McGraw-Hill Book Co., 1968.

Sadofsky, David. *Knowledge as Power: Political and Legal Control of Information.* New York: Praeger, 1990.

Schick, Frank L., Renee Schick and Mark Carroll. *Records of the*

Presidency: Presidential Papers and Libraries from Washington to Reagan. Phoenix: Oryx Press, 1989.

Schmeckebier, Laurence F. *The Government Printing Office: Its History, Activities and Organization.* Service Monographs of the United States Government, No. 36. Baltimore: Johns Hopkins Press, 1925.

Schuck, Peter H. *Foundations of Administrative Law.* Edited by Roberta Romano. Interdisciplinary Readers in Law. Oxford: Oxford University Press, 1994.

Sirica, John J. *To Set the Record Straight: The Break-in, the Tapes, the Conspirators, the Pardon.* New York: W. W. Norton and Co., 1979.

Smith, Curt. *Windows on the White House: The Story of Presidential Libraries.* South Bend, IN: Diamond Communications, 1997.

Smith, Myron J., Jr. *Watergate: An Annotated Bibliography of Sources in English, 1972-1982.* Metuchen, NJ: Scarecrow Press, 1983.

Stephens, Otis H. and Gregory J. Rathjen. *The Supreme Court and the Allocation of Constitutional Powers: Introductory Essays and Selected Cases.* San Francisco: W. H. Freeman and Co., 1980.

Strober, Gerald S. and Deborah H. Strober. *Nixon: An Oral History of His Presidency.* New York: HarperCollins, 1994.

Stuckey, Mary E. *The President as Interpreter-In-Chief.* Edited by George J. Graham Jr. Chatham House Studies in Political Thinking. Chatham, NJ: Chatham House Publishers, 1991.

Taft, William Howard. *Our Chief Magistrate and His Powers.* Reprint, with a foreword by Nicholas Murray Butler. New York: Columbia University Press, 1925.

Veit, Frank. *Presidential Libraries and Collections.* Westport, CT: Greenwood Press, 1987.

Veysey, Laurence R. *The Emergence of the American University.* Chicago: University of Chicago Press, 1970.

Viola, Herman. *The National Archives of the United States.* New York: Harry N. Abrams, 1984.

Warner, Robert M. *Diary of a Dream: A History of the National Archives Independence Movement, 1980-1985.* Metuchen, NJ: Scarecrow Press, 1995.

Weinberg, Steve. *For Their Eyes Only: How Presidential Appointees Treat Public Documents as Personal Property.* Washington, DC: Center for Public Integrity, 1992.

White, Theodore H. *Breach of Faith: The Fall of Richard Nixon.* New York: Atheneum and Reader's Digest Press, 1975.

Willets, Gilson. *Inside History of the White House: The Complete History of the Domestic and Official Life in Washington of the Nation's Presidents and Their Families*. New York: Christian Herald, 1908.

Wise, David. *The Politics of Lying: Government Deception, Secrecy and Power*. New York: Random House, 1973.

Unpublished Works

Dissertations

Cochrane, Lynn Scott. "The Presidential Library System: A Quiescent Policy System." Ph.D. diss., Virginia Polytechnic Institute and State University, 1998.

Hufbauer, Benjamin. "The Father in the Temple: Memory and Masculinity in Presidential Commemoration." Ph.D. diss., University of California, Santa Barbara, 1999.

Paul, Gary Norman. "The Development of the Hoover Institution on War, Revolution and Peace Library, 1919-1944." Ph.D. diss., University of California, Berkeley, 1974.

Wallace, David A. "The Public's Use of Recordkeeping Statutes to Shape Federal Information Policy: A Study of the PROFS Case." Ph.D. diss., University of Pittsburgh, 1997.

Woestman, Kelly Alicia. "Mr. Citizen: Harry S. Truman and the Institutionalization of the Ex-Presidency." Ph.D. diss., University of North Texas, 1993.

Theses

Bromiley, Frances. "The History and Organization of the Franklin D. Roosevelt Library, Hyde Park, New York." M.L.S. thesis, Western Reserve University, 1959.

Grove, Myrna J. "Rutherford B. Hayes Presidential Center, Library and Archives: Patron Use of Collections and Services." M.L.S. thesis, Kent State University, 1999.

Student Papers

Bartel, Cheryl and Inna Ilinskaya. "Paperwork Reduction Act of 1995." Bill tracing exercise for Information Studies 455: Government Information, UCLA, Fall 2001.

McCool, Kristin. "Time Line of Events Leading to the Passage of the Presidential Records Act of 1978 by the United States 95th Congress, 2nd Session." Bill tracing exercise for Information Studies 455: Government Information, UCLA, Fall 2001.

Sezzi, Peter H. "Presidential Records: Access Delayed Equals Access Denied?" Research paper for Information Studies 455: Government Information, UCLA, Fall 2001.

Weinreich, Jill and Peter H. Sezzi. "Verification or Duplication? An Evaluation of the Process and Tools Used in Bill Tracing the Presidential Records Act of 1978 as a Case Study." Bill tracing exercise for Information Studies 455: Government Information, UCLA, Fall 2001.

Published Conference Proceedings

Hamby, Alonzo L. and Edward Weldon, eds. *Access to the Papers of Recent Public Figures: The New Harmony Conference.* Bloomington, IN: Organization of American Historians, 1977.

Hoxie, R. Gordon, ed. *The White House: Organization and Operations.* Proceedings. Vol. 1, No. 1. New York: Center for the Study of the Presidency, 1971.

———. *The Presidency of the 1970's.* Proceedings. Vol. 2, No. 1. New York: Center for the Study of the Presidency, 1973.

Relyea, Harold C., ed. *The Presidency and Information Policy.* Proceedings. Vol. 4, No. 1. Foreword by R. Gordon Hoxie. New York: Center for the Study of the Presidency, 1981.

"Symposium on Presidential Libraries." *Government Information Quarterly* 11: 1 (1994).

"Symposium on Presidential Libraries and Materials." *Government Information Quarterly* 12: 1 (1995).

"*United States v. Nixon*: Presidential Power and Executive Privilege Twenty-Five Years Later." *Minnesota Law Review* 83: 5 (May 1999).

Webb, John, ed. *The Presidential Libraries.* Institute in Archival Librarianship. University of Oregon, September 22, 1969-August 14, 1970. ERIC Doc. No. ED 053 736.

Nongovernmental Reports

Committee on the Records of Government. *Report.* Reprint. Malabar, FL: Robert E. Krieger Publishing Co., 1988. Originally published by the Committee on the Records of Government.

Fischer, Linda. "The Role and Function of Presidential Libraries." Simi Valley, CA: Ronald Reagan Library, 1991. ERIC Doc. No. ED 344 612.

Heclo, Hugh. *Studying the Presidency: A Report to the Ford Foundation*. N.p.: [Ford Foundation], 1977.

Joint AHA-OAH Ad Hoc Committee. *Final Report of the Joint AHA-OAH Ad Hoc Committee to Investigate the Charges against the Franklin D. Roosevelt Library and Related Matters*. N.p.: N.pub., 1970.

Loewenheim, Francis L. *A Statement in Rebuttal [to the Final Report by the Joint AHA-OAH Ad Hoc Committee to Investigate the Charges Against the Franklin D. Roosevelt Library and Related Matters]*. [Houston]: N. pub., 1970.

Signed Book Sections

Armstrong, Scott. "The War Over Secrecy: Democracy's Most Important Low-Intensity Conflict." In *A Culture of Secrecy: The Government Versus the People's Right to Know*, edited by Athan G. Theoharis, 140-185. Lawrence, KS: University Press of Kansas, 1998.

Berkeley, Edmund, Jr. "The Archivist and Access Restrictions." In *Access to the Papers of Recent Public Figures: The New Harmony Conference*, edited by Alonzo L. Hamby and Edward Weldon, 57-59. Bloomington, IN: Organization of American Historians, 1977.

Berman, Larry. "The Evolution and Value of Presidential Libraries." In *The Presidency and Information Policy*, edited by Harold C. Relyea, 79-91. New York: Center for the Study of the Presidency, 1981.

————. "Presidential Libraries: How Not to Be a Stranger in a Strange Land." In *Studying the Presidency*, edited by George C. Edwards, III and Stephen J. Wayne, 225-256. Knoxville, TN: University of Tennessee Press, 1983.

Bernstein, Barton J. "A Plea for Opening the Door." In *Access to the Papers of Recent Public Figures: The New Harmony Conference*, edited by Alonzo L. Hamby and Edward Weldon, 83-90. Bloomington, IN: Organization of American Historians, 1977.

Braunstein, Yale M. "Economic Considerations of Federal Information Policies." In *United States Government Information Policies: Views and Perspectives*, edited by Charles R. McClure, Peter Hernon and Harold C. Relyea, 190-204. Norwood, NJ: Ablex Publish ing Corp., 1989.

Broderick, John C. "Access to Manuscript Collegions [Sic] in the Library of Congress." In *Access to the Papers of Recent Public Figures: The New Harmony Conference*, edited by Alonzo L. Hamby and Edward Weldon, 60-63. Bloomington, IN: Organization of American Historians, 1977.

Burns, James MacGregor. "Roosevelt: The Lion and the Fox." In *Franklin D. Roosevelt: A Profile*, edited by William E. Leuchtenburg. American Profiles. New York: Hill and Wang, 1967.

Caudle, Sharon L. and Karen B. Levitan. "Improving the Role of Information Resources Management in Federal Information Policies." In *United States Government Information Policies: Views and Perspectives*, edited by Charles R. McClure, Peter Hernon and Harold C. Relyea, 296-314. Norwood, NJ: Ablex Publishing Corp., 1989.

Chalou, George C. "National Archives." In *A Historical Guide to the U.S. Government*, edited by George T. Kurian, 396-403. New York: Oxford University Press, 1998.

Cook, Blanche Wiessen. "The Dwight David Eisenhower Library: The Manuscript Fiefdom at Abilene." In *Access to the Papers of Recent Public Figures: The New Harmony Conference*, edited by Alonzo L. Hamby and Edward Weldon, 77-82. Bloomington, IN: Organization of American Historians, 1977.

Dunigan, Peter. "The Hoover Institution: Origin and Growth." In *The Library of the Hoover Institution on War, Revolution and Peace*, edited by Peter Dunigan, 3-12. Hoover Press Publication No. 316. Palo Alto, CA: Hoover Institution on War, Revolution and Peace and Stanford University, 1985.

Gosden, John and Jon Turner. "The President and Information Management." In *The Presidency and Information Policy*, edited by Harold C. Relyea, 34-47. New York: Center for the Study of the Presidency, 1981.

Grossman, Michael B. and Martha J. Kumar. "The Refracting Lens: The President as He Appears Through the Media." In *The Presidency and Information Policy*, edited by Harold C. Relyea, 102-139. New York: Center for the Study of the Presidency, 1981.

Halperin, Morton. "The President and National Security Information." In *The Presidency and Information Policy*, edited by Harold C. Relyea, 66-78. New York: Center for the Study of the Presidency, 1981.

Hamby, Alonzo L. "Unseen Sources: A Historian's Dilemna [Sic]." In *Access to the Papers of Recent Public Figures: The New Harmony*

Conference, edited by Alonzo L. Hamby and Edward Weldon, 14-24. Bloomington, IN: Organization of American Historians, 1977.

Hawley, Ellis W. "Some Thoughts on and Experiences with Presidential Libraries and the Library of Congress." In *Access to the Papers of Recent Public Figures: The New Harmony Conference*, edited by Alonzo L. Hamby and Edward Weldon, 72-76. Bloomington, IN: Organization of American Historians, 1977.

Heclo, Hugh. "The Changing Presidential Office." In *Politics and the Oval Office: Toward Presidential Governance*, edited by Arnold J. Meltsner, 161-183. San Francisco: Institute for Contemporary Studies, 1981.

Hernon, Peter. "Government Information: A Field in Need of Research and Analytical Studies." In *United States Government Information Policies: Views and Perspectives*, edited by Charles R. McClure, Peter Hernon and Harold C. Relyea, 3-24. Norwood, NJ: Ablex Publishing Corp., 1989.

————. "Protected Government Information: A Maze of Statutes, Directives and Safety Nets." In *United States Government Information Policies: Views and Perspectives*, edited by Charles R. McClure, Peter Hernon and Harold C. Relyea, 245-268. Norwood, NJ: Ablex Publishing Corp., 1989.

Hernon, Peter and Charles R. McClure. "The Study of Federal Government Information and Information Policy: Needs and Concerns." In *United States Government Information Policies: Views and Perspectives*, edited by Charles R. McClure, Peter Hernon and Harold C. Relyea, 315-332. Norwood, NJ: Ablex Publishing Corp., 1989.

Hewlett, Richard. "Experiences of a Government Historian." In *Access to the Papers of Recent Public Figures: The New Harmony Conference*, edited by Alonzo L. Hamby and Edward Weldon, 47-49. Bloomington, IN: Organization of American Historians, 1977.

Hoff, Joan. "The Endless Saga of the Nixon Tapes." In *A Culture of Secrecy: The Government Versus the People's Right to Know*, edited by Athan G. Theoharis, 115-139. Lawrence, KS: University Press of Kansas, 1998.

Katz, Steven L. and David Plocher. "Federal Information Policy Development: A Citizen's Perspective." In *United States Government Information Policies: Views and Perspectives*, edited by Charles R. McClure, Peter Hernon and Harold C. Relyea, 115-138. Norwood, NJ: Ablex Publishing Corp., 1989.

Krislov, Samuel. "*Nixon v. Administrator of General Services*." In *Oxford Companion to the Supreme Court*, edited by Kermit L. Hall, 594-595. New York: Oxford University Press, 1992.

———. "*United States v. Nixon.*" In *Oxford Companion to the Supreme Court,* edited by Kermit L. Hall, 593-594. New York: Oxford University Press, 1992.

Kumar, Martha Joynt. "Presidential Libraries: Gold Mine, Booby Trap, or Both?" In *Studying the Presidency,* edited by George C. Edwards, III and Stephen J. Wayne, 199-224. Knoxville, TN: University of Tennessee Press, 1983.

Mason, Philip P. "The Archivist's Responsibility to Researchers and Donors: A Delicate Balance." In *Access to the Papers of Recent Public Figures: The New Harmony Conference,* edited by Alonzo L. Hamby and Edward Weldon, 25-37. Bloomington, IN: Organization of American Historians, 1977.

McClure, Charles R. "Frameworks for Studying Federal Information Policies: The Role of Graphic Modeling." In *United States Government Information Policies: Views and Perspectives,* edited by Charles R. McClure, Peter Hernon and Harold C. Relyea, 271-295. Norwood, NJ: Ablex Publishing Corp., 1989.

McClure, Charles R., Ann Bishop and Philip Doty. "Federal Information Policy Development: The Role of the Office of Management and Budget." In *United States Government Information Policies: Views and Perspectives,* edited by Charles R. McClure, Peter Hernon and Harold C. Relyea, 51-76. Norwood, NJ: Ablex Publishing Corp., 1989.

McCoy, Donald R. "National Archives and Records Service (NARS)." In *Government Agencies,* edited by Donald R. Whitnah, 309-314. The Greenwood Encyclopedia of American Institutions, No. 7. Westport, CT: Greenwood Press, 1983.

McGranery, Regina C. "A Donor's View." In *Access to the Papers of Recent Public Figures: The New Harmony Conference,* edited by Alonzo L. Hamby and Edward Weldon, 54-56. Bloomington, IN: Organization of American Historians, 1977.

Middleton, Harry. "A President and His Library: My Recollections of Working with Lyndon B. Johnson." In *Farewell to the Chief: Former Presidents in American Public Life,* edited by Richard Norton Smith and Timothy Walch, 109-114. Worland, WY: High Plains Publishing Co., 1990.

Miller, Arthur S. "Executive Privilege: A Political Theory Masquerading as Law." In *The Presidency and Information Policy,* edited by Harold C. Relyea, 48-65. New York: Center for the Study of the Presidency, 1981.

Morehead, Joe. "Tennis Elbow of the Soul: The Public Papers of Richard Nixon, 1973-1974." In *Essays on Public Documents and Government Policies*, 139-148. New York: Haworth Press, 1986. Reprint, *Serials Librarian* 1: 3 (Spring 1977). Also published in *Technical Services Quarterly* 3: 3/4 (Spring/Summer 1986).

O'Neill, James E. "Federal Law and Access to Federal Records." In *Access to the Papers of Recent Public Figures: The New Harmony Conference*, edited by Alonzo L. Hamby and Edward Weldon, 38-43. Bloomington, IN: Organization of American Historians, 1977.

Pemberton, William E. "General Services Administration (GSA)." In *Government Agencies*, edited by Donald R. Whitnah, 268-272. The Greenwood Encyclopedia of American Institutions, No. 7. Westport, CT: Greenwood Press, 1983.

Peyton, David. "Federal Information Policy Development: A Private-Sector Perspective." In *United States Government Information Policies: Views and Perspectives*, edited by Charles R. McClure, Peter Hernon and Harold C. Relyea, 100-114. Norwood, NJ: Ablex Publishing Corp., 1989.

Potter, David M. "Sketches of the Roosevelt Program." In *Franklin D. Roosevelt: A Profile*, edited by William E. Leuchtenburg. New York: Hill and Wang, 1967.

Powell, H. Jefferson. "Joseph Story." In *The Supreme Court Justices: A Biographical Dictionary*, edited by Melvin I. Urofsky, 435-444. New York: Garland Publishing, 1994.

Reed, Daniel J. "A Matter of Time." In *Access to the Papers of Recent Public Figures: The New Harmony Conference*, edited by Alonzo L. Hamby and Edward Weldon, 64-71. Bloomington, IN: Organization of American Historians, 1977.

Reedy, George E. "The President and the Media: An Adversarial but Helpful Relationship." In *The White House: The First Two Hundred Years*, edited by Frank Freidel and William Penack, 141-154. Boston: Northeastern University Press, 1994.

Relyea, Harold C. "The Presidency and the People's Right to Know." In *The Presidency and Information Policy*, edited by Harold C. Relyea, 1-33. New York: Center for the Study of the Presidency, 1981.

————. "Historical Development of Federal Information Policy." In *United States Government Information Policies: Views and Perspectives*, edited by Charles R. McClure, Peter Hernon and Harold C. Relyea, 25-48. Norwood, NJ: Ablex Publishing Corp., 1989.

————. "Access to Government Information: Rights and Restrictions." In *United States Government Information Policies: Views and Per-*

spectives, edited by Charles R. McClure, Peter Hernon and Harold C. Relyea, 141-160. Norwood, NJ: Ablex Publishing Corp., 1989.

Riley, Thomas B. "Intellectual Trends in Dissemination of Government Information." In *United States Government Information Policies: Views and Perspectives*, edited by Charles R. McClure, Peter Hernon and Harold C. Relyea, 234-244. Norwood, NJ: Ablex Publishing Corp., 1989.

Shill, Harold B. "NTIS and the Privatization of Government Information." In *United States Government Information Policies: Views and Perspectives*, edited by Charles R. McClure, Peter Hernon and Harold C. Relyea, 205-233. Norwood, NJ: Ablex Publishing Corp., 1989.

Tate, Thad W. "Bushrod Washington." In *The Supreme Court Justices: A Biographical Dictionary*, edited by Melvin I. Urofsky, 511-513. New York: Garland Publishing, 1994.

U.S. Congress. House. Committee on Government Operations. "Electronic Collection and Dissemination of Information by Federal Agencies: A Policy Overview." In *United States Government Information Policies: Views and Perspectives*, edited by Charles R. McClure, Peter Hernon and Harold C. Relyea, 161-189. Norwood, NJ: Ablex Publishing Corp., 1989.

Weingarten, Fred W. "Federal Information Policy Development: The Congressional Perspective." In *United States Government Information Policies: Views and Perspectives*, edited by Charles R. McClure, Peter Hernon and Harold C. Relyea, 77-99. Norwood, NJ: Ablex Publishing Corp., 1989.

Weinstein, Allen. "A Plaintiff's Perspective." In *Access to the Papers of Recent Public Figures: The New Harmony Conference*, edited by Alonzo L. Hamby and Edward Weldon, 50-53. Bloomington, IN: Organization of American Historians, 1977.

Weldon, Edward. "Some Legal Considerations Affecting Access." In *Access to the Papers of Recent Public Figures: The New Harmony Conference*, edited by Alonzo L. Hamby and Edward Weldon, 44-46. Bloomington, IN: Organization of American Historians, 1977.

Wigdor, David and Alexandra K. Wigdor. "The Future of Presidential Papers." In *The Presidency and Information Policy*, edited by Harold C. Relyea, 92-101. New York: Center for the Study of the Presidency, 1981.

Unsigned Journal Articles

"Ex-Presidencies Often Reveal More Than Presidency Itself Can." *National Journal* 22: 28 (July 14, 1990): 1734.

"A Government Threat to Manuscript Collections." *Manuscripts* 7: 4 (Summer 1955): 214-215.

"Hutchinson Papers." *Proceedings of the Massachusetts Historical Society* 13 (January 1874): 217-232.

"In the Matter of the Lewis and Clark Papers." *Manuscripts* 9: 1 (Winter 1957): 1-19.

"Johnson Presidential Library Will Feature Museum." *Texas Libraries* 29: 3 (Fall 1967): 172-180.

"Johnson Presidential Library Plans Announced." *Texas Libraries* 29: 1 (Spring 1967): 3-7.

"News Notes." *American Archivist* 2: 1 (January 1939): 58-59.

"News Notes." *American Archivist* 2: 2 (April 1939): 132.

"News Notes." *American Archivist* 15: 4 (October 1952): 375-377.

"Prologue in Portfolio." *Prologue* 21: 2 (Spring 1989): 146-153.

"The Records of Public Officials: Final Report of the Forty-Eighth American Assembly." *American Archivist* 38: 3 (July 1975): 329-336.

"U.S. Archivist Discusses Presidential Libraries, Papers." *Texas Libraries* 29: 3 (Fall 1967): 169-171.

"Who Owns Presidential Documents?" *Editorial Research Reports Daily Reminders*, September 16, 1975.

Signed Journal Articles

Abbot, W. W. "An Uncommon Awareness of Self: The Papers of George Washington." *Prologue* 21: 1 (Spring 1989): 7-19.

Aeschbacher, William D. "Presidential Libraries: New Dimension in Research Facilities." *Midwest Quarterly* 6: 2 (Winter 1965): 205-214.

Alsobrook, David E. "The Birth of the Tenth Presidential Library: The Bush Presidential Materials Project, 1993-1994." *Government Information Quarterly* 12: 1 (1995): 33-41.

Andreassen, John C. L. "Archives in the Library of Congress." *American Archivist* 12: 1 (January 1949): 20-26.

Bahmer, Robert H. "The Case of the Clark Papers." *American Archivist* 19: 1 (January 1956): 19-22.

Baker, Richard Allan. "Documenting the History of the United States Senate." *Government Publications Review* 10: 5 (September/October 1983): 415-426.

Bane, Suda L. "The Dedicatory Exercises of the Hoover Library." *American Archivist* 5: 3 (July 1942): 179-184.

Bassanese, Lynn A. "The Franklin D. Roosevelt Library: Looking to the Future." *Government Information Quarterly* 12: 1 (1995): 103-112.

Beale, Howard K. "The Professional Historian: His Theory and His Practice." *Pacific Historical Review* 22: 3 (August 1953): 227-255.

Bearman, David. "The Implications of *Armstrong v. Executive* [Sic] *of the President* for the Archival Management of Electronic Records." *American Archivist* 56: 4 (Fall 1993): 674-689.

Becker, Lawrence C. "Too Much Property." *Philosophy and Public Affairs* 21: 2 (Spring 1992): 196-206.

Bonafide, Dom. "The Other Side of the Transition: Leaving Office Isn't as Much Fun." *National Journal* 12: 51-52 (December 20, 1980): 2158.

Bowles, Nigel. "Studying the Presidency." *Annual Review of Political Science* 2 (1999): 1-23.

Boyd, Julian P. "'These Precious Monuments of . . . Our History.'" *American Archivist* 22: 2 (April 1959): 147-180.

Bradsher, James Gregory. "A Brief History of the Growth of the Federal Government Records, Archives, and Information, 1789-1985." *Government Publications Review* 13: 4 (July/August 1986): 491-505.

————. "Discussion Forum: Federal Records and Archives." *Government Information Quarterly* 4: 2 (1987): 127-134.

Bridges, Roger D. "Our Purpose and Direction." *Hayes Historical Journal* 10: 1 (Winter 1991): 6-7.

Broeker, Galen. "Jared Sparks, Robert Peel and the State Paper Office." *American Quarterly* 13: 2 (Summer 1961): 140-152.

Brooks, Philip C. "The Historian's Stake in Federal Records." *Mississippi Valley Historical Review* 43: 2 (September 1956): 259-274.

————. "The Harry S. Truman Library." *Social Education* 22: 7 (November 1958): 363-364.

————. "The Harry S. Truman Library—Plans and Reality." *American Archivist* 25: 1 (January 1962): 25-37.

————. "A Special Library for the Presidency." *MLA: Missouri Library Association Quarterly* 23: 2 (June 1962): 41-52.

————. "Understanding the Presidency: The Harry S. Truman Library." *Prologue* 1: 3 (Winter 1969): 3-12.

Brown, Thomas Elton. "The Freedom of Information Act in the Information Age: The Electronic Challenge to the People's Right to

Know." *American Archivist* 58: 2 (Spring 1995): 202-211.

Bullock, Helen Duprey. "The Robert Todd Lincoln Collection of the Papers of Abraham Lincoln." *The Library of Congress Quarterly Journal of Current Acquisitions* 5: 1 (November 1947): 3-8.

Burk, Robert F. "New Perspectives for Presidential Libraries." *Presidential Studies Quarterly* 21: 3 (Summer 1991): 399-410.

Butterfield, Lyman H. "The Papers of Thomas Jefferson: Progress and Procedures in the Enterprise at Princeton." *American Archivist* 12: 2 (April 1949): 131-145.

———. "The Adams Papers: 'Whaterever You Write Preserve'." *American Heritage* 10: 3 (April 1959): 26-33, 88-93.

———. "The Papers of the Adams Family: Some Account of Their History." *Proceedings of the Massachusetts Historical Society* 71 (October 1953-May 1957): 328-356.

Campbell, Douglas G. "The Lyndon Baines Johnson Library: A Museum-Library-Monument." *Journal of the West* 23: 1 (January 1984): 97-102.

Cannon, Carl M. "Improving the White House Memory." *National Journal* 32: 20 (May 13, 2000): 1529-1530.

———. "Why Reagan Papers Aren't Being Released." *National Journal* 33: 20 (May 19, 2001): 1503.

Cappon, Lester J. "The National Archives and the Historical Profession." *Journal of Southern History* 35: 4 (November 1969): 477-499.

———. "Why Presidential Libraries?" *Yale Review* 68: 1 (October 1978): 11-34.

———. "Jared Sparks: The Preparation of an Editor." *Proceedings of the Massachusetts Historical Society* 90 (1978): 3-21.

Carney, Eliza Newlin. "At the Archives, Controversy's Routine." *National Journal* 25: 11 (March 13, 1993): 628-630.

Catanzariti, John. "'The Richest Treasure House of Information': The Papers of Thomas Jefferson." *Prologue* 21: 1 (Spring 1989): 39-55.

Chambers, John Whiteclay, II. "Presidents Emeritus." *American Heritage* 30: 4 (June/July 1979): 16-25.

Cochrane, James L. "The U.S. Presidential Libraries and the History of Political Economy." *History of Political Economy* 8: 3 (Fall 1976): 412-427.

Cole, Garold L. "Presidential Libraries." *Journal of Librarianship: Quarterly of the Library Association* 4: 2 (April 1972): 115-129.

Cole, John Y. "The Library of Congress and the Presidential Parade,

1800-1984." *Library of Congress Information Bulletin* 43: 42 (October 15, 1984): 343-348.

Colket, Meredith B., Jr. "The Preservation of Consular and Diplomatic Post Records of the United States." *American Archivist* 6: 4 (October 1943): 193-205.

Connor, R. D. W. "The Franklin D. Roosevelt Library." *American Archivist* 3: 2 (April 1940): 81-92.

————. "FDR Visits the National Archives." *American Archivist* 12: 4 (October 1949): 323-332.

Conway, Pat. "Research in Presidential Libraries: A User Survey." *Midwestern Archivist* 11: 1 (Winter 1986): 35-56.

Cook, Blanche Wiessen. "Presidential Papers in Crisis: Some Thoughts on Lies, Secrets and Silence." *Presidential Studies Quarterly* 26: 1 (Winter 1996): 285-292.

Cook, J. Frank. "'Private Papers' of Public Officials." *American Archivist* 38: 3 (July 1975): 299-324.

Cooper, Phillip J. "By Order of the President: Administration by Executive Order and Proclamation." *Administration and Society* 18: 2 (August 1986): 233-262.

Culbertson, Thomas J. "The Hayes Presidential Center Library and Archives." *Hayes Historical Journal* 10: 2 (Winter 1991): 40-44.

Cullen, Charles T. "Casual Observer Beware: The Need for Using Scholarly Editions." *Prologue* 21: 1 (Spring 1989): 68-73.

Daellenbach, Dennis A. "The Ronald Reagan Presidential Library." *Government Information Quarterly* 11: 1 (1994): 23-35.

Danilov, Victor J. "Presidential Libraries and Museums." *Curator* 34: 3 (1991): 222-238.

Davison, Kenneth. "Presidential Libraries." *Hayes Historical Journal* 10: 2 (Winter 1991): 8-11.

Drewry, Elizabeth B. "The Role of Presidential Libraries." *Midwest Quarterly* 7: 1 (October 1965): 53-65.

Duckett, Kenneth W. "The Harding Papers: How Some Were Burned." *American Heritage* 16: 2 (February 1965): 25-31, 102-109.

Edgerton, Jay. "Lewis and Clark Sequel." *Manuscripts* 9: 2 (Spring 1957): 110-111.

Epstein, F.T. "Die Hoover Library der Stanford-Universitat (USA) (The Hoover Library of Stanford University (USA))." *Nachrichten fur Wissenschaftliche Bibliotheken* 3: 7/8 (July/August 1950): 105-106.

Farrand, Max. "The Records of the Federal Convention." *American*

Historical Review 13: 1 (October 1907): 44-65.

Fenn, Dan H., Jr. "Launching the John F. Kennedy Library." *American Archivist* 42: 4 (October 1979): 429-442.

Ford, Frederick W. "Some Legal Problems in Preserving Records for Public Use." *American Archivist* 20: 1 (January 1957): 41-47.

Freidel, Frank. "Roosevelt to Reagan: The Birth and Growth of Presidential Libraries." *Prologue* 21: 2 (1989): 103-113.

Fridley, Russell. "Should Public Papers Be Private Property?" *Minnesota History* 44: 1 (Spring 1974): 37-39.

Garber, Marc N. and Kurt A. Wimmer. "Presidential Signing Statements as Interpretations as Legislative Intent: An Executive Aggrandizement of Power." *Harvard Journal on Legislation* 24: 2 (Summer 1987): 363.

Garrison, Curtis W. "The Relation of Historical Manuscripts to Archival Materials." *American Archivist* 2: 2 (April 1939): 97-105.

———. "A President's Library." *Ohio State Archaeological and Historical Society Quarterly* 48: 2 (April 1939): 127-133.

Gellman, Robert. "Public Records—Access, Privacy, and Public Policy: A Discussion Paper." *Government Information Quarterly* 12: 4 (1995): 391-426.

Geselbracht, Raymond H. "Archivist's Perspective: The Four Eras in the History of Presidential Papers." *Prologue* 15: 1 (Spring 1983): 37-42.

———. "The Origins of Restrictions on Access to Personal Papers at the Library of Congress and the National Archives." *American Archivist* 49: 2 (Spring 1986): 142-162.

———. "Harry S. Truman and His Library: Past Accomplishments and Plans for the Future." *Government Information Quarterly* 12: 1 (1995): 93-102.

Geselbracht, Raymond H. and Daniel J. Reed. "The Presidential Library and the White House Liaison Office." *American Archivist* 46: 1 (Winter 1983): 69-72.

Giglio, James N. "Past Frustrations and New Opportunities: Researching the Kennedy Presidency at the Kennedy Library." *Presidential Studies Quarterly* 22: 2 (Spring 1992): 371-379.

Glenn, Bess. "The Taft Commission and the Government's Record Practices." *American Archivist* 21: 3 (July 1958): 277-303.

Greenwell, Regina. "The Oral History Collections of the Presidential Libraries." *Journal of American History* 84: 2 (September 1997): 596-603.

Grover, Wayne C. "Federal Government Archives." *Library Trends* 5: 3 (January 1957): 390-396.

Gustafson, Milton O. "The Presidential Libraries: Some Impressions." *Manuscripta* 18: 3 (November 1974): 155-165.

———. "The Empty Shrine: The Transfer of the Declaration of Independence and the Constitution to the National Archives." *American Archivist* 39: 3 (July 1976): 271-285.

Hagedorn, Hermann. "The Roosevelt Library." *Library Journal* 54: 18 (October 15, 1929): 841-843.

Haldeman, H. R. "The Nixon White House Tapes: The Decision to Record Presidential Conversations." *Prologue* 20: 2 (Summer 1988): 78-87.

Hamer, Philip M. "'Authentic Documents Tending to Elucidate Our History'." *American Archivist* 25: 1 (January 1962): 3-13.

Hanson, Robert. "Hail to the Chiefs: Our Presidential Libraries." *Wilson Library Bulletin* 55: 8 (April 1981): 576-583.

Hart, John. "Neglected Aspects of the Study of the Presidency." *Annual Review of Political Science* 1 (1998): 379-399.

Hirshon, Arnold. "The Scope, Accessability [*sic*] and History of Presidential Papers." *Government Publications Review* 1: 4 (Fall 1974): 363-390.

———. "Recent Developments in the Accessibility of Presidential Papers and Other Presidential Historical Materials." *Government Publications Review* 6: 4 (Fall 1979): 343-357.

Hoff, Joan. "Researchers' Nightmare: Studying the Nixon Presidency." *Presidential Studies Quarterly* 26: 1 (Winter 1996): 259-276.

Holmes, Oliver W. "'Public Records'—Who Knows What They Are?" *American Archivist* 23: 1 (January 1960): 3-26.

Horrocks, David A. "Access and Accessibility at the Gerald R. Ford Library." *Government Information Quarterly* 11: 1 (Winter 1994): 47-65.

Jacobs, Richard F. "The Status of the Nixon Presidential Historical Materials." *American Archivist* 38: 3 (July 1975): 337.

Jones, H. G. "Presidential Papers: Is There a Case for a National Presidential Library?" *American Archivist* 38: 3 (July 1975): 325-328.

Kahn, Herman. "World War II and Its Background: Research Materials at the Franklin D. Roosevelt Library and Policies Concerning Their Use." *American Archivist* 17: 2 (April 1954): 149-162.

———. "The Presidential Library—A New Institution." *Special Libraries* 50: 3 (March 1959): 106-113.

———. "The Long-Range Implications for Historians and Archivist of the Charges Against the Franklin D. Roosevelt Library." *American Archivist* 34: 3 (July 1971): 265-275.

Kamath, P. M. "Presidential Libraries of United States." *Herald of Library Science* 33: 3/4 (July/October 1994): 200-204.

Kirkendall, Richard S. "Presidential Libraries—One Researcher's Point of View." *American Archivist* 25: 4 (October 1962): 441-448.

———. "A Second Look at Presidential Libraries." *American Archivist* 29: 3 (July 1966): 371-386.

Knill, Mary K. "The Lyndon B. Johnson Library in the Information Age." *Government Information Quarterly* 12: 1 (1995): 57-70.

Knowlton, John D. "'Properly Arranged and So Correctly Recorded'." *American Archivist* 27: 3 (July 1964): 371-374.

Krauskopf, Robert W. "The Hoover Commissions and Federal Record-keeping." *American Archivist* 21: 4 (October 1958): 371-399.

Krusten, Maarja. "Watergate's Last Victim." *Presidential Studies Quarterly* 26: 1 (Winter 1996): 277.

Kumar, Martha Joynt. "News Notes: The Presidential Libraries Act of 1986." *Presidential Studies Quarterly* 16: 3 (Summer 1986): 614-619.

Lagerquist, Philip D. "The Harry S. Truman Library." *Library Journal* 83: 2 (January 15, 1958): 144-147.

———. "The Harry S. Truman Library as a Center for Research on the American Presidency." *College and Research Libraries* 25: 1 (January 1964): 32-36.

Leland, Waldo Gifford. "The National Archives: A Programme." *American Historical Review* 18: 1 (October 1912): 1-28.

———. "The Creation of the Franklin D. Roosevelt Library: A Personal Narrative." *American Archivist* 18: 1 (January 1955): 11-29.

———. "Recollections of the Man Who Rang the Bell." *American Archivist* 21: 1 (January 1958): 55-57.

Leopold, Richard W. "The Historian and the Federal Government." *Journal of American History* 64: 1 (June 1977): 5-23.

Liebmann, Alfred J. "Presidents and Books: A unique collection is being formed with all the excitement known only to a true collector." *Manuscripts* 7: 2 (Winter 1955): 72-84.

Lloyd, David Demarest." Presidential Papers and Presidential Libraries." *Manuscripts* 8: 1 (Fall 1955): 4-15.

———. "The Harry S. Truman Library." *American Archivist* 18: 2 (April 1955): 99-110.

Lovely, Sister Louise. "The Evolution of Presidential Libraries." *Government Publications Review* 6: 1 (1979): 27-35.

Lubar, Steven. "Information Culture and the Archival Record." *American Archivist* 62: 2 (Spring 1999): 10-22.

Lyandres, Natasha and Olga Leontieva. "Developing International Cataloging Standards for Archival Holdings: Rosarkhiv-RLG-Hoover Project, 1994-1997." *American Archivist* 61: 2 (Fall 1998): 441-452.

Lyons, Charles F., Jr. "The Nixon Presidential Materials Staff." *Government Information Quarterly* 12: 1 (1995): 43-56.

Maass, Richard. "Arguments Heard in the Clark Case: Verdict Awaited in the Dispute." *Manuscripts* 8: 2 (Winter 1956): 113-116.

Mackaman, Frank H. "Human Drama: Presidential Museums Tell the Story." *Prologue* 21: 2 (Summer 1989): 135-145.

Marchman, Watt Pearson and James H. Rodabaugh. "Collections of the Rutherford B. Hayes State Memorial." *Ohio History* 71: 2 (July 1962): 151-157.

McCoy, Donald R. "The Beginnings of the Franklin D. Roosevelt Library." *Prologue* 7: 3 (Fall 1975): 137-150.

———. "And Launched the Office the Presidential Libraries in the National Archives." *American Libraries* 7: 3 (March 1976): 154-155.

———. "'Be Yourself': Harry S. Truman as Former President." *American Archivist* 22: 3 (Fall 1990): 261-264.

McDonough, John, R. Gordon Hoxie and Richard Jacobs. "Who Owns Presidential Papers?" *Manuscripts* 27: 1 (Winter 1975): 2-11.

McKay, Pamela R. "Presidential Papers: A Property Issue." *Library Quarterly* 52: 1 (January 1982): 21-40.

McLean, Philip T. "The Hoover Library on War, Revolution, and Peace." *College and Research Libraries* 1: 2 (March 1940): 154-158.

Mearns, David C. "The Lincoln Papers." *Abraham Lincoln Quarterly* 4: 8 (December 1947): 369-385.

Menez, Joseph F. "Presidential Papers and Presidential Libraries." *Social Science* 47: 1 (Winter 1972): 34-39.

Metzdorf, Robert F. "Lewis and Clark I: A Librarian's Point of View." *Manuscripts* 9: 4 (Fall 1957): 226-230.

Miller, Harold L. "Will Access Restrictions Hold Up in Court? The FBI's Attempt to Use the Braden Papers at the State Historical Society of Wisconsin." *American Archivist* 52: 2 (Spring 1989): 180-190.

Miller, Nancy. "Public Access to Public Records: Some Threatening Reforms." *Wilson Library Bulletin* 56: 2 (October 1981): 95-99.

Miller, Randall K. "Presidential Sanctuaries after the Clinton Sex Scandals." *Harvard Journal of Law and Public Policy* 22: 2

(Spring 1999): 647-734.

Montgomery, Bruce P. "Nixon's Legal Legacy: White House Papers and the Constitution." *American Archivist* 56: 4 (Fall 1993): 586-613.

Morgan, Donald G. "The Origin of Supreme Court Dissent." *William and Mary Quarterly, Third Series* 10: 3 (July 1953): 353-377.

Morgan, Ruth P. "Nixon, Watergate and the Study of the Presidency." *Presidential Studies Quarterly* 26: 1 (Winter 1996): 217.

Morrissey, Charles T. "Truman and the Presidency: Records and Oral Recollections." *American Archivist* 28: 1 (January 1965): 53-61.

Nash, George H. "Achieving Post-Presidential Greatness: Lessons from Herbert Hoover." *Prologue* 22: 3 (Fall 1990): 257-260.

Naulty, Susan. "Creating an Archives at the Richard Nixon Library and Birthplace." *Government Information Quarterly* 11: 1 (1994): 37-45.

Nelson, Anna Kasten. "The Public Documents Commission: Politics and Presidential Records." *Government Publications Review* 9: 5 (September-October 1982): 443-451.

———. "Historian's Perspective: Challenge of Documenting the Federal Government in the Latter 20th Century." *Prologue* 14: 2 (Summer 1982): 89-92.

———. "The 1985 Report of the Committee on the Records of Government: An Assessment." *Government Information Quarterly* 4: 2 (1987): 143-150.

O'Neill, James E. "Will Success Spoil the Presidential Libraries." *American Archivist* 36: 3 (July 1973): 339-351.

Peterson, Trudy Huskamp. "Foreword." *Government Information Quarterly* 12: 1 (1995): 15-16.

Pfiffner, James P. "White House Staff versus the Cabinet: Centripetal and Centrifugal Roles." *Presidential Studies Quarterly* 16: 4 (Fall 1986): 666-690.

Phillips, Faye. "Congressional Papers: Collection Development Policies." *American Archivist* 58: 3 (Summer 1995): 258-269.

Pinkett, Harold T. "Accessioning Public Records: Anglo-American Practices and Possible Improvements." *American Archivist* 41: 4 (October 1978): 413-421.

Plantinga, S. F. M. "Watergate en de Archieven: De Presidential Records Act [Sic] 1978." *Nederlands Archieven Bald* 86: 4 (December 1982): 348-358.

Polenberg, Richard. "The Roosevelt Library Case: A Review Article." *American Archivist* 34: 3 (July 1971): 277-284.

Reid, Warren R. "Public Papers of the Presidents." *American Archivist* 25: 4 (October 1962): 435-440.

Relyea, Harold C. "Public Access to Congressional Records: Present Policy and Reform Considerations." *Government Information Quarterly* 2: 3 (1985): 235-256.

———. "The Federal Presidential Library System." *Government Information Quarterly* 11: 1 (1994): 7-21.

Rhoads, James B. "Who Should Own the Documents of Public Officials?" *Prologue* 7: 1 (Spring 1975): 32-35.

———. "The Papers of the Presidents." *Proceedings of the Massachusetts Historical Society* 88 (1976): 94-104.

Richardson, John V., Jr. and Margaret R. Zarnosky. "A State Transition Model of United States Congressional Information." *Journal of Government Information* 21 (January/February 1994): 25-35.

Riddlesperger, James W., Jr. and James D. King. "Presidential Appointments to the Cabinet, Executive Office, and White House Staff." *Presidential Studies Quarterly* 16: 4 (Fall 1986): 691-699.

Rigg, Frank. "The John F. Kennedy Library." *Government Information Quarterly* 12: 1 (1995): 71-81.

Roberts, Patricia S. and Sarah T. Kadec. "Discussion Forum: The Effects of Electronic Recordkeeping on the Historic Record of the U.S. Government." *Government Information Quarterly* 7: 4 (1990): 383-387.

Rosenbach, A. S. W. "The Libraries of Presidents of the United States." *American Antiquarian Society Proceedings* 44: 2 (October 1934): 337-364.

Rowland, Buford. "The Papers of the Presidents." *American Archivist* 13: 3 (July 1950): 195-211.

Rozell, Mark J. "President Nixon's Conception of Executive Privilege: Defining the Scope and Limits of Executive Branch Secrecy." *Presidential Studies Quarterly* 22: 2 (Spring 1992): 323-335.

Rulon, Philip R. "Education Research Opportunities at the Eisenhower Library." *Prologue* 10: 4 (Winter 1978): 242-251.

Russell, Francis. "The Harding Papers: . . . And Some Were Saved." *American Heritage* 16: 2 (February 1965): 25-31, 102-110.

———. "The Shadow of Warren Harding." *Antioch Review* 36: 1 (Winter 1978): 57-76.

Ruthwell, C. Easton. "Resources and Research in the Hoover Institution and Library." *American Archivist* 18: 2 (April 1955): 141-150.

Ryerson, Richard Alan. "Documenting the Presidency of John Adams: The Adams Papers Project." *Prologue* 21: 1 (Spring 1989): 21-37.

Samuels, Helen Willa. "Who Controls the Past." *American Archivist* 49: 2 (Spring 1986): 109-124.

Schewe, Donald B. "Establishing a Presidential Library: The Jimmy Carter Experience." *Prologue* 21: 2 (Summer 1989): 125-133.

———. "The Jimmy Carter Library." *Government Information Quarterly* 6: 3 (1989): 237-246.

———. "The Jimmy Carter Library: An Update." *Government Information Quarterly* 11: 1 (1994): 67-69.

Schlesinger, Arthur, Jr. "Who Owns a President's Papers?" *Manuscripts* 27: 3 (Summer 1975): 178-182.

Schmertz, Mildred F. "Getting Ready for the John F. Kennedy Library: Not Everyone Wants to Make It Go Away." *Architectural Record* 156: 12 (December 1974): 98-105.

Schubert, Glendon A., Jr. "Judicial Review of the Subdelegation of Presidential Power." *Journal of Politics* 12: 4 (November 1950): 668-693.

Schur, Susan E. "Library/Conservation Profile: The John Fitzgerald Kennedy Library." *Technology and Conservation* 5: 1 (Spring 1980): 32-39.

Shaffer, Helen B. "Presidential Accountability." *Editorial Research Reports* 1: 9 (March 7, 1973): 165-184.

———. "Separation of Powers." *Editorial Research Reports* 2: 10 (September 12, 1973): 689-708.

Sheldon, Richard N. "Editing a Historical Manuscript: Jared Sparks, Douglas Southall Freeman and the Battle of Brandywine." *William and Mary Quarterly, Third Series* 36: 2 (April 1979): 255-263.

Shelley, Fred. "The Interest of J. Franklin Jameson in the National Archives: 1908-1934." *American Archivist* 12: 2 (April 1949): 99-130.

———. "The Presidential Papers Program of the Library of Congress." *American Archivist* 25: 4 (October 1962): 429-434.

Shipman, Fred W. "The Franklin D. Roosevelt Library." *Library Journal* 66: 19 (November 1, 1941): 936-937.

———. "Franklin Delano Roosevelt, 1882-1945." *American Archivist* 8: 4 (October 1945): 229-232.

Smith, Nancy Kegan. "Private Reflections on a Public Life: The Papers on Lady Bird Johnson at the LBJ Library." *Presidential Studies Quarterly* 20: 4 (Fall 1990): 737-744.

Smith, Richard Norton. "A Presidential Revival: How the Hoover Library Overcame a Mid-Life Crisis." *Prologue* 21: 2 (Summer 1989): 115-123.

Smith, Thomas A. "Before Hyde Park: The Rutherford B. Hayes Library." *American Archivist* 43: 4 (Fall 1980): 485-488.

Snyder, Charles M. "Forgotten Fillmore Papers Examined: Sources for Reinterpretation of a Little-Known President." *American Archivist* 32: 1 (January 1969): 11-14.

Stagg, J. C. A. "Setting the Stage for Reappraisal: The Papers of James Madison." *Prologue* 21: 1 (Spring 1989): 57-67.

Starostin, Ye V. and T. S. Kabochkina. "Prezidentskiye biblioteki v sisteme arkhivnoy sluzhby SSHA (Presidential libraries in the system of U.S. depository archives)." *Sovetskiye arkhivy* 6 (1978): 78-86.

Stathis, Stephen W. "Former Presidents as Congressional Witnesses." *Presidential Studies Quarterly* 13: 3 (Summer 1983): 458-481.

Stein, Nathaniel E. "Plain Paper $5 — Parchment $7: Subscription book for the first facsimile of Declaration of Independence has had an interesting history—with a happy ending." *Manuscripts* 7: 3 (Spring 1955): 160-162.

Steinwall, Susan D. "Appraisal and the FBI Files Case: For Whom Do Archivists Retain Records?" *American Archivist* 49: 1 (Winter 1986): 52-63.

Stewart, Kate. "James Madison as an Archivist." *American Archivist* 21: 3 (July 1958): 243-257.

Stewart, William J. "Opening Closed Material in the Roosevelt Library." *Prologue* 7: 4 (Winter 1975): 239-241.

Stewart, William J. and Charyl C. Pollard. "Franklin D. Roosevelt, Collector." *Prologue* 1: 3 (Winter 1969): 13-28.

Teasley, Martin M. "German Language Study at the Dwight D. Eisenhower Library." *Foreign Language Annals* 20: 1 (February 1987): 39-41.

———. "No Signs of Mid-Life Crisis: The Eisenhower Library at Thirty-Something." *Government Information Quarterly* 12: 1 (1995): 83-92.

Thompson, Brian Chandler. "The Sitting Modern President and the National Archives." *Government Information Quarterly* 12: 1 (1995): 17-32.

Vaughn, Joseph F., ed. "Senate Debate on Public Records." *American Archivist* 10: 3 (July 1947): 258-262.

Vose, Clement E. "Presidential Papers as a Political Science Concern." *PS* 8: 1 (Winter 1975): 8-18.

———. "Nixon's Archival Legacy." *PS* 10: 4 (Fall 1977): 432-438.

———. "The Nixon Project." *PS* 16: 3 (Summer 1983): 512-521.

Wagner, D. O. "Some Antecedents of the American Doctrine of Judicial Review." *Political Science Quarterly* 40: 4 (December 1925): 561-593.

Walch, Timothy. "Reinventing the Herbert Hoover Presidential Library." *Government Information Quarterly* 12: 1 (1995): 113-125.

Ward, Geoffrey. "'Future Historians Will Curse as Well as Praise Me'." *Smithsonian* 20: 9 (December 1989): 58-69.

Warner, Robert M. "The Prologue Is Past." *American Archivist* 41: 1 (January 1978): 5-15.

Webster, Charles K. "Some Early Applications from American Historians to Use the British Archives." *Journal of Modern History* 1: 3 (September 1929): 416-419.

Weisberger, Bernard A. "The Paper Trust." *American Heritage* 22: 3 (April 1971): 38-41, 104-107.

Weldon, Edward. "Lest We Forget: Setting Priorities for the Preservation and Use of Historical Records." *American Archivist* 40: 3 (July 1977): 295-300.

Whitfield, Stephen J. "Richard Nixon as a Comic Figure." *American Quarterly* 37: 1 (Spring 1985): 114-132.

Wickman, John E. "John Foster Dulles' 'Letter of Gift'." *American Archivist* 31: 4 (October 1968): 355-363.

————. "The Dwight D. Eisenhower Library." *Special Libraries* 60: 9 (November 1969): 590-595.

Wilhelm, Kristen. "Making History: Tracing Retrospective U.S. Legislative Histories." *Journal of Government Information* 26: 5 (September/October 1999): 485-499.

Wilson, Don W. "Prologue in Perspective: Presidential Libraries." *Prologue* 21: 2 (Summer 1989): 100-101.

————. "Prologue in Perspective: The Legacy of Ebenezer Hazard, America's First Documentary Editor." *American Archivist* 21: 1 (Spring 1989): 4-5.

————. "Not So Buried Treasures: Primary Sources from the National Archives and Presidential Libraries." *Journal of Youth Services in Libraries* 4: 4 (Summer 1991): 377-382.

————. "Presidential Libraries: Developing to Maturity." *Presidential Studies Quarterly* 21: 4 (Fall 1991): 771-779.

————. "Presidential Records: Evidence for Historians or Ammunition for Prosecutors." *Government Information Quarterly* 14: 4 (1997): 339-349.

Wilson, Don W. and Michael J. Brodhead. "GPR Interview: The Nation's Memory, an Interview with Don W. Wilson." *Government Publications Review* 20: 1 (January/February 1993): 1-19.

Wolff, Cynthia J. "Necessary Monuments: The Making of the Presidential Library System." *Government Publications Review* 16: 1 (January/February 1989): 47-62.

Worsnop, Richard L. "Libraries for Ex-Presidents." *Editorial Research Reports Daily Reminders*, September 11, 1981.

Wright, Conrad Edick. "Constant Aims, Changing Technologies: Photostat and Microfilm Publishing at the Massachusetts Historical Society." *Microform Review* 24: 2 (Spring 1995): 61-63.

Zobrist, Benedict K. "Resources of Presidential Libraries for the History of the Second World War." *Military Affairs* 39: 2 (April 1975): 82-85.

————. "Resources of Presidential Libraries for the History of Post World War II American Military Government in Germany and Japan." *Military Affairs* 42: 1 (February 1978): 17-19.

Unsigned Legal Journal Articles

"The Authority of Administrative Agencies to Consider the Constitutionality of Statutes." *Harvard Law Review* 90: 8 (June 1977): 1682-1707.

"Congressional Standing to Challenge Executive Action." *University of Pennsylvania Law Review* 122: 5 (May 1974): 1366-1381.

"Executive Privilege and the Freedom of Information Act: Constitutional Foundation of the Amended National Security Exemption." *Washington University Law Quarterly* 1976: 4 (Fall 1976): 609-666.

"The Freedom of Information Act: A Seven-Year Assessment." *Columbia Law Review* 74: 5 (June 1974): 895-959.

"Government Control of Richard Nixon's Presidential Material." *Yale Law Journal* 87: 8 (July 1978): 1601-1635.

"The Military and State Secrets Privilege: Protection for the National Security or Immunity for the Executive." *Yale Law Journal* 91: 3 (January 1982): 570.

"Recent Case: Constitutional Law—Executive Privilege—D.C. Circuit Defines Scope of Presidential Communications Privilege, *In Re Sealed Case*, 116 F.3d 550 (D.C. Cir. 1997)." *Harvard Law Review* 111: 3 (January 1998): 861-866.

"Recent Cases—Executive Privilege: The President Does Not Have an Absolute Privilege to Withold Evidence from a Grand Jury, *Nixon v. Sirica*, 487 F.2d 700 (D.C. Cir. 1973)." *Harvard Law Review* 87: 7 (May 1974): 1557-1568.

"The Right to Privacy in Nineteenth Century America." *Harvard Law Review* 94: 8 (June 1981): 1892-1910.

"The Supreme Court, 1973 Term: Judicial Claims of Executive Privilege." *Harvard Law Review* 88: 1 (November 1974): 50-61.

"The Supreme Court, 1979 Term: Freedom of Information Act, Threshold Definitional Barriers to Disclosure." *Harvard Law Review* 94: 1 (November 1980): 232-241.

"The Supreme Court, 1996 Term Leading Cases—Constitutional Law: Separation of Powers—Presidential Immunity." *Harvard Law Review* 111: 1 (November 1997): 227-237.

"What Constitutes a Public Record or Document within Statute Making Falsification, Forgery, Mutilation, Removal or Other Misuse Thereof an Offense." *American Law Reports 4th* 75 (1990, August 2001 Supp.): 1067-1102.

Signed Legal Journal Articles

Amar, Akhil Reed. "*Nixon*'s Shadow." *Minnesota Law Review* 83: 5 (May 1999): 1405-1420.

Bailey, R. Kevin. "'Did I Miss Anything?' Excising the National Security Council from FOIA Coverage." *Duke Law Journal* 46: 6 (April 1997): 1475-1516.

Barron, James H. "Warren and Brandeis, *The Right to Privacy*, 4 Harv. L. Rev. 193 (1890): Demystifying a Landmark Citation." *Suffolk University Law Review* 13: 4 (Summer 1979): 875-922.

Berger, Michael M. "Land Use Institute: Planning, Regulation, Litigation, Eminent Domain and Compensation, Recent Takings and Eminent Domain Cases." *American Law Institute - American Bar Association Continuing Legal Education* (August 18, 1993): 343-356.

Berger, Raoul. "The President, Congress, and the Courts." *Yale Law Journal* 83: 6 (May 1974): 1111-1155.

———. "The Incarnation of Executive Privilege." *UCLA Law Review* 22: 1 (October 1974): 4-29.

Bilder, Mary Sarah. "The Shrinking Back: The Law of Biography." *Stanford Law Review* 42: 2 (January 1991): 299-360.

Bishop, Joseph W., Jr. "The Executive's Right of Privacy: An Unresolved Constitutional Question." *Yale Law Journal* 66: 4 (February 1957): 477-491.

Bleich, Jeffrey L. and Eric B. Wolff. "Executive Privilege and Immunity: The Questionable Role of the Independent Counsel and the

Courts." *St. John's Journal of Legal Commentary* 14: 1 (Summer 1999): 15-50.

Bretscher, Carl. "Presidential Records Act: The President and Judicial Review Under the Records Acts." *George Washington Law Review* 60: 5 (June 1992): 1477-1508.

Brown, Rebecca L. "Caging the Wolf: Seeking a Constitutional Home for the Independent Counsel." *Minnesota Law Review* 83: 5 (May 1999): 1269-1284.

Brownell, Herbert. "Who Really Owns the Papers of Departing Federal Officials?" *New York State Bar Journal* 50: 3 (April 1978): 193-195, 230-234.

Bruff, Harold H. "Judicial Review and the President's Statutory Powers." *Virginia Law Review Association* 68: 1 (January 1982): 1-61.

Bruff, Harold H. and Ernest Gellhorn. "Congressional Control of Administrative Regulation: A Study of Legislative Vetoes." *Harvard Law Review* 90: 7 (May 1977): 1369-1440.

Calabresi, Steven G. "The President, the Supreme Court, and the Constitution: A Brief Positive Account of the Role of Government Lawyers in the Development of Constitutional Law." *Law and Contemporary Problems* 61: 1 (Winter 1998): 61.

———. "Caesarism, Departmentalism and Professor Paulsen." *Minnesota Law Review* 83: 5 (May 1999): 1421-1434.

Cannon, Mark W. "Administrative Change and the Supreme Court." *Judicature* 57: 8 (March 1974): 334-341.

Carrington, Paul D. "Political Questions: The Judicial Check on the Executive." *Virginia Law Review* 42: 2 (February 1956): 175-201.

Castano, Sylvia E. "Disclosure of Federal Officials' Documents Under the Freedom of Information Act: A Limited Application." *Houston Law Review* 18: 3 (March 1981): 641-654.

Charlton, Diana L. "Secret Service Testimony Regarding Presidential Activities: The Piracy of Privacy?" *Saint Louis University Law Journal* 43: 2 (Spring 1999): 591-620.

Chemerinsky, Erwin. "Controlling Inherent Presidential Power: Providing a Framework for Judicial Review." *Southern California Law Review* 56: 4 (May 1983): 863-911.

Choper, Jesse H. "The Supreme Court and the Political Branches: Democratic Theory and Practice." *University of Pennsylvania Law Review* 122: 4 (April 1974): 810-858.

Chung, Christine Sgarlata and David J. Byer. "The Electronic Paper Trail: Evidentiary Obstacles to Discovery and Admission of Electronic Evidence." *Boston University Journal of Science and Technology Law* 4: 1 (Spring 1998): 5-45.

Cox, Archibald. "Executive Privilege." *University of Pennsylvania Law Review* 122: 6 (June 1974): 1383-1438.

Currie, David P. "The President's Evidence." *Green Bag 2nd* 1 (Winter 1998): 131.

Danielson, George E. "Presidential Immunity from Criminal Prosecution." *Georgetown Law Journal* 63: 5 (May 1975): 1065-1069.

Davenport, Frederick M. "The Growing Power of the Presidency." *Boston University Law Review* 14: 3 (June 1934): 655-667.

Davis, Kenneth Culp. "Administrative Arbitrariness: A Postscript." *University of Pennsylvania Law Review* 114: 6 (April 1966): 823-833.

Dionisopoulos, P. Allan. "New Patterns in Judicial Control of the Presidency: 1950's to 1970's." *Akron Law Review* 10: 1 (Summer 1976): 1-38.

Entin, Jonathan L. "Separation of Powers, the Political Branches and the Limits of Judicial Review." *Ohio State Law Journal* 51 (Winter 1990): 175-227.

Ervin, Sam, Jr. "Controlling 'Executive Privilege.'" *Loyola Law Review* 20: 1 (Fall 1974): 11-31.

Ford, William D. and Daniel H. Pollitt. "Who Owns the Tapes?" *North Carolina Central Law Journal* 6: 2 (Spring 1975): 197-203.

Freund, Paul A. "The Supreme Court, 1973 Term: Foreword—On Presidential Privilege." *Harvard Law Review* 88: 1 (November 1974): 13-39.

Gerstenblith, Patty. "Identity and Cultural Property: The Protection of Cultural Property in the United States." *Boston University Law Review* 75: 3 (May 1995): 559-688.

Glancy, Dorothy. "Getting Government Off the Backs of People: The Right of Privacy and Freedom of Expression in the Opinions of Justice William O. Douglas." *Santa Clara Law Review* 21: 4 (Fall 1981): 1047-1067.

Gunther, Gerald. "Judicial Hegemony and Legislative Autonomy: The *Nixon* Case and the Impeachment Process." *UCLA Law Review* 22: 1 (October 1974): 30-39.

Hadley, Herbert Spencer. "The Right to Privacy." *Northwestern Law Review* 3: 1 (October 1894): 9-21.

Hager, L. Michael. "The Constitution, the Court, and the Cover-Up: Reflections on *United States v. Nixon*." *Oklahoma Law Review* 29: 3 (Summer 1976): 591-606.

Hannigan, Michael J. and Francis J. Nealon. "The Freedom of Information Act: The Parameters of the Exemptions." *Georgetown Law*

Journal 62: 1 (October 1973): 177-207.

Henkin, Louis. "Executive Privilege: Mr. Nixon Loses, But the Presidency Largely Prevails." *UCLA Law Review* 22: 1 (October 1974): 40-46.

Hobbs, D.S. "*United States v. Nixon*: An Historical Perspective." *Loyola of Los Angeles Law Review* 9: 1 (December 1975): 11-66.

Hogan, Lawrence J. "The Impeachment Inquiry of 1974: A Personal View." *Georgetown Law Journal* 63: 5 (May 1975): 1051-1063.

Jaffe, Louis L. "Judicial Review: Question of Law." *Harvard Law Review* 69: 2 (December 1955): 239-276.

―――. "Judicial Review: Question of Fact." *Harvard Law Review* 69: 6 (April 1956): 1020-1056.

―――. "Judicial Review: Constitutional and Jurisdictional Fact." *Harvard Law Review* 70: 6 (April 1957): 963-985.

―――. "The Right to Judicial Review Part I." *Harvard Law Review* 71 (January 1958): 401-437.

Jaworski, Leon. "The Most Lustrous Branch: Watergate and the Judiciary." *Fordham Law Review* 65: 6 (May 1977): 1267-1280.

Johnsen, Dawn. "Executive Privilege Since *United States v. Nixon*: Issues in Motivation and Accommodation." *Minnesota Law Review* 83: 5 (May 1999): 1127-1142.

Karst, Kenneth L. and Harold W. Horowitz. "Presidential Prerogative and Judicial Review." *UCLA Law Review* 22: 1 (October 1974): 47-67.

Kelley, William K. "The Constitutional Dilemma of Litigation Under the Independent Counsel System." *Minnesota Law Review* 83: 5 (May 1999): 1197-1268.

Kurland, Philip B. "*United States v. Nixon*: Who Killed Cock Robin?" *UCLA Law Review* 22: 1 (October 1974): 68-75.

Kutner, Luis. "Executive Privilege . . . Growth of Power Over a Declining Congress." *Loyola Law Review* 20: 1 (Fall 1974): 33-44.

Lacovara, Philip Allen. "*United States v. Nixon*: The Prelude." *Minnesota Law Review* 83: 5 (May 1999): 1061-1068.

Leahy, William F. "Recent Developments in Administrative Law: Congressional Supervision of Agency Action, the Fate of the Legislative Veto after Chadha." *George Washington Law Review* 53: 1 (November 1984/January 1985): 168-190.

Lee, Rex E. "Executive Privilege, Congressional Subpoena Power, and Judicial Review: Three Branches, Three Powers, and Some Relationships." *Brigham Young University Law Review* 1978: 2 (1978): 231-297.

Lewis, James D. "White House Electronic Mail and Federal Record keeping Law: Press "D" to Delete History." *Michigan Law Review* 93: 4 (February 1995): 794-849.

Logan, Wayne A. "The Ex Post Facto Clause and the Jurisprudence of Punishment." *American Criminal Law Review* 35: 4 (1998): 1261-1318.

Manning, John F. "The Independent Counsel Statute: Reading "Good Cause" in Light of Article II." *Minnesota Law Review* 83: 5 (May 1999): 1285-1336.

Martinelli, John K. "*United States v. Armstrong*: The United States Supreme Court's First 'Crack' at the Standard for Discovery in Selective Prosecution Challenges." *George Mason University Civil Rights Law Journal* 7: 1 (Spring 1997): 49-81.

Mason, Sasha A. "The D.C. Circuit Review, August 1996-July 1997—Freedom of Information Act: The National Security Council Is Not an Agency Under the Freedom of Information Act." *George Washington Law Review* 66: 4 (April 1998): 996-1006.

McGlaughon, H. King, Jr. "Constitutional Law—Executive Privilege: Tilting the Scales in Favor of Secrecy." *North Carolina Law Review* 53: 2 (December 1974): 419-430.

McGowan, Carl. "Presidents and Their Papers." *Minnesota Law Review* 68: 2 (December 1983): 409-437.

McNeely-Johnson, K. A. "*United States v. Nixon*, Twenty Years After: The Good, the Bad and the Ugly—An Exploration of Executive Privilege." *Northern Illinois University Law Review* 14 (Fall 1993): 251.

Merrill, Thomas W. "The Landscape of Constitutional Property." *Virginia Law Review* 86: 5 (August 2000): 885-999.

Mezvinsky, Edward M. and Doris S. Freedman. "Federal Income Tax Evasion as an Impeachable Offense." *Georgetown Law Journal* 63: 5 (May 1975): 1071-1081.

Miller, Arthur Selwynn. "Implications of Watergate: Some Proposals for Cutting the Presidency Down to Size." *Hastings Constitutional Law Quarterly* 2: 1 (Winter 1975): 33-74.

Miller, Randall K. "Congressional Inquests: Suffocating the Constitutional Prerogative of Executive Privilege." *Minnesota Law Review* 81 (February 1997): 631-692.

Mishkin, Paul J. "Great Cases and Soft Law: A Comment on *United States v. Nixon*." *UCLA Law Review* 22: 1 (October 1974): 76-91.

Moore, Adam D. "A Lockean Theory of Intellectual Property." *Hamline Law Review* 21 (Fall 1997): 65-108.

Nathanson, Nathaniel L. "From Watergate to *Marbury v. Madison*:

Some Reflections on Presidential Privilege in Current Historical Perspectives." *Arizona Law Review* 16: 1 (1974): 59-77.

Noonan, Michael M. "*Kissinger v. Reporters Committee for Freedom of the Press*: The Supreme Court Denies FOIA Access to 'Lost' Documents." *Loyola Law Review* 26: 3 (Summer 1980): 706-716.

O'Connor, Thomas H. "Privacy in Historical Perspective." *Massachusetts Law Quarterly* 53: 2 (June 1968): 101-115.

Owens, Dennis J. "The Establishment of a Doctrine: Executive Privilege after *United States v. Nixon*." *Texas Southern University Law Review* 4: 1 (Fall 1976): 22-49.

Patterson, L. Ray. "*Folsom v. Marsh* and Its Legacy." *Journal of Intellectual Property Law* 5: 2 (Spring 1998): 431-452.

Paulsen, Michael Stokes. "*Nixon* Now: The Courts and the Presidency after Twenty-five Years." *Minnesota Law Review* 83: 5 (May 1999): 1337-1404.

Perritt, Henry H., Jr. "Electronic Records Management and Archives." *University of Pittsburgh Law Review* 53: 4 (Summer 1992): 963-1024.

Prakash, Saikrishna Bangalore. "A Critical Comment on the Constitutionality of Executive Privilege." *Minnesota Law Review* 83: 5 (May 1999): 1143-1190.

Pratt, Walter F. "The Warren and Brandeis Argument for a Right to Privacy." *Public Law* 1975 (Summer 1975): 161-179.

Ratner, Leonard G. "Executive Privilege, Self-Incrimination, and the Separation of Powers Illusion." *UCLA Law Review* 22: 1 (October 1974): 92-115.

Reich, Charles A. "The New Property." *Yale Law Journal* 73: 5 (April 1964): 733-787.

Richardson, Elliot L. "Freedom of Information." *Loyola Law Review* 20: 1 (Fall 1974): 45-64.

Richetti, Sandra E. "Congressional Power Vìs a Vìs the President and Presidential Papers." *Duquesne Law Review* 32: 4 (Summer 1994): 773-798.

Rogers, William P. "Constitutional Law: The Papers of the Executive Branch." *American Bar Association Journal* 44: 10 (October 1958): 941-944, 1007-1014.

Rosenberg, Morton. "Congress's Prerogative Over Agencies and Agency Decisionmakers: The Rise and Demise of the Reagan Administration's Theory of the Unitary Executive." *George Washington Law Review* 57 (January 1989): 627-702.

Rozell, Mark J. "Executive Privilege and the Modern Presidents: In

Nixon's Shadow." *Minnesota Law Review* 83: 5 (May 1999): 1069-1126.

———. "Restoring Balance to the Debate Over Executive Privilege: A Response to Berger." *William and Mary Bill of Rights Journal* 8 (April 2000): 541.

Salyers, Lance. "Invaluable Tool vs. Unfair Use of Private Information: Examining Prosecutors' Use of Juror's Criminal History in Voir Dire." *Washington and Lee Law Review* 56: 3 (Summer 1999): 1079-1124.

Schlei, Jeffrey Alan. "Copyright: The Unauthorized Use of Verbatim Quotes from a Public Figure's Manuscript Prior to Its Publication for Use in a News Story Constituted an Appropriation of the Right of First Publication and Is Not Protected by the Fair Use Privilege of the Copyright Act, *Harper & Row Publishers, Inc. v. Nation Enterprises* (U.S. Sup. Ct. 1985)." *Drake Law Review* 35: 2 (1985/1986): 445-461.

Schlesinger, Arthur, Jr. "The Constitution and Presidential Leadership." *Maryland Law Review* 47: 1 (Fall 1987): 54-74.

Schrag, Philip G. "Working Papers as Federal Records: The Need for New Legislation to Preserve the History of National Policy." *Administrative Law Review* 46: 2 (Spring 1994): 95-140.

Schubiner, Steven P. "Administrative Law—Freedom of Information Act—Agency Under No Duty to Retrieve Wrongfully Removed Records: *Kissinger v. Reporters Committee for Freedom of the Press*, 445 U.S. 136 (1980)." *Wayne Law Review* 27: 3 (Spring 1981): 1315-1332.

Schwartz, Bernard. "A Reply to Mr. Rogers: The Papers of the Executive Branch." *American Bar Association Journal* 45: 5 (May 1959): 467-470, 525, 526.

Sheehan, Catherine F. "Opening the Government's Electronic Mail: Public Access to National Security Council Records." *Boston College Law Review* 35: 5 (September 1994): 1145-1201.

Simon, Andrea. "A Constitutional Analysis of Copyrighting Government-Commissioned Work." *Columbia Law Review* 84 (March 1984): 425-465.

Simones, Anthony. "The Iran-Contra Affair: Ten Years Later." *UMKC Law Review* 67: 1 (Fall 1998): 61-75.

Sofaer, Abraham D. "Executive Power and the Control of Information: Practice Under the Framers." *Duke Law Journal* 26: 1 (March 1977): 1-57.

Sorensen, Theodore C. "Making the President More Accountable to the

People." *Human Rights* 5: 1 (Fall 1975): 47-61.

Spencer, Patricia L. "Recent Cases, Constitutional Law: *Nixon v. Administrator of General Services*, 97 S.Ct. 2777 (1977)." *Akron Law Review* 11: 2 (Fall 1977): 373-386.

Stein, Theodore P. "*Nixon v. Fitzgerald*: Presidential Immunity as a Constitutional Imperative." *Catholic University Law Review* 32: 3 (Spring 1983): 759-785.

Thatcher, C. Marshall. "*United States v. Nixon*: What Price Unanimity?" *Ohio Northern Law Review* 2: 2 (1974): 303-317.

Turley, Jonathan. "'From Pillar to Post': The Prosecution of American Presidents." *American Criminal Law Review* 37: 3 (Summer 2000): 1049-1106.

―――. "Presidential Papers and Popular Government: The Convergence of Constitutional and Property Theory in Claims of Ownership and Control of Presidential Records." *Cornell Law Review* 88 (2003): 651-732.

Van Alstyne, William. "A Political and Constitutional Review of *United States v. Nixon*." *UCLA Law Review* 22: 1 (October 1974): 116-140.

Wald, Patricia M. "The Freedom of Information Act: A Short Case Study in the Perils and Paybacks of Legislating Democratic Values." *Emory Law Journal* 33: 3 (Summer 1984): 649-683.

Warren, Samuel D. and Louis D. Brandeis. "The Right to Privacy." *Harvard Law Review* 4: 5 (December 1890): 193-220.

Weingart, Lee C. "Who Keeps the Secrets? A Framework and Analysis of the Separation of Powers Dispute in *American Foreign Service Association v. Garfinkel*." *George Washington Law Review* 59: 1 (November 1990): 193-238.

Williams, Jennifer R. "Beyond *Nixon*: The Application of the Takings Clause to the Papers of Constitutional Officeholders." *Washington University Law Quarterly* 71: 3 (Fall 1993): 871-898.

Wolkinson, Herman. "Demands of Congressional Committee for Executive Papers, Part I." *Federal Bar Journal* 10: 2 (April 1949): 103-149.

―――. "Demands of Congressional Committees for Executive Papers, Part II." *Federal Bar Journal* 10: 2 (July 1949): 223-259.

Yang, John C. "Standing . . . In the Doorway of Justice." *George Washington Law Review* 59: 5 (June 1991): 1356-1394.

Yoo, John C. "The First Claim: The Burr Trial, *United States v. Nixon*, and Presidential Power." *Minnesota Law Review* 83: 5 (May 1999): 1435-1480.

Zan, Myint. "The Three Nixon Cases and Their Parallels in Malaysia."

St. Thomas Law Review 13: 3 (Spring 2001): 743-784.

ALR Articles

Kramer, Donald T. "Executive Privilege with Respect to Presidential
Papers and Recordings." *American Law Reports Federal* 19 (1974,
October 2001 Supp.): 472-484.
Shields, Marjorie A. "What Constitutes 'Agency' for Purposes of Freedom of Information Act (5 U.S.C.A. 552)." *American Law Reports Federal* 165 (2000, Oct. 2001 Supp.): 591-624.
Wasil, Jo Ann F. "What Is 'Record' within the Meaning of Privacy Act
of 1974 (5 U.S.C.A. 552A)." *American Law Reports Federal* 121
(1994, Oct. 2001 Supp): 465.

Unsigned Magazine Articles

"All Recorded History." *Insight on the News* 13: 44 (December 1,
1997): 10-14.
"Bush Violated Law and U.S. Constitution." *Editor and Publisher*,
April 15, 1995: 17.
"Engineers Probe Nixon Tape." *Popular Mechanics* 177: 11 (Novem-
ber 2000): 20.
"Nixon Documents: More Court Fights Ahead." *U.S. News and World
Report*, July 11, 1977, 22
"Presidential Libraries: Where Tourists, Scholars Brush Elbows." *U.S.
News and World Report*, July 11, 1977, 23-25.
"Presidents Who Testified: Tyler, Teddy Roosevelt Gave Facts to
Congress." *U.S. News and World Report*, November 27, 1957, 32.
"Raiding the White House Files: Papers Sold, Burned, Given to
World." *U.S. News and World Report*, November 27, 1953, 29-31.
"Taping for Posterity." *The Economist*, January 9, 1999, 77.
"Watergate: Nixon Agrees to Pay $467,000 Tax Bill." *Congressional
Quarterly Weekly*, April 6, 1974, 863-888?

Signed Magazine Articles

Bates, Leonard, et al. "Presidential Papers." *New York Times Book Review*, September 7, 1969: 26.
Corn, David. "Nixon's Tapes, Dole's Record." *The Nation*, May 20,
1996: 23-25.
Deitch, Joseph. "Portrait: James O'Neill." *Wilson Library Bulletin* 59:

7 (March 1985): 479-481.

Feeney, Mark. "In the Nixon Archives." *Boston Globe Magazine*, May 6, 1990, 16.

Feis, Herbert. "Speaking of Books: Unpublic Public Papers." *New York Times Book Review*, April 21, 1968, 2, 58.

Flanagan, Suzan. "The Other Presidential Library." *Civil War Times Illustrated* 39: 4 (August 1, 2000): 18-21, 66-67.

Gasparello, Linda. "Abshire: History Keeps Presidential Ship Afloat." *White House Weekly*, July 19, 1999.

Graff, Henry F. "Preserving the Secrets of the White House." *New York Times Magazine*, December 29, 1963, 9, 30-31.

Gustafson, Milton O. "Public Papers." *New York Times Book Review*, May 1968, 50.

Helicher, Karl. "The Once-Secret History." *Library Journal* 126: 15 (September 15, 2001): 96.

Hersh, Seymour. "Nixon's Last Cover-Up: The Tapes He Wants the Archives to Suppress." *New Yorker* (December 14, 1989): 76-95.

Lewis, Finlay. "Presidential Papers: An Attempt to Own History." *The Nation*, October 19, 1974, 366-369.

Livernash, Bob. "Presidential Papers to Be Public Property." *Congressional Quarterly Weekly*, October 21, 1978, 3052.

McCarthy, Joe. "A Walk Through History with Harry Truman, Part I." *Holiday*, November 1963, 56-61, 101, 102, 104, 107.

———. "A Walk Through History With Harry Truman, Part II." *Holiday*, December 1963, 96, 97, 230-234.

Nadel, Gerry. "Johnny, When Will We Get Your Library?" *Esquire*, January 1975, 92-99, 130.

Nevins, Allan. "The President's Papers—Private or Public?" *New York Times Magazine*, October 19, 1947, 11, 52-54, 56.

Phillips, Andrew. "The Voices of History." *Maclean's* (November 17, 1997): 38-41.

Rhoads, James B. "Presidential Papers: A Reply." *New York Times Book Review*, September 7, 1969, 26, 28.

Rovere, Richard H. "Mr. Truman Shows Off His Library." *New York Times Magazine*, June 30, 1957, 5, 20, 22.

Siegel, Matt. "Getting Nixon Paid for Watergate Tapes." *American Lawyer*, January/February 1993, 111.

Sorel, Edward. "The Richard M. Nixon Library: Some Modest Proposals." *Atlantic* 227: 2 (February 1971): 85-92.

Stone, I.F. "The Fix." *New York Times Review of Books*, October 3, 1974, 6, 7.

Theoharis, Athan G. "The Culture of Secrecy: Can It Be Cracked Open?" Review of *Secrecy: The American Experience*, by Daniel Patrick Moynihan and *A Culture of Secrecy*, edited by Athan G. Theoharis. *Nieman Reports*, Spring 1999, 67-68.

Unsigned Legal Magazine Articles

"Bush Signs Agreement on Papers." *News Media and the Law* 17: 1 (Winter 1993): 5.

"Computer Tapes Are Public Information." *News Media and the Law* 7: 2 (Spring 1983): 30.

"Court Holds E-mail Is Federal Record." *News Media and the Law* 17: 4 (Fall 1993): 6-7.

"Judge Halts Destruction of Bush's Records." *News Media and the Law* 17: 1 (Winter 1993): 3-6.

Signed Legal Magazine Articles

Brams, Steven J. and Douglas Muzzio. "Game Theory and the White House Tapes Case." *Trial* 13: 5 (May 1977): 48-53.

Callen, Earl. "A Freedom-of-Information Act Fable . . . What's in a Name File?" *Civil Liberties Review* 3: 2 (June/July 1976): 58-66.

Gillers, Stephen. "Secret Government and What to Do About It." *Civil Liberties Review* 1: 2 (Winter/Spring 1974): 68-74.

Preston, William. "Historians and Presidents." *Civil Liberties Review* 3: 6 (February/March 1977): 58-61.

Taylor, Phillip. "Reagan's White House Papers Stay Delayed." *News Media and the Law* 25: 4 (Fall 2001): 34.

Young, Rowland L. "Supreme Court Report: Court Upholds Constitutionality of Presidential Papers Act." *American Bar Association Journal* 63: 10 (October 1977): 1446-1448.

Unsigned Newspaper Articles

"Bill Assumes Control of Nixon Tapes." *Christian Science Monitor*, September 25, 1974: 6.

"Broadcast Case Argued." *New York Times*, December 20, 1974 (IV), 75.

"Carter Is Against a Bill on Disclosure of Papers." *New York Times*, March 8, 1978, A16.

"Court OKs Erasing of White House Records." *Chicago Daily Law*

Bulletin, January 15, 1993, 1.

"Court Ruling May Mean Millions for Nixon." *Buffalo News*, November 18, 1992, 8.

"Decades-Old Struggle Over Nixon Papers Could End." *State Journal-Register* (Springfield, IL), April 6, 1997, 8.

"First Lady's Papers to Go to Repository." *New York Times*, December 24, 1938, 13.

"Ford Gives Nixon Full Pardon." *Editorials on File* (New York), 5: 17 (September 1-15, 1974).

"Ford Signs Bill on Nixon Papers." *New York Times*, December 20, 1974 (IV), 75.

"History, Declassified." *Christian Science Monitor*, November 14, 2001, 8.

"Hundreds of Nixon Tapes in National Archives Left in 'Legal Limbo'." *Los Angeles Times* (Orange County Edition), July 6, 1995, B1.

"Judge Rules Against Effort by Bush to Control His Records." *New York Times*, February 28, 1995, A20.

"Kissinger Phone Calls to Be Released." *New York Times*, February 11, 2002.

"Messe Overruled on Nixon Papers." *New York Times*, March 7, 1987, A7.

"Mr. Roosevelt's Archives." *New York Times*, December 13, 1938: 24.

"Nixon Blocks Release of Some of His Papers." *Los Angeles Times*, April 23, 1987, A15.

"Nixon Estate Is Seeking Millions for Documents U.S. Confiscated." *New York Times*, November 17, 1999, A24.

"Nixon Library: Library Chronology." *Los Angeles Times* (Orange County Edition), July 17, 1990 (Special Section), 5.

"Nixon Loses 1980 Lawsuit Seeking Payment for Papers." December 15, 1991, A31.

"Nixon Must Be Paid for Tapes, Papers." *Legal Times*, November 23, 1992, 16.

"Nixon Sues on U.S. Control of Presidential Records." *New York Times*, December 19, 1980, A24.

"Nixon Upheld on Access to Papers." *New York Times*, April 15, 1978.

"Overdue Notice." *Legal Times*, November 23, 1992, 3.

"Papers of the President Become Public Property." *Washington Post*, November 6, 1978, A11.

"President Starts Archives Project." *New York Times*, December 23, 1938: 15.

"Presidential Papers Measure Signed." *Christian Science Monitor*, November 7, 1978, 2.

"Presidents' Data Sought for U.S." *New York Times*, July 6, 1955: 17.

"Roosevelt Estate to House Archives, Go to Public Later." *New York Times*, December 11, 1938, 1, 49.

"Richard Nixon: 1913-1994; The Nixon Chronology." *Los Angeles Times*, April 27, 1994 (Special Section), V7.

"Security Council Permitted by Court to Shield Records." *Washington Post*, May 28, 1997, A8.

"Some Coolidge Papers Were Kept in an Attic." *New York Times*, March 14, 1985, A21.

"U.S. Library Plan Is Put Into Effect." *New York Times*, August 21, 1955, L75.

Signed Newspaper Articles

Allen, Mike and George Lardner, Jr. "A Veto Over Presidential Papers." *Washington Post*, November 2, 2001, A1.

Apple, R.W., Jr. "Nixon Tapes Must Be Kept Three Years for Use in Court." *New York Times*, September 9, 1974, A1.

Berger, Michael M. "Even Nixon Gets Property Rights Protection." *Chicago Daily Law Bulletin*, December 10, 1992, 6.

———. "Nixon's the One—Again—This Time, on Property Rights." *Los Angeles Daily Journal*, December 2, 1992, 7.

Berkman, Harvey. "Tapes: Burger's Secret Call to Nixon." *National Law Journal*, December 16, 1996, A10.

Bredemeier, Kenneth. "Appeals Court Allows Suits for Release of Nixon Papers." *Washington Post*, December 22, 1978, A7.

Bumiller, Elisabeth. "November 2, 2001." *New York Times*, November 2, 2001, A22.

Burnham, David. "Library of Congress: Facts? Let Them East Docudrama." *New York Times*, June 4, 1984, A16.

Cowan, Alison Leigh. "Battling Over Records of Bush's Governorship." *New York Times*, February 11, 2002.

Frammolino, Ralph and John Needham. "Library May Bring Nixon a Measure of Redemption." *Los Angeles Times*, July 17, 1990, A1.

Hey, Robert P. "Congress Plans to Keep Grip on Nixon Papers and Tapes." *Christian Science Monitor*, September 26, 1974, 1, 4.

Hurd, Charles W. "Roosevelt Papers a Rare Legacy." *New York Times*, December 18, 1938.

Huxtable, Ada Louise. "The Museum Upstages the Library." *New York*

Times, October 28, 1979, D31, D39.

Jackson, Robert L. "Nixon Is Owed for His Tapes, Court Rules." *Los Angeles Times*, November 18, 1992, A1.

———. "Nixon Saw Watergate as 'Routine,' Tapes Show." *Los Angeles Times*, May 18, 1993, A12.

———. "More of Nixon Tapes to Be Sold to Public." *Los Angeles Times*, April 18, 2001, A12.

Kamen, Al. "Court Diminishes 'Executive Privilege': Nixon Can't Automatically Block Papers' Release, Panel Rules." *Washington Post*, April 13, 1988, A23.

Kiefer, Francine. "A Fight Brews Over Ex-Presidents' Papers." *Christian Science Monitor*, November 6, 2001, 2.

Klaidman, Stephen. "Nine Trucks Convoy Ford Presidential Papers to Michigan." *Washington Post*, January 21, 1977, A9.

Kutler, Stanley I. "Presidential Materials: Nixon's Ghost at Justice." *Wall Street Journal*, April 1, 1986, 1.

Lardner, George, Jr. "Pricing the Nixon Records." *Washington Post*, December 3, 1998, A21.

———. "Nixon to Get Day in Court on Tapes Compensation." *Washington Post*, March 29, 1998, A3.

———. "Release of Reagan Documents Put on Hold." *Washington Post*, June 10, 2001, A5.

———. "Bush Urged to Rescind Order on Presidential Materials." *Washington Post*, November 7, 2001, A27.

Lauter, David. "Nixon's Plea to Shield Tapes, Records Rejected." *National Law Journal*, February 22, 1982.

Lesher, Dave and Richard M. Nixon. "Nixon Believes Public Will Give Him Kinder Judgment." *Los Angeles Times*, July 15, 1990, A1.

Lewis, Nancy. "Archives Can Decide Release of Nixon Papers." *Washington Post*, March 7, 1987, A3.

Locy, Toni. "Bush Denied Control of His Records: Judge Voids Deal Signed with Archivist." *Washington Post*, February 28, 1995, A17.

Lyons, Richard D. "Papers and Tapes Issues in Capital." *New York Times*, August 10, 1974, A1.

Marquis, Christopher. "Legal Victory for Nixon." *New York Times*, June 18, 2000, WK2.

———. "White House Again Delays Reagan Files' Release." *New York Times*, September 1, 2001, A10.

McAllister, Bill and Al Kamen. "Archives Is Dedicated, Sans Leader." *Washington Post*, May 13, 1994, A21.

Miller, Bill. "Records Order Spurs Lawsuit." *Washington Post*, November 29, 200, A31.

Mintz, Morton. "Court Denies Nixon's Bid for Papers." *Washington Post*, June 29, 1977, A1.

Mouat, Lucia. "Presidential Papers—Who Should Own Them?" *Christian Science Monitor*, September 17, 1974, A1.

Needham, John. "Nixon Library: Controversy Dogs Creation, Content." *Los Angeles Times* (Orange County Edition), July 17, 1990 (Special Section), 5.

O'Brien, Linda, Frederick J. Graboske and Jesse Berney. "More Secrets?" *Washington Post*, November 9, 2001 (Letters to the Editor), A36.

Reinert, Patty. "Bush Signs Executive Order Granting Power to Keep Papers Secret." *Houston Chronicle*, November 2, 2001, A4.

Rich, Spencer. "Plan for Public Access to Nixon Papers Gains." *Washington Post*, September 17, 1974, A2.

Riechmann, Deb. "Reagan Papers to Be Available Friday in Simi." *Ventura County Star*, March 13, 2002, A3.

Robinson, Timothy S. "Nixon to Allow Access to Some of His Papers." *Washington Post*, A6.

Rodriguez, Eva M. "Disquieting Times at the Federal Courts." *Legal Times*, December 28, 1992, 15.

Roosevelt, Franklin D. "Roosevelt's Explanation of the Repository Plan." *New York Times*, December 11, 1938, 49.

Rosenberg, William G. "Shredding Pieces of History." *Washington Post*, October 15, 1996, A15.

Rubin, James H. "Court Hears Debate on Who Owns Nixon Tapes." *Chicago Daily Law Bulletin*, September 14, 1992, 1.

Sammon, Bill. "Web Sites Told to Delete Data." *Washington Times*, March 21, 2002.

Saperstein, Saundra. "Highlights of Opinions, Dissents, Speeches by Justice Rehnquist." *Washington Post*, June 19, 1986, A10.

Saunders, Doug. "Nixon Library at Heart of Bitter Family Feud." *Ventura County Star*, April 26, 2002, A6.

Scheibe, John. "Reagan Library Looks for 'Wows.'" *Ventura County Star*, March 10, 2002, A1, A8.

Schorr, Daniel. "Undercutting History." *Christian Science Monitor*, November 16, 2001, 11.

Sterngold, James. "Nixon Daughters Battle Over $19 Million Library Bequest." *New York Times*, March 16, 2002, A10.

Sullivan, T. J. "Private Papers." *Ventura County Star*, March 3, 2002, A1.

Taylor, Stuart, Jr. "Judge Bars Access to Nixon Papers." *New York Times*, December 31, 1983, A1.

Wagner, Michael G. "Court Rules Some Nixon Tapes Are Private." *Los Angeles Times*, April 1, 1998, 3.

Weikel, Dan. "More Papers on Nixon's Career Will Go on View." *Los Angeles Times* (Orange County Edition), March 24, 1994, B1.

Weiner, Tim. "The 37th President: White House Tapes." *New York Times*, April 25, 1994, A1.

————. "Historian Wins Battle Over Nixon Tapes." *New York Times*, April 13, 1996, 12.

————. "After Long Litigation Agreement Is Near on Release of Tapes from Nixon White House." *New York Times*, March 26, 1996, A17.

————. "Return of a Recording Artist." *New York Times*, March 31, 1996, E2.

Weiss, Kenneth R. "Nothing to Read at Reagan Library." *Los Angeles Times*, February 10, 1991, A3.

Weiss, Kenneth R. and Paul Feldman. "Paper Blizzard: Reagan Library Releases Six Million Pages, Calls Them 'Routine'." *Los Angeles Times*, November 13, 1991, 1.

Wohl, Alexander. "High Crimes and Misdemeanors." *Legal Times*, November 23, 1992, 46.

York, Michael. "White House Disputes Impacts of Tapes Order." *Washington Post*, December 10, 1992, A10.

Unsigned Newspaper Editorials

"And Mr. Nixon's Taxes." *New York Times*, January 8, 1974, 32.

"A Coda to Nixon's Battles." *Los Angeles Times*, June 14, 2000, B8.

"Congress and the Tapes." *Christian Science Monitor*, September 26, 1974.

"Correcting a Blunder." *New York Times*, September 19, 1974, 42.

"A Curious Claim by the Nixon Estate." *New York Times*, February 22, 1999, A16.

"Presidential Papers . . . " *New York Times*, January 8, 1974, 32.

"President's Papers Now Are Yours." *Christian Science Monitor*, November 8, 1978, 24.

"Protecting Mr. Nixon's Records." *Washington Post*, July 3, 1977, C6.

"Release of Nixon Papers, Tapes." *Buffalo News*, April 28, 1994, 2.

"Take the Records and Run?" *New York Times*, November 25, 1992, A20.

"Today's Debate: Presidential Documents, Self-Serving Secrecy." *USA Today*, November 12, 2001, A16.

"Trouble in the Files." *Washington Post*, May 14, 1995, C6.

Signed Newspaper Editorials / Opinion Pieces

Boyd, Julian P. "Records of the Presidency." *New York Times*, May 1, 1960, E10.

Bryant, Irving. "Care of Presidents' Papers." *New York Times*, December 19, 1954 (IV), 6.

Dallek, Robert. "All the Presidents' Words Hushed." *Los Angeles Times*, November 25, 2001.

Gonzales, Alberto R. "Today's Debate: Presidential Documents, Protect Sensitive Documents." *USA Today*, November 12, 2001, A16.

Hamby, Alonzo L. "How to Frustrate Historians." *New York Times*, October 13, 1974 (IV), 16.

Hensen, Steven J. "The President's Papers Are the People's Business." *Washington Post*, December 16, 2001, B1.

Kutler, Stanley I. "Liberation of the Nixon Tapes." *Legal Times*, May 6, 1996, 24.

Lewis, Anthony. "The President's Papers, But Everybody's Business." *New York Times*, September 29, 1974 (IV), 2.

Miller, Arthur Selwynn. "Who Owns the Nixon Tapes and Papers?" *Washington Post*, September 21, 1974, 16.

Reeves, Richard. "Writing History to Executive Order." *New York Times*, November 16, 2001, A25.

Reston, James. "The President's Papers." *New York Times*, August 16, 1974, 29.

Safire, William. "Executive Privilege, Again." *New York Times*, January 3, 2002, A23.

Schnapper, M.B. "Reagan Gets the Last Word." *Manhattan Lawyer*, July 25, 1989, 16.

Teepen, Tom. "White House Invokes 'Selective' Privilege in Enron Investigation." *Ventura County Star*, 2002, B8.

Vose, Clement E. "In a Gift-Horse's Mouth." *New York Times*, December 28, 1973, 29.

Weingarten, Gene. "Just What Was He Smoking?" *Washington Post*, March 21, 2002, C1.

Radio Broadcasts

Edwards, Bob and Nina Totenberg. "Executive Order barring release of presidential papers if a former or current president wishes is coming under fire from historians and others." *Morning Edition.* National Public Radio, November 19, 2001.

Hansen, Liane. "Editing Nixon's Tapes." *NPR Weekend Sunday.* National Public Radio, September 6, 1998.

Bibliographies

The American Presidency: A Historical Bibliography. Clio Bibliography Series No. 15. Santa Barbara, CA: ABC-Clio Information Services, 1984.

deVergie, Adrienne and Mary Kate Kell. *Location Guide to the Manuscripts of Supreme Court Justices.* Rev. ed. Legal Bibliography Series No. 24. Austin, Texas: Tarlton Law Library, University of Texas School of Law, 1981.

Lambert, Jeffrey M. *Monumental Memorials: The Architecture and Design of Presidential Libraries.* Bibliography No. A 1520. Monticello, IL: Vance Bibliographies, 1986.

Martin, Fenton S. and Robert U. Goehlert. *How to Research the Presidency.* Washington, DC: Congressional Quarterly, 1996.

Unsigned Book Sections (Biographical)

"Bushrod Washington, 1799-1829." In *The Supreme Court Justices: Illustrated Biographies, 1789-1995,* edited by Clare Cushman, 51-55. Washington, DC: Congressional Quarterly, 1995.

"Herbert Brownell, Jr." In *Biographical Directory of the United States Executive Branch, 1774-1989,* edited by Robert Sobel, 47-48. New York: Greenwood Press, 1990.

"Herbert Brownell, Jr., 1904-1996." In *Encyclopedia of the United States Cabinet,* edited by Mark Grossman, vol. 1, 119-120. Santa Barbara, CA: ABC-CLIO, 2000.

"Joseph Story, 1812-1845." In *The Supreme Court Justices: Illustrated Biographies, 1789-1995,* edited by Clare Cushman, 86-90. Washington, DC: Congressional Quarterly, 1995.

Unsigned Book Sections (Non-biographical)

"Congress Votes to Retain Nixon Tapes." In *Congressional Quarterly Almanac 30 (1974)*. Washington, DC: Congressional Quarterly, 1974.
"Presidential Papers." In *Congressional Quarterly Almanac 34 (1978)*. Washington, DC: Congressional Quarterly, 1978.

Authored Electronic Resources

American Political Science Association. *Bush Signs Presidential Records Act Executive Order; Restricts Release of Documents.* [Electronic resource]. 2001 [cited December 22, 2001]. Available from 209.235.241.4/new/pra.cfm.
Carlin, John W. *Opening the Reagan Records.* [Electronic resource]. National Archives and Records Administration, December 10, 2001 [cited February 3, 2004]. Available from www.archives. gov/presidential_libraries/presidential_records/opening_reagan_ records.html.
Dean, John. *Hiding Past and Present Presidencies.* [Electronic resource]. Tom Paine.Com, 2001 [cited January 15, 2002]. Available from 205.252.23.176/features/2001/11/30/3.htm.
Hensen, Steve. *SAA Responds to Executive Order 13233 on Presidential Papers.* [Electronic resource]. November 6, 2001 [cited February 3, 2004]. Available from www.archivists.org/news/ actnow.asp.
Judson, Richard. *Standards for Permanent Records Storage and Presidential Libraries.* [Electronic resource]. National Archives and Records Administration, December 26, 2001 [cited February   3, 2004]. Available   from   www.archives.gov/preservation/ conferences/standards_permanent_storage.html.
Wolff, Cindi. *From the Chair.* [Electronic resource]. ALA/GODORT, Winter 2001 [cited February 3, 2004]. Available from sunsite.berkeley.edu/GODORT/columns/chr_200112.html.

Other Electronic Resources

Bush Gubernatorial Records Should Be Available Under Texas Law, Not Kept Secret in Father's Library. [Electronic resource]. Public Citizen, January 7, 2002 [cited February 3, 2004]. Available from www.citizen.org/pressroom/release.cfm?ID=988.

Department of Justice Freedom of Information Act Reference Guide. [Electronic resource]. Department of Justice, August 2000 [cited February 3, 2004]. Available from www.usdoj.gov/04foia/ referenceguidemay99.htm.

Freedom of Information Act Guide. [Electronic resource]. Department of Justice, May 2000 [cited February 3, 2004]. Available from www.usdoj.gov/oip/introduc.htm.

Judges of the United States Courts: John Joseph Sirica. [Electronic resource]. Federal Judiciary Commission, 2002 [cited February 3, 2004]. Available from air.fjc.gov/servlet/uGetInfo?jid=2200.

Judges of the United States Courts: Joseph Story. [Electronic resource]. Federal Judiciary Commission, 2002 [cited February 3, 2004]. Available from air.fdj.gov/servlet/uGetInfo?jid=2302.

Judges of the United States Courts: Charles Robert Richey. [Electronic resource]. Federal Judiciary Commission, 2002 [cited February 3, 2004]. Available from air.fjc.gov/servlet/uGetInfo/ jid=2004.

Memorandum of Understanding between the National Archives and Records Administration and the Executive Office of the President Concerning the Continuation and Completion, after January 20, 2001, of the Tape Restoration, Multi Host, and Reformatting Projects for the Clinton-Gore Administration Electronic Mail Records Associated with Automatic Records Management System. [Electronic resource]. National Archives and Records Administration, December 10, 2001 [cited February 3, 2004]. Available from www.archives.gov/presidential_libraries/presidential_records/clint on_gore_email_records_memo.html.

Presidential Libraries of the National Archives and Records Administration. [Electronic resource]. National Archives and Records Administration, March 14, 2001 [cited February 3, 2004]. Available from www.archives.gov/presidential_libraries/about/ about.html.

Press Briefing by Ari Fleischer: Excerpts on Access to Presidential Records. [Electronic resource]. [cited February 3, 2004]. Available from www.fas.org/sgp/news/2001/11/wh110101.html.

Press Release: Public Citizen Sues to Block Implementation of Executive Order on Presidential Records. [Electronic resource]. Public Citizen, November 28, 2001 [cited February 3, 2004]. Available from www.citizen.org/pressroom/release.cfm?ID=941.

Public Citizen has sued the Bush administration to overturn an executive order that would severely limit access to presidential records.

[Electronic resource]. Public Citizen, November 28, 2001 [cited February 3, 2004]. Available from www.citizen.org/ hot_issues/issue.cfm?ID=168.

APPENDICES

Appendix A

Executive Orders that Apply to Presidential Records 1789-2001

Executive orders, documents signed by the president that have the force of law but are not sanctioned by any statute, including the ones listed in the following section, can often be difficult to track down if issued before 1936, when they first became codified in the *Federal Register*. Orders issued prior to 1936 are most easily located using Clifford Lee's *Presidential Executive Orders* (New Jersey, 1943; New York, 1944). Even more comprehensive is CIS's *Index to Presidential Executive Orders and Proclamations* (Washington, DC, 1986), which covers the years 1789-1983 and acts as an index to 8,000+ microfiche set of the orders.

*EO 206   March 9, 1903   T. Roosevelt
Revolutionary and Continental Congress archives and the papers of George Washington, Thomas Jefferson, James Madison, James Monroe and Alexander Hamilton transferred from the State Dept. to the Library of Congress.

*EO 449   May 23, 1906   T. Roosevelt
Papers of Burr Conspiracy, Jefferson Davis and others transferred from State Dept. to the Library of Congress.

*EO 1499   March 16, 1912   W. H. Taft
"Useless" government papers, documents, etc. are to be submitted to the "Librarian of Congress" before destruction.

*EO 3554   Sept. 29, 1921   W. G. Harding
The Declaration of Independence and the Constitution are transferred from the custody of the State Dept. to the Library of Congress.

*EO 3594   Dec. 19, 1921   W. G. Harding
Papers of James Madison transferred from State Dept. to Library of
Congress.

EO 12667   Jan. 18, 1989   R. W. Reagan
"Presidential Records" *Fed. Reg.* 54: 13 (Jan. 23, 1989): 3403. Signed
Jan. 18, 1989; filed Jan. 19, 1989, 11:07 am (c. 25 hours before inaugu-
ration ceremony of George Herbert Walker Bush.)

EO 13233   Nov. 1, 2001   G. W. Bush
"Further Implementation of the Presidential Records Act" of 1978 *Fed.
Reg.* 66: 214 (Nov. 5, 2001): 56025-56029. Signed Nov. 1, 2001; filed
Nov. 2, 2001, 11:23 am.

* Numbering taken from *Presidential Executive Orders Numbered 1-8030:
1862-1938.* Clifford L. Lord, et al., ed. 2 vols. New York: [Books, Inc. ?],
1940.

Appendix B

Legislative Bill Tracings

The following section provides complete legislative histories to six acts that relate to the history and development of public ownership of and access to the records of federal officials. This section includes legislative histories, complete citations to all relevant congressional documents (hearings, prints and reports), to the following acts: the creation of the FDR presidential library; the Presidential Libraries Act (PLA); the Microfilming of Presidential Papers Act; the Presidential Recordings and Materials and Preservation Act (PRMPA); the extension of the Public Documents Commission; and the Presidential Records Act (PRA). Also included as a legislative history, but nearly as comprehensive as the other bill tracings, are histories of the various cost-reducing measures aimed at former presidents that were introduced throughout the 1980s as well as pending legislation in Congress concerning the current initial funding situation of presidential libraries.

Turning to the documents, reports and daily digests produced by Congress itself often are the best place to go for any legislative history. However, subject access to congressional documents often must be effected by using the breadth of products and services of the *Congressional Information Service (CIS)*, especially for Congresses from 1970. However, for materials produced by Congresses predating 1970, consulting the yearly indexes for the *Congressional Record*, the *House Journal* and the *Senate Journal* was essential. Consulting the *United States Congressional Code and Administrative News* (*USCCAN*) also proved useful in compiling legislative histories and final editions of bills enacted into law. Of course, *USCCAN*'s usefulness only extended to bills enacted into law, and I turned to the congressional *Journals* for failed legislation. Also of great help in finding legislative information was Nancy Johnson's *Compiled Legislative Histories*, which pointed to places where already compiled legislative histories for selected acts could be found.

Each legislative history includes citations to the various publishing organs of Congress, the *Congressional Record* (*Con. Rec.*), the *House Journal* (*H.Jrnl.*) and the *Senate Journal* (*S.Jrnl.*). Although omitted from any of the bibliographies in the second half of this thesis, citations to the *Congressional Record,* the *House Journal* and the *Senate Journal* where the acts mentioned in the above paragraph are supplied, even when the cite mentions only where bills were referred or reported to or from committees. Citations included in the bibliographic portions of this thesis to the *Record* and the *Journals* are only to instances where each respective organ includes substantial text about the bill in question (i.e., citations to referred and reported notices are not included in the bibliographies, but are supplied in the bill tracings that follow).

These bill tracings are as comprehensive as can be without access to primary materials or interviews with persons associated with each bill. Further insights to each bill are no doubt available, but the purpose of these tracings is only to supply the reader with references to historical and legislative timelines for each bill. The bill number in bold face indicates the version of the bill that eventually became law. Also supplied in this section are descriptions of several significant executive orders that relate to the ownership and access to presidential records and other federal records and documents.

Franklin D. Roosevelt Library Act of 1939
76th Congress, 1st Session

	S.J. Res. 118	H.J. Res. 268 H.Res. 238
April 19	S.J. Res. 118 (D-KY) intro. by Mr. Barkley and referred to Sen. Comm. on the Lib. (*Con. Rec.* 4431)	H.J. Res 268 intro by Mr. Keller (D-IL); companion bill to S.J. Res. 118. (*Con. Rec.*4513)
April 20	Reptd back from Comm. without amendment and passed on to Senate. No objection from floor. Engrosssed, third reading given. [No debate, no vote] (*Con. Rec.* 4543)	
April 24	Referred to House Comm. on the Lib. (*Con. Rec.* 4704)	
May 10		Reptd back from Comm. with H.Rept. 76-612 (*Con. Rec.* 5408)
June 5	Read in House and debated. Roll call vote taken on motion to suspend rules and pass the res. but super req. maj. not met (*Con. Rec.* 6622-6628)	Debated on House floor, objections from the floor prevented bill from passage over without prejudice. (*Con. Rec.* 6607)
June/July		Mr. Sabath (D-IL) intro. H.Res. 238 for the consideration of S.J. Res. 118, along with H.Rept. 76-1019 (*Con. Rec.* 8514)

July 12	Comm. on the Lib. refers res. to the Comm. of the Whole House, without amendment, with H. 76- Rept. 1098. (*Con. Rec.* 8987)	
July 13	Made special order (H.Res. 238)	H.Res. 238, to consider S.J. Res. 118. Debated, called up. Amendment agreed to, read a third time, motion to recommit bill to House Comm. on the Lib. failed and bill passed. (*Con. Rec.* 9037-9066)
July 14	House amendment. to S.J. Res. 118 (carried in H.Res. 238) announced and agreed to in Sen. (*Con. Rec.*9141-9142)	
July 17		Laid on table in lieu of passage of S.J. Res. 118 (*Con. Rec.* 9282)
July 18	Bill enrolled and presented to Pres. (but notice appears in July 19 *Con. Rec.* 9465) along with two other bills (*Con. Rec.* 9373, 9459 and 9465)	
July 30	Reptd back to Sen *sine die* by Presidential Secretary, Mrs. Latta, that signed by Pres. on July 27 (*Con. Rec.*10145)	

S.J. Res. 118 became Pub. Res. No. 30, 53 Stat. 1062-66.
Not codified in the U.S.C.

S.J. Res. 81

H.J. Res. 330
H.J. Res. 331
H.J. Res. 332

June 2

H.J. Res. 330 intro by Mr. McCormack (D-MA). H.J. Res. 331 intro by Mr. Martin (R-MA). H.J. Res. 332 intro by Mr. Rees (R-KS). All three bills referred to House Comm. on Gov. Operations. *Con. Rec.* 7550)

June 20

S.J. Res. 81 intro by Mr. Symington (D-MO), Mr. Carlson (R-KS) and Mr. Schoeppel (R-KS). Read twice and referred to Comm. on Gov. Operations. (*Con. Rec.* 8655)

June 29

Mr. Moss (D-CA) of House Comm. on Gov. Operations. referred bill to Comm. of the Whole House with amendment and H.Rept. 84-998. (*Con. Rec.* 9520)

June 30

Mr. Hoffman (R-MI) of Comm. on Gov. Operations referred bill to Comm. of the Whole House without amendment and Minority View (Pt. 2) of H.Rept. 84-998. (*Con. Rec.* 9677)

July 5   Mr. Moss moves to sus-
                                                         pend rules and pass bill.
                                                         Second req'd. Super-maj.
                                                         req. met on voice vote.

July 5 (cont'd)   Motion to reconsider laid
                                                         on the table. (*Con. Rec.*
                                                         9938)

July 6   Referred to Sen. Comm.
                                                         on Gov. Operations. (*Con.
                                                         Rec.* 9979)

July 28   Rept'd with amendments
                                                         and S.Rept. 84-1189 (*Con.
                                                         Rec.* 11752)

July 30   Amendments agreed to,
                                                         engrossed and bill read a
                                                         third time. (*Con. Rec.*
                                                         12230)

Aug. 1   House agrees to Sen.
                                                         amendments without ob-
                                                         jections. Motion to recon-
                                                         sider laid on the table.
                                                         (*Con. Rec.* 12649-12650)

Aug. 2   Examined and signed by
                                                         both chambers (*Con. Rec.*
                                                         12839 and 13075, Sen.
                                                         and House, respectively)

Aug. 4   LAST SESSION DAY   Presented to President Ei-
                                                         senhower (*Con. Rec.*
                                                         13078)

Aug. 12   Signed by Pres. and re-
                                                         ported back to Congress
                                                         (*Con. Rec.* 13081)

H.J. Res. 330 became P.L. 84-373, 69 Stat. 695.

Codified at 44 U.S.C. § 2101-2114.
Presidential Recordings and Materials Preservation Act of 1974
93rd Congress, 2nd Session

	H.R. 14939
	H.R. 15378
	H.R. 15773
	H.R. 16454
S. 2951	H.R. 16719
	H.R. 16803
	H.R. 16858
	H.R. 16902
S. 4016	H.R. 16948
	H.R. 16954
	H.R. 17025
	H.R. 17080
S. 4053	H.R. 17091
	H.R. 17116
	H.R. 17242
	H.R. 17278
S. 4080	H.R. 17279
	H.R. 17403
	H.R. 17404
	H.R. 17484

Feb. 4	S. 2951 intro by Mr. Bayh (D-IN) and referred to Sen. Comm. on Gov. Operations. (*Sen. Journal* 100)	
May 21		H.R. 14939 intro by Mr. Luken (D-OH) and referred to Comm. on House Admin.
June 13		H.R. 15378 intro by Mr. Luken and referred to Comm. on House Admin (same as H.R. 14939)
July 2		H.R. 15773 intro by Mr. Luken and referred to Comm. on House Admin (same as H.R. 14939)

August 15   H.R. 16454 intro by Mr.
                                                   Bingham (D-NY) and re-
                                                   ferred to Comm. on House
                                                   Admin.

Sept. 18   S. 4016 intro by Mr.   H.R. 16719 intro by
                  Nelson (D-WI), Mr.   Mr. Luken and referred
                  Ervin (D-NC) and Mr.   to Comm. on House Admin
                  Javits (R-NY) and re-   (same as H.R. 14939)
                  ferred to Comm. on Gov.
                  Operations (*Con. Rec.*
                  31549-31551)

                  Mr. Mondale (D-MN)
                  added as cosponsor of
                  S. 2951 (*Sen. Journal*
                  1015).

Sept. 23   H.R. 16803 intro by Mr.
                                                   Robison (R-NY) and re-
                                                   ferred to House Comm. on
                                                   Gov. Operations. (same
                                                   as H.R. 16454)

Sept. 24   H.R. 16858 intro by Mr.
                                                   Luken and referred to
                                                   Comm. on House Admin.

Sept. 26   S. 4016 reptd with   H.R. 16902 intro By Mr.
                  amendment and S.   Brademas (D-IN) and
                  Rept. 93-1181 (*Con.*.   referred to Comm. on
                  Rec. 32703)   House Admin.

                  Eleven additional co-
                  sponsors also added to
                  the bill. Cosponsors
                  added at Mr. Ervin's re-
                  quest included: Mr.
                  Ribicoff (D-CT), Mr.
                  Metcalf (D-MT), Mr.

Huddleston (D-KY),
Mr. Chiles (D-FL),
Mr. Percy (R-IL). Co-
sponsors added by re-
quest of Mr. Robert C.
Byrd (for Mr. Nelson)
included: Mr. Muskie
(D-ME), Mr. Hatfield
(R-OR), Mr. Dole
(R-KS), Mr. Montoya
(D-NM) and Mr.
Stevenson (D-IL).
(*Con. Rec.* 32717)

S. 4053 intro by Mr.
Pell (D-RI) and referred
to Sen. Comm. on Gov.
Operations.

Sept. 30		H.R. 16948 intro by Mr. Lagomarsino (R-CA) and referred to Comm. on House Admin. (*House Journal* 1775)
		H.R. 16954 intro. by Mr. Seiberling (D-OH) and referred to Comm. on House Admin.
Oct. 2	S. 4080 intro by Mr. Hruska (R-NE) and referred to Sen. Comm. on Gov. Operations.	H.R. 17025 intro by Ms. Grasso (D-CT and referred to Comm. on House Admin.
Oct. 3	Debate in Sen. on S. 4016 over agreement with amendment (*Con. Rec.* 33849-33878)	H.R. 17080 intro. by Mr. Moorhead (D-PA) and referred to Comm. on House Admin. (*House Journal* 1884)

Oct. 4   S. 4016 debated. Vote to
                  send the bill to the Sen.
                  Com. on the Jud. failed
                  (Roll call No. 451; 15-51).
                  Motion to table amend-
                  ment that would strike out
                  section 3(b) and sections
                  5 and 6 entirely passed.
                  Com. amendment agreed to.
                  Bill engrossed and read a
                  third time. Bill passed
                  (Roll Call No. 454; 56-7).
                  (*Con. Rec.* 33958-33976
                  & *House Journal* 1816)

Oct. 7   Referred to Comm. on House   H.R. 17091 intro by
                  Admin. (*Con. Rec.* 34256 &   Mr. Burke (D-MA)
                  House Journal 1835)   and referred to Com
                                                    on House Admin.
                                                    (same as H.R.
                                                    16454)

                                                    H.R. 17116 intro by
                                                    Mr. Gilman (R-NY)
                                                    referred to Comm.
                                                    on House Admin.
                                                    (same as H.R.
                                                    16454)

Oct. 8   Mr. Gravel (D-AK) and Mr.
                  Ribicoff (D-CT) added as
                  cosponsors of S. 2951 (*Sen.
                  Journal* 1284)

Oct. 10   H.R. 17242 intro by
                                                    Mr. Roybal (D-CA)
                                                    and referred to Comm.
                                                    on House Admin.
                                                    (*House Journal* 1972)

Oct. 10

H.R. 17278 intro by Mr. Luken and referred to Comm. on House Admin. (See H.R. 16858)

H.R. 17279 intro by Mr. Luken and referred to Comm. on House Admin. (See H.R. 16858)

Oct. 16

H.R. 17403 intro by My. Roybal and referred to Com. on House Admin. (*House Journal* 2035)

Nov. 19

House Subcomm. on Printing unanimous voice vote. (*Con. Rec.* 37900)

Nov. 20

H.R. 17484 intro by Mr. Brademas , Mr. Gettys (D-SC), Mr. Gaydos (D-PA), Mr. Jones (D-TN), Mr. Koch (D-NY), Mr. Cleveland (R-NH) and Mr. Hansen (R-ID). Referred to Comm. on House Admin. (*House Journal* 2094)

Nov. 26

Unanimous vote in House Comm. on Admin. (*Con. Rec.* 37900)

Nov. 27

Mr. Hays (D-OH) from
Comm. on House
Admin. reported S.
4016 to Com. of
the Whole House,
with amendment and
H. Rept. 93-1507.
(Omitted from the Rec.
of Nov.26) (*Con. Rec.*
37955 & *House Journal*
2150)

Dec. 3

Read in House. Second
demanded. House rules
suspended and amended
S. 4016 passed with
super maj. vote (*Con.
Rec.* 37898-37906 &
House Journal 2141)

Dec. 9

House approved amendment
to S. 4016 laid before the
Sen., agreed to and amended. (*Con. Rec.* 38529-
38537 & *House Journal*
2197)

House agrees to Sen.
amendments to House
amend. to S. 4016.
(*Con. Rec.* 37898-
37906 & *House Journ-
al* 2197)

Dec. 10

S. 4016 enrolled and signed
by Acting Speaker Pro Tem.
of the Sen. (*Con. Rec.* 38812
& *House Journal* 2202)

House message to Sen. read
that House agreed to Sen.
amendments of the House
amendment to S. 4016. (*Con. Rec.*
38818)

Sec. of Sen. reported that
enrolled bill S. 4016 presented
to Pres. (*Con. Rec.* 38820)

Dec. 19

Omitted in Record:
Approved and signed by Pres.
(*House Journal* 2564)

S. 4016 became P.L. 93-526, 88 Stat. 1695. Codified at 44 U.S.C.
§ 2111.

Act Extending the Life of the National Study Commission on the Records and Documents of Federal Officials
94th Congress, 2nd Session

S. 3060

March 11	S. 3060 intro by Mr. Nelson (D-WI) and referred to Sen. Comm. on Gov. Operations.	
March 26	Reported to Sen. from Comm. on Gov. Oprtations with S. Rept. 94-713.	
March 30	Considered, engrossed and read a third time in Sen. (*Con. Rec.* 8621)	
	Bill passes Senate.	
March 31		S. 3060 called up in House, considered, read a third time and passed. Motion to reconsider laid on the table. (*Con. Rec.* 8884-8885)
April 1	Measure enrolled in House.	Measure enrolled in Senate.
	Measure presented to the Pres.	
April 11		
	Measure approved and signed by the Pres.	

S. 4016 became PL 94-261, 90 Stat. 326; 44 U.S.C. § 3318, § 3322

	H.R. 9130
	H.R. 10998
S. 2596	H.R. 11001
S. 3494	H.R. 13364
	H.R. 13500
	H.R. 14299

1st Session
1977

Sept. 15

H.R. 9130 intro by Mr. Preyer (D-NC) and referred jointly to Comm. on House Admin. and Comm. on Gov. Operations. (*Con. Rec.* H 9118)

Dec. 15

END FIRST SESSION

2nd Session
1978

Feb. 16

H.R. 10998 intro by Mr. Preyer and referred jointly to Comm. on House Admin. and Comm. on Gov. Operations. (*Con. Rec.* 3662)

Feb. 20

H.R. 11001 intro. by Mr. Ertel (D-PA). Cosponsored by Mr. Brademas (D-IN). Ref. jointly to Comm. on House Admin. and Comm. on Gov. Operations. (*Con. Rec.* 3681)

Feb. 23		Subcomm. on Gov. Info. and Indiv. Rights, House Comm. on Gov. Operations began hearings on H.R. 10998 and 11001 (*Con. Rec. Daily Digest* D110)
Feb. 27	S. 2596 intro by Mr. Nelson (D-WI). Companion bill to H.R. 11001. Read twice and referred to Sen. Comm. on Gov. Affairs. (*Sen. Journal* 893).	
Feb. 28		Hearings cont'd (*Con. Rec. Daily Digest* D128)
March 2		Hearings cont'd (*Con. Rec. Daily Digest* D 143)
March 7		Hearings cont'd (*Con. Rec. Daily Digest* D160)
May 4	Mr. Riegle (D-MI) added as cosponsor to S. 2596 (*Sen. Journal* 893)	
June 8	Mr. Moynihan (D-NY) added as co sponsor (*Sen. Journal* 893)	
June 29		H.R. 13364 intro by Mr. Pryer as compromise bill to H.R. 10998 and 11001. Cosponsored by Mr. Brademas and Ertel. Referred jointly to Comm. on House Admin. and Comm. on Gov. Operations. (*Con. Rec.* 19565 & *House Journal* 1206)

July 13 | Subcom. on Gov Info. and Indiv. Rights, House Comm. on Gov. Operations approve full comm. action H.R. 13364 and S. 1265. (*Con. Rec. Daily Digest* D580)

July 17 | H.R. 13500 intro by Mr. Pryer as clean bill to all others hitherto into. Thirteen cosponsors: Mr. Brademas, Mr. Ertel, Mr. Brooks (D-TX), Mr. Fountain (D-NC), Mr. Harrington (D-MA), Miss Jordan (D-TX), Mr. Moss (D-CA), Mr. Ryan (D-CA), Mr. Weiss (D-NY), Mr. Horton (R-NY), Mr. Erlenborn (R-IL), Mr. McCloskey (R-CA) and Mr. Quayle (R-IN). Referred jointly to Com. on House Admin. and Comm. on Gov. Operations. (*Con. Rec.* 21225 & *House Journal* 1376)

July 19 | Comm. on Gov. Operations reports to House Comm. as the Whole H.R. 13500 by vote of 33 to 2 (*Con. Rec. Daily Digest* D599)

Aug. 14 | Amended rept. on H.R. 13500, H.Rept. 95-1487, pt. 1, reported to the House and ordered to be

printed. (*Con. Rec.* 25999
& *House Journal* 1615)

Sept. 12   S. 3494 intro, read a sec-
ond time and referred to
Sen. Comm. on Gov.
Affairs. Mr. Nelson
(D-WI) sponsor, Mr. Percy
(R-IL) cosponsor. (*Sen.
Journal* & *Con. Rec. Daily
Digest* D780)

Oct. 5   H.R. 14249 intro by Mr.
Brooks. The bill is al-
most the same as H.R.
13500, but with some
minor alterations. Thir-
teen cosponsors: Mr.
Preyer, Mr. Brademas,
Mr. Ertel, Mr. Fountain,
Mr. Harrington, Miss
Jordan, Mr. Ryan, Mr.
Weiss, Mr. Horton, Mr.
Erlenborn , Mr.
McCloskey, Mr. Quayle
and Mr. Thompson
(D-NJ). Referred jointly
to Comm. on House
Admin. and Comm. on
Gov. Operations. (*Con.
Rec.* 33860 & *House
Journal* 2631)

Oct. 10   H.R. 13500 received in Sen.   House suspended rules to
pass amended H.R. 13500
by super maj. voice vote.
Amendment incorp.
changes of H.R. 14249.
Motion to reconsider
laid on the desk. (*Con.
Rec.* 34892-34897 &
Con. Rec. Daily Digest

D888 & *House Journal*
2716-2718)

Oct. 13	H.R. 13500 called up, considered, amended and passed in Sen. Engrossed and passes Sen. by voice vote. (*Con. Rec.*36843 & *Con. Rec. Daily Digest* D905 & *House Journal* 2960)	
Oct. 14	H.R. 13500 examined, enrolled and signed by Speaker Pro. Tem. of of Sen. (*Con. Rec.* 38084)	House concurred in Sen. 13500. (*Con. Rec.* 38283 & *House Journal* 3002)
	[*Sen. Journal* says Sen. passed H.R. 13500 with its amendment on Oct. 14 and it was agreed to by the House the same day. *Sen. Journal* 1017]	Bill examined and signed by Speaker of the House. (*Con. Rec.* 38778 & *Con. Rec. Daily Digest* D921 & *House Journal* 3559)
Oct. 25	Measure signed in Sen. and delivered to Pres. (*Sen. Journal* 1017)	H.R. 13500 presented to Pres. (*Con. Rec.* 38780 *House Journal* 3562)
Nov. 4		H.R. 13500 approved as P.L. 95-591 (*Con. Rec.* 38783 & *Con. Rec. Daily Digest* D947 & *House Journal* 3565 & *Sen. Journal* 1017)
Nov. 6	President signs H.R. 13500 into law with signing statement (*Weekly Comp. of Pres. Docs.* 1965)	

H.R. 13500 became PL 95-591; 92 Stat. 2523. 44 U.S.C. § 2200-2205.

Bills Related to the Presidential Libraries Act of 1986

NOTE: Due to the long and complex history of
the Presidential Libraries Act of 1986 , instead of listing
complete legislative histories for all of the bills that
led up to the 1986 act, only the bill numbers
have been listed. However, for the 1986 act
itself, a full legislative history is included.

96th Congress

H.R. 7224
H.R. 7713
S. 2408

97th Congress

H.R. 3904
H.R. 4671
S. 1325

98th Congress

H.R. 2446
H.R. 5478
H.R. 5843
H.R. 6335
S. 563
S. 2567

99th Congress

H.R. 1236
H.R. 1349
H.R. 2113
H.R. 4890
S. 1047

Presidential Libraries Act of 1986
99th Congress, 1st and 2nd Sessions

H.R. 1349

1st Session
1985

Feb. 28

H.R. 1349, "a bill to re-duce the costs of operating Presidential libraries," intro by Mr. English (D-OK). Referred to House Comm. on Gov. Operations. Co-sponsors include: Mr. Kindness (R-OH), Mr. Wise (D-WV), Mr. Spratt (D-SC), Mr. MacKay (D-FL), Mr. Reid (D-NV), Mr. Bilirakis (R-FL), Mr. Neal (D-NC), Mr. Towns (D-NY), Mr. Miller (R-NJ), Mr. Burton (R-IN), Mr. Rinaldo (R-WA) and Mr. DioGuardi (R-NY).

March 11

Bill referred to Subcomm. on Gov. Info., Justice and Agric. Exec. comment requested on the bill from OMB, NARS, Nt'nl Capital Planning Comm. and Smith. Inst.

March 26

Subcomm. hearings held. Consideration and mark-up session held by sub-comm. Amended bill referred back to full Comm.

April 2	Amended bill ordered to be reported.
April 23	Additional cosponsors added for H.R. 1349 include: Mr. Lightfoot (R-IA), Mr. Clinger (R-PA), Mr. Pursell (R-MI), Mr. Horton (R-NY), Mr. McCandless (R-CA) and Mr. Monson (R-UT).
April 25	Comm. on House Admin. referred H.R. 2113 to Subcom. on Procurement and Printing.
April 29	House Comm. on Gov. Operations referred H.R. 2113 jointly to Subcom. on Gov. Info., Justice and Agric. and Subcomm. on Leg. and Nt'nl Security. Executive comment requested by from OMB, GSA, Treasury Dept., GAO and NARA.
May 7	Last additional cosponsor added for H.R. 1349, Mr. Brooks (D-TX).
May 13	House Comm. on Post Office and Civil Service jointly referred H.R. 2113 to Subcomm. on Compensation and Emp. Benefits and Subcomm. on Civil Serv.

May 15

Amended H.R. 1349 reported to House by Comm. on Gov. Operations with House Report no. 99-125. Placed on Union Calendar No. 79.

May 20

Executive comment on H.R. 2113 requested from the following agencies: OMB, OPM, GSA, Treasury Dept. and NARA.

June 4

H.R. 1349 rose to the floor of the House under suspension of the rules, amended and passed via voice vote.

June 6

H.R. 1349 received in Sen., read twice and referred to the Sen. Comm. on Gov. Affairs.

June 28

Comm. requests executive comment on bill from NARA, GSA, OMB and Nt'nl Capital Planning Comm.

July 30

Comm. receives executive comment from Nt'nl Capital Planninng Comm.

Oct. 2

H.R. 1349 ordered reported favorably with amendments in lieu of Title I of S. 1047.

END FIRST SESSION

2nd Session
1986

March 7   H.R. 1349 reported to
           Sen. by Mr. Roth
           (R-DE) with amend-
           ments. Senate Report
           99-257. Placed on Sen.
           Leg. Calendar 555.

March 21   Measure laid before
           Sen. with unanimous
           consent. Sen. agrees
           by voice vote to amend-
           ment proposed by Mr.
           Simpson (R-WY) for
           Mr. Roth. Amended
           measure then agreed to
           by voice vote.

May 13   House agreed to Sen.
                                           amendments unani-
                                           mously and cleared for
                                           Pres.

May 15   Measure signed and en-   Measure enrolled in
           rolled in Senate and   House.
           presented to Pres.

May 27
                        Act signed into law
                        by Pres.

H.R. 1349 became PL 99-323; 100 Stat. 495 ; 44 U.S.C. § 2101,
                        § 2112.

Accountability for Presidential Gifts Bill
107th Congress, 1st and 2nd Sessions

H.R. 577
H.R. 1081

1st Session
2001

Feb. 13	Mr. Duncan (R-TN) intro. H.R. 577 and referred to House Comm. on Gov. Reform.
March 6	Mr. Burton (R-IN), Mr. Petri (R-WI), Mr. Sessions (R-TX) and Mr. Smith (R-NJ) added as a cosponsors to H.R. 577.
March 7	H.R. 577 referred to Subcom. on Gov. Efficiency, Financial Mgmt and Intergov. Relations.
	Mr. Wamp (R-TN) added as cosponsor to H.R. 577.
March 8	Mr. Goode (D-VA) added as cosponsor to H.R. 577.
March 13	The following cosponsors added to H.R. 577: Ms. Davis (R-VA), Mr. Hood (R-IL) and Mr. Schaffer (R-CO).
March 15	Mr. Ose (R-CA) intro. H.R. 1081 and referred to House Comm. on Gov. Reform.

March 23

H.R. 1081 referred to Subcomm. on Gov. efficiency, Financial Mgmt and Intergov. Relations.

April 3

Mr. Clement (D-TN) added as cosponsor to H.R. 577.

April 4

Ms. Thurman (D-FL) added as cosponsor to H.R. 577.

Dec. 20

END FIRST SESSION

2nd Session
2002

Feb. 5

Mr. Horn (R-CA) moved that H.R. 577 be considered under suspension of the rules (*Con. Rec.* H115-118). Bill debated and roll call vote taken on super maj. Vote (Roll Call No. 6; 392-3) (*Con. Rec.* H115-116). Motion to reconsider laid on the table and title of measure amended.

Feb. 6 H.R. 577 received in Sen., read twice and referred to Comm. on Gov. Affairs.

Feb. 26

Mr. Burton (R-IN), Mr. Cannon (R-UT), Mr. Duncan (R-TN), Mr. La-Tourette (R-OH), Mr. Otter (R-ID) and Mr. Shays (R-CT) are all added as cosponsors to H.R. 1081.

Feb. 28

Mr. Terry (R-NE) added as cosponsor to H.R. 1081.

March 21   Comm. on Gov. Affairs reports favorably and without amendment on H.R. 577.

March 15

H.R. 1081, the "Accountability for Presidential Gifts Act" intro. by Doug Ose (R-CA). Referred to House Comm. on Gov. Reform.

March 18

Ms. Morella (R-MD) added as cosponsor to H.R. 1081.

March 23

Referred to Subcom. on Gov. Efficiency, Financial Mgmt and Intergov. Relations.

April 16

Mr. Petri (R-WI) added as cosponsor to H.R. 1081.

April 30

Added as cosponsors to H.R. 1081 are Mr. Wolf (R-VA) and Mr. Taylor (D-MS).

Appendix B

June 11   Reported without amend-
ment from Comm. on Gov.
Affairs by Mr. Lieberman
(D-CT). Senate Report 107-
160. Placed on Sen. Leg.
Calendar 413.

June 18   Subcomm. on Gov. Efficiency, Financial Mgmt
and Intergov. Relations
holds hearings. No doc
produced.

Nov. 22

LAST SESSION DAY

Appendix C

Table of Cases

What follows is an index to all of the judicial cases listed in the previous bibliographies. In italics are the proper case names, while all other items listed in roman type are see references to the proper names of the cases. See references have been included for each inverted case name (Nixon, U.S. v., *see U.S. v. Nixon*). Personal names are also included as see references (e.g., Richard Nixon v. United States, *see Nixon v. U.S.*). All references to the United States are listed as U.S. Cross-references have been listed for United States but not for United States of America, however. Compound and complex compound names (e.g., Department of Justice) have been cross-referenced in multiple places (e.g., Dept. of Justice, DOJ). For full bibliographic information on each of these citations, please consult pages the relevant pages in the bibliography (Part 3).

Armstrong v. EOP (1996)

Arthur Sampson, Richard M. Nixon v., *see Nixon v. Sampson*

Arthur Sampson, Public Citizen v., *see Public Citizen v. Sampson* (1974a)

Arthur Sampson, Public Citizen v., *see Public Citizen v. Sampson* (1974b)

Bela Marsh, Charles Folsom v., *see Folsom v. Marsh*

Brandon v. Eckard

Burr, U.S. v., *see U.S. v. Burr*

Bush, Armstrong v. (1989), *see Armstrong v. Bush* (1989)

Bush, Armstrong v. (1991), *see Armstrong v. Bush* (1991)

Campaign Activities, Senate Select Committee on Presidential, v., Richard M. Nixon, *see Senate Select Committee v. Nixon*

Carlin, Kutler and Public Citizen v., *see Kutler v. Carlin*

Carlin, Public Citizen v., *see Public Citizen v. Carlin*

Carmen, Allen v., *see Allen v. Carmen*

Chadha, INS v., *see INS v. Chadha*

Charles Folsom v. Bela Marsh, *see Folsom v. Marsh*

Charles R. Richey, Richard M. Nixon v., *see Nixon v. Richey*

Citizen, Public, v. Arthur Sampson, *see Public Citizen v. Sampson* (1974a)

Citizen, Public, v. Arthur Sampson, *see Public Citizen v. Sampson* (1974b)

Citizen, Public, v. John W. Carlin, *see Public Citizen v. Carlin*

Citizen, Public, v. Department of Justice, *see Public Citizen v. DOJ*

City of New York v. Dewitt C. Lent, *see New York v. Dewitt*

Clark Papers Case, *see U.S. v. First Trust Company of Saint Paul*

Committee on Presidential Campaign Activities, Senate Select, v. Richard M. Nixon, *see Senate Select Committee v. Nixon*

Cox, Sirica and, Nixon v., *see Nixon v. Sirica*

Dellums v. Powell

Department of Health and Human Services, Sidney M. Wolfe v., *see Wolfe v. Dept. of Health and Human Serv.*

Department of Justice, Public Citizen v., *see Public Citizen v. DOJ*

Dewitt C. Lent, New York v., *see New York v. Dewitt*

DOJ, Public Citizen v., *see Public Citizen v. DOJ*

Eckard, Brandon v., *see Brandon v. Eckard*

Edward Y. Higbee, Wilson Eyre v., *see Eyre v. Higbee*

EOP, Armstrong v. (1993a), *see Armstrong v. EOP* (1993a)

EOP, Armstrong v. (1993b), *see Armstrong v. EOP* (1993b)

EOP, Armstrong v. (1995), *see Armstrong v. EOP* (1995)

Dellums v. Powell
Roosevelt's Will, In re, *see In re Roosevelt's Will*
Rowland G. Freeman, Richard M. Nixon v., *see Nixon v. Freeman*
St. Paul, First Trust Company of, United States v., *see U.S. v. First Trust Company of Saint Paul*
Saint Paul, First Trust Company of, United States v., *see U.S. v. First Trust Company of Saint Paul*
Sampson, Nixon v., *see Nixon v. Sampson*
Sampson, Public Citizen v., *see Public Citizen v. Sampson* (1974a)
Sampson, Public Citizen v., *see Public Citizen v. Sampson* (1974b)
Samuel Z. Montoya, Historical Society of New Mexico v., *see Hist. Soc. of New Mex. v. Montoya*
Samuel Z. Montoya, Kenneth D. Sender v., *see Sender v. Montoya*
Sawyer, Youngstown v., *see Youngstown v. Sawyer*
Scott Armstrong v. Executive Office of the President (1993a), *see Armstrong v. EOP* (1993a)
Scott Armstrong v. Executive Office of the President (1993b), *see Armstrong v. EOP* (1993b)
Scott Armstrong v. Executive Office of the President (1995), *see Armstrong v. EOP* (1995)
Scott Armstrong v. Executive Office of the President (1996), *see Armstrong v. EOP* (1996)
Scott Armstrong v. George Bush (1989), *see Armstrong v. Bush* (1989)
Scott Armstrong v. George Bush (1991), *see Armstrong v. Bush* (1991)
Sealed Case, In re, *see In re Sealed Case*
Select Committee on Presidential Campaign Activities, Senate, v. Richard M. Nixon, *see Senate Select Committee v. Nixon*
Senate Select Committee v. Nixon
Senate Select Committee on Presidential Campaign Activities v. Richard M. Nixon, *see Senate Select Committee v. Nixon*
Sender v. Montoya
Sidney M. Wolfe v. Department of Health and Human Services, *see Wolfe v. Dept. of Health and Human Serv.*
Sirica, Nixon v., *see Nixon v. Sirica*
Stanley I. Kutler and Public Citizen v. John W. Carlin, *see Kutler v. Carlin*
Taylor, Griffin and, v. U.S., *see Nixon v. U.S.* (1995)
Title to Pres. Papers (Att'y Gen. Op.)
Title to Presidential Papers, *see Title to Pres. Papers* (Att'y Gen. Op.)
Trudy Peterson, AHA v. , *see AHA v. Peterson*
Trust Company of Saint Paul, First, United States v., *see U.S. v. First*

Appendix D

Archives with Presidential Records

What follows is a list of and contact information for archival institutions that contain significant holdings of materials related to the ownership of, preservation of and access to presidential materials. By no means comprehensive, the list contains listings of all federal presidential libraries, the Library of Congress and a few other private institutions. Listed first are presidential libraries (both federal and otherwise), followed by other pertinent institutions, both public and private. The list that follows should be treated as a starting point for scholars interested in the recorded history of the U.S. presidency and the records created by that institution over the decades.

Presidential Libraries

Rutherford B. Hayes Presidential Center
www.rbhayes.org
Spiegel Grove
Fremont, OH 43420
Toll Free Phone: 1-800-998-7737
Phone: 419-332-4952
Fax: 419-332-4952
E-Mail hayeslib@rbhayes.org

Hoover Institution on War, Revolution & Peace
Stanford University
www-hoover.stanford.edu
Stanford, CA 94305-6010
Toll Free Phone: 1-877-466-8374
Phone: 650-723-1754
Fax: 650-723-1687
E-Mail: horaney@hoover.stanford.edu

Herbert Hoover Library
hoover.archives.gov
210 Parkside Drive
P.O. Box 488
West Branch, IA 52358-0488
Phone: 319-643-5301
Fax: 319-643-6045
E-Mail: hoover.library@nara.gov

Franklin D. Roosevelt Library
www.fdrlibrary.marist.edu
4079 Albany Post Road
Hyde Park, NY 12538-1999
Toll Free Phone: 1-800-337-8474
Phone: 845-486-7770
Fax: 845-486-1147
E-Mail: roosevelt.library@nara.gov

Harry S. Truman Library
www.trumanlibrary.org
500 West U.S. Highway 24
Independence, MO 64050-1798
Toll Free Phone: 1-800-833-1225
Phone: 816-268-8200
Fax: 816-268-8295
E-Mail: truman.library@nara.gov

Dwight D. Eisenhower Library
www.eisenhower.utexas.edu/
200 SE 4th Street
Abilene, KS 67410-2900
Toll Free Phone: 1-877-746-4453
Phone: 785-263-6700
Fax: 785-263-6718
E-Mail: eisenhower.library@nara.gov

John F. Kennedy Library

www.jfklibrary.org
Columbia Point
Boston, MA 02125-3398
Toll Free Phone: 1-877-616-4599
Phone: 617-514-1600
TTY: 617-514-1573
Fax: 617-929-4538
E-Mail: kennedy.library@nara.gov

Lyndon B. Johnson Library

www.lbjlib.utexas.edu
2313 Red River Street
Austin, TX 78705-5702
Phone: 512-721-0200
Fax: 512-712-0236
E-Mail: johnson.library@nara.gov

Nixon Presidential Materials Staff

National Archives at College Park
nixon.archives.gov
8601 Adelphi Road
College Park, MD 20740-6001
Phone: 301-837-3290
Fax: 301-837-3202
E-Mail: nixon@nara.gov

Richard Nixon Library and Birthplace

www.nixonfoundation.org
18001 Yorba Linda Blvd.
Yorba Linda, CA 92886
Phone: 714-993-3393
Fax: 714-528-0544
E-Mail: revjht@msn.com

Gerald R. Ford Library

www.ford.utexas.edu
1000 Beal Avenue
Ann Arbor, MI 48109-2114
Phone: 734-741-2218
Fax: 734-741-2341
E-Mail: ford.library@nara.gov

Gerald R. Ford Museum
www.ford.utexas.edu
303 Pearl Street, NW
Grand Rapids, MI 49504-5353
Phone: 616-254-0400
Fax: 616-254-0386
E-Mail: ford.museum@nara.gov

Jimmy Carter Library
www.jimmycarterlibrary.org
441 Freedom Parkway
Atlanta, GA 30307-1498
Phone: 404-331-3942
Fax: 404-730-2215
E-Mail: carter.library@nara.gov

Ronald Reagan Library
www.reagan.utexas.edu
40 Presidential Drive
Simi Valley, CA 93065-0600
Toll Free Phone: 800-410-8354
Fax: 805-522-9621
E-Mail: reagan.library@nara.gov

George Bush Library
bushlibrary.tamu.edu
1000 George Bush Drive West
College Station, TX 77845
Phone: 979-691-4000
Fax: 979-691-4050
E-Mail: bush.library@nara.gov

William J. Clinton Presidential Library
http://www.clintonlibrary.gov/
1200 President Clinton Avenue
Little Rock, AR 72201
Phone: 501- 374-4242
Fax: 501-244-2883
E-Mail: clinton.library@nara.gov

Other Institutions

Office of Presidential Libraries
National Archives at College Park
8601 Adelphi Road
College Park, MD 20740-6001
Phone: 301-713-6050
Fax: 301-713-6045

The Adams Papers
Massachusetts Historical Society
www.masshist.org/adams_editorial
1154 Boylston Street
Boston, MA 02215
Phone: 617-536-1608
Fax: 617-859-0074
E-Mail: masshist@masshist.org

The Fillmore Papers
Buffalo and Erie County Historical Society
bechs.org
25 Nottingham Court
Buffalo, NY 14202-3199
Phone: 716-873-9644, ext. 306

The Buchanan Papers
Historical Society of Pennsylvania
www.hsp.org
1300 Locust Street
Philadelphia, PA 19107
Phone: 215-732-6200
Fax: 215-732-2680

The Harding Papers
Ohio Historical Society
www.ohiohistory.org
I-71 and 17th Avenue
Columbus, OH 43085
Phone: 614-297-2510

Manuscript Reading Room, Library of Congress
www.loc.gov/rr/mss
Room LM101, James Madison Building
101 Independence Ave., SE
Washington, DC 20540-4680
Phone (Reading Room): 202-707-5387
Fax: 202-707-6336
E-Mail: To e-mail, go to the following website:
        www.loc.gov/rr/askalib/ask-mss.html

Mailing Address:
Manuscript Division
Library of Congress
101 Independence Avenue, SE
Washington, DC 20540-4680

Index

About the Author

Peter H. Sezzi is an associate librarian at Ventura College. This is his first book. Mr. Sezzi was born, raised and educated in Ventura, California. He is a graduate of Ventura College as well as the University of California, Los Angeles. His B.A. is in English and history, the latter of which he graduated with Departmental Honors for his senior honors thesis, "Woodrow Wilson and the Origins of Progressive Thought, 1879-1910." After a short hiatus from the academe, Mr. Sezzi returned to UCLA as a graduate student in the Department of Information Studies. This book is based on his master's thesis. Mr. Sezzi is currently working on compiling bibliographies on the African campaigns of World War I and the U.S. Channel Islands.